THE
BATTLE
OF
BRITAIN

JULY – OCTOBER 1940

AN ORAL HISTORY OF BRITAIN'S 'FINEST HOUR'

MATTHEW PARKER

headline

First published in 2000
by HEADLINE PUBLISHING GROUP

First published in paperback in 2001
by HEADLINE PUBLISHING GROUP

6

This book accompanies the television series produced by
United Productions for ITV and first broadcast in 2000
Series Producer and Director: Steven Clarke
Director: Nicholas White
Assistant Producer: Louise Osborne
Researcher: Jacqui Mitchell
Production Manager: Liz Stevens

ISBN 978 0 7472 3452 4

Typeset by Letterpart Limited, Reigate, Surrey

Printed and bound in Great Britain by
CPI Mackays, Chatham ME5 8TD

HEADLINE PUBLISHING GROUP
An Hachette Livre UK Company
338 Euston Road
London NW1 3BH

www.headline.co.uk
www.hachettelivre.co.uk

www.matthewparker.co.uk

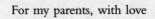

For my parents, with love

Contents

Acknowledgements

M Y FIRST DEBT OF THANKS IS TO ALL THOSE WHO HAVE allowed me to use their testimonies of the summer of 1940. As far as possible I have avoided 'novelising' their experiences and allowed them to talk directly to the reader. I hope this has enabled them to tell the story to a large extent themselves. Their experiences are not supposed to be typical of airman, soldier or civilian, but they remain a fascinating first-hand account of the extraordinary events of that year.

I am also indebted to all at United Productions. This book came about as a result of their work for their two-part television series for ITV. I am grateful for all the advice and support I received from Steven Clarke, Nick White and Louise Osborne, and would like to specially thank Jacqui Mitchell, whose patience, intelligence and hard work made this project possible.

Heather Holden-Brown and Lindsay Symons at Headline have given me encouragement and advice for which I am grateful. The translation of German material for this book was by Sheila Parker, and I am also indebted to my father for his research work, particularly on local airfields in the south of England. Finally, and most important of all, thanks and love to Hannah and Oliver.

Preface

THE SUMMER AND EARLY AUTUMN OF 1940 WAS, FOR Britain, the most intense moment of the twentieth century. For millions of ordinary young people it seemed that the great, impersonal forces of history had barged into their lives. Priorities were warped out of recognition: instead of being concerned with work, children, fun or love, everyone's purpose now had to be to fight and win the war. Where people had belonged to a class or race, to communities or towns, now they were forced, as never before, to unite as a nation.

Many thought they might never see their loved ones again, and as the cold, wet winter gave way to a glorious spring and summer, there was a rush of weddings. But not all young couples tied the knot in the moments before the war swept their normal lives away. Londoner Sid Wakeling decided that he and his girlfriend Daphne – whom he called 'Pinkie' – should wait until after the war. 'I wanted very much to get engaged,' Daphne remembers, 'but he said, "No, I don't want you being left behind if I go," and was insistent on that.' They had met two years before the war at a scout group when Daphne was fifteen and Sid eighteen. Soon after, Daphne had left school to work in an insurance company on City Road and Sid started a job as a trainee stockbroker. Sometimes they would meet in their lunch breaks and go to the Whispering Gallery in St Paul's Cathedral. In their free time, like thousands of other young couples, they cycled together or went for walks or to the cinema. Daphne remembers Sid as 'very jokey, but very firm in beliefs and opinions. He had a good head on his shoulders.'

Sid Wakeling hadn't believed his leaders' promises that war could be avoided, that there would be 'peace for our time'. He joined the RAF Volunteer Reserve in April 1939. There would be no trenches, distant generals, mud and blood for him; instead he sought the freedom and excitement of the clean, open skies. At weekends he learnt to fly, and when war broke out he was immediately called up and started combat training. In early July 1940 he joined 87 Squadron based at Church Fenton, near Leeds. But by the middle of August the squadron had gone south, and was in the thick of the action, flying from an airfield just outside Exeter.

On 8 August, Sid had a few days' leave and took Daphne to see *Gone with the Wind* at the Ritz cinema in Leicester Square as a belated eighteenth birthday celebration. For her present, he gave her a gold bracelet engraved with '*Amor Vincit Omnia*' – 'Love conquers all'. They parted at Paddington station.

On 22 August, Sid wrote to Daphne:

My darling,
  Many thanks for your long letter but I am sorry that our first letters crossed. Well dear, I have at last got my own machine. It is brand new and will be super when I have flown it for a few hours. At the moment I am having a 'Felix the Cat' painted on it. My pal [Laurence 'Rubber' Thorogood, Sid's best friend on the squadron] also has his own machine now so the 'Heavenly Twins' are quite happy . . .
  I hope you do not get too bored with life now mother is away but please darling, look after yourself and get as

much rest as you can. You know sweetheart I worry quite a lot about your health so please look after yourself . . .

I have been shifted back to my old flight again so I am still in the same flight as Rubber. Well dear please give my regards to everyone and I hope you are feeling fit.

So, Cheerio Darling

Yours as Ever

Sid xxxxxxxx

Three days later, a force of German dive-bombers was spotted once more assembling over Cherbourg on the northern French coast. Soon they were joined by a swarm of 200 fighters. The thirteen Hurricanes of 87 Squadron were the first to the interception 20,000 feet over Portland. Flying with Wakeling, 'Widge' Gleed wrote later of that moment: 'My mouth feels hellishly dry; there is a strong sinking feeling in my breast. Thank God a doctor isn't listening to my heart. It's absolutely banging away.'[1] The pilots hear a familiar cry over their radios: 'Christ! There they are. Tally-ho,' and swing into attack formation, 'Line astern, line astern, go!' With closing speeds of upwards of 600 miles an hour, the opposing fighters are amongst each other in seconds. The Hurricanes open fire with their eight wing-mounted machine-guns. The Germans respond with cannon – thin-shelled explosive bullets. After the first pass, the fighters wheel about, desperately trying to shake an enemy off their tail or to bring one into their sights. Within moments, there is smoke and flames; an aircraft explodes violently; now there are parachutes drifting through the thickening combat. Sid Wakeling, throwing his aircraft around in the sky, is turning to face an attacker when a cannon shell rips into his cockpit. His comrades hear him over the radio saying his hand's been blown off, but he's going to try to get back to base. But his aircraft is now on fire, and spiralling down towards the Dorset countryside. At the last moment, they see him jump clear, but he falls on a roadside and lies there, the silk of his unopened parachute flapping forlornly in the wind.

On the same day, in west London, Daphne sits down to reply to Sid's last letter:

My darling

Thank you very much for your letter, it's funny how our letters cross, isn't it?

I'm so pleased you've got your own plane dear. I'd be thrilled to bits if I were in your place. Daddy said can't you think of something more original than Felix . . .

Since I last wrote we have had several air-raids. Three yesterday, one caused me to be half an hour late for work . . .

Well dearest I hope you and Rubber are very happy with your new babies, take care of them and I hope they take care of you. How did Rubber get on with that girl you left him with?

Cheerio darling, write as soon as you can spare a minute.

Love from Pinko xxxxxxxxx

Two days later, Daphne was visiting Sid's invalid father as usual. 'I went into the house and there were several people there. They took me home and told my family.' The same day, her last letter to Sid was returned to her. Daphne was sent away to stay with an aunt and uncle and was not allowed by the families to go to the funeral at the Holy Trinity church in Warmwell. A month later she was back at home, and going to work. Everything might have been back to normal, except that she kept thinking she saw Sid walking past her on the street or getting off a bus. 'It was a very long, deep bereavement for me,' she says. 'I suppose I should have been more prepared, but you can't ever really be prepared to hear of the death of someone you're fond of.'

The 'Spitfire Summer' of 1940 would change the lives of virtually everyone living in Britain at the time. The country, and the wider world, too, would by the end of the year be a very different place.

CHAPTER ONE

Blitzkrieg

NO SCENES OF REJOICING MET THE BRITISH DECLARATION of war on 3 September 1939. Unlike in August 1914, there were no patriotic crowds in the streets. Much had changed in the intervening period. The terrible legacy of the First World War, when millions had been maimed or killed, together with the social divisions caused by the Depression and the General Strike, had destroyed the mood of 1914 forever. Moreover, the few years preceding the war had seen the leadership of Britain dithering in the face of aggression from the Fascist states of Italy and Germany. Mussolini, the Italian dictator, had invaded Ethiopia in 1935, and the western democracies had had neither the will nor the means to oppose him. In the same year, Hitler had, by rearming, begun the process of overturning the Versailles Treaty signed by Germany at the end of the First World War. The French and British, pursuing a popular policy of 'appeasement' and wishing to avoid another war at all costs, did nothing to prevent him. The next year Hitler ordered German troops into the demilitarised Rhineland bordering France and in March 1938 Austria was occupied to become part of a Greater Germany. Then, ostensibly to protect the large German population in northern Czechoslovakia, Hitler threatened to invade his neighbour to the south-east.

In September the British Prime Minister Neville Chamberlain travelled to Munich to discuss the crisis, and agreed, along with the French, to Hitler's occupation of the German-speaking area of Czechoslovakia, the Sudetenland. Chamberlain returned to London brandishing his famous 'peace for our time' scrap of paper. But it became apparent almost immediately that Hitler should never have been trusted. By March 1939 the rest of northern Czechoslovakia was occupied and a client state, Slovakia, established in the south. At last France and Britain began to wake up to the threat and rearmament was accelerated, air-raid shelters built and gas masks distributed. In March, Britain and France pledged to defend Belgium, Holland and Poland against attack. In response to this growing firmness, in August 1939 Hitler concluded a non-aggression pact with his bitter ideological enemy the Soviet Union, which included a secret clause that agreed the partition of Poland between the two states.

Having staged a supposed aggression by Poland on the border, Hitler ordered German tanks to cross the frontier on 1 September and Britain and France reluctantly declared war two days later. Against a Polish army of some forty divisions still in the process of mobilisation, the Germans fielded sixty-two battle-ready divisions, of which six were armoured and ten mechanised. The Germans also had a new style of warfare, Blitzkrieg or 'lightning war', in which fast-moving tanks and armoured divisions smashed through front lines supported by synchronised attacks by Luftwaffe (German air force) dive-bombers. Many of the German pilots had had combat experience fighting in the Spanish Civil War (1936–39) on the side of Franco, and the Luftwaffe attacked with some 1,300 modern combat aircraft. To stop this the Poles had only a few hundred PZL fighters and light bombers. The PZL single-seater aircraft, with an open cockpit and a fixed undercarriage, was obsolete compared with the Germans' Messerschmitt Bf 109 fighter.

The Luftwaffe struck hard and fast on the first day of the invasion. By the end of 1 September much of the Polish air force had been destroyed on the ground by bombing attacks. The Polish pilots fought bravely and skilfully, using the PZL's great manoeuvrability to good effect. Two hundred and eighty-five German aircraft were destroyed in the course of the campaign, but it was not enough to prevent the German bombers and dive-bombers from attacking lines of communication and command centres to devastating effect. The Polish army, although determined, was poorly equipped and badly placed to defend the 1,750-mile frontier with East Prussia and Nazi-occupied Czechoslovakia. The pride of its forces, the cavalry, was no match for the modern tanks and Blitzkrieg tactics of the Germans. By 17 September Warsaw was surrounded and Luftwaffe aircraft were in place to bomb the city into submission. On the same day Red Army units entered Poland from the east, as had been agreed. The defenders of Warsaw gave up on 27 September. By 6 October the battle for Poland was over and the victorious German divisions were heading back westwards towards France and Britain. The only setback for the Germans had been the escape of some 100,000 Polish soldiers and pilots through Romania. These men were to fight hard against the Nazis throughout the war, most famously at Monte Cassino in Italy and during the Battle of Britain. Pole Wladyslaw Gnys, who had been the first fighter pilot of the war to shoot down a German aircraft, would, within ten months, be flying Hurricanes out of Northolt in England.

But even in Berlin, there had been few celebrations of the start of the war, and when Poland was defeated and the disputed Danzig corridor was back in German hands, many expected the war to end. There was more concern about newly introduced rationing on textiles and clothing and about shortages of coal and potatoes. But without a withdrawal from

Poland there was no prospect of peace for the British and French, and American efforts through President Roosevelt's envoy Sumner Welles found favour in neither Berlin nor Rome.

The Poles had hoped that their agreement with the western powers would have led to an attack into the west of Germany on the part of Britain and France. But apart from a half-hearted offensive towards the Saarland between 8 September and 1 October, the Allies, expecting a replay of the events of 1914–15, busied themselves with defensive measures. Along the Franco-German border, the massive Maginot Line, a series of underground forts considered impregnable, was further strengthened. Whole armies were garrisoned within the deep bunkers and tunnels to man the network of artillery emplacements and machine-gun nests.

The line of defences ended, however, at the Belgian border. Here the rest of the French divisions and the British Expeditionary Force were to be waiting, prepared to move to positions in Holland and Belgium to counter what seemed to be the inevitable attack through the neutral Low Countries. However, co-operation with the Belgians and Dutch could not be properly established because the small countries wanted to preserve their neutrality and avoid provoking an attack from Germany.

The first British presence in France was the RAF, which had been divided into two sections: the Advanced Air Striking Force (AASF), based in Rheims; and the Air Component of the British Expeditionary Force. The former were to reinforce the French army along the frontier with Germany, while the latter were to operate in conjunction with the BEF. The AASF consisted of ten bomber and two fighter squadrons. The bombers were Fairey Battles, an obsolete three-seater type; the fighters, though, were Hurricanes. The Air Component consisted of four squadrons of Lysanders, two-seaters mainly for observation purposes; four squadrons of Blenheims, two-engined fighter-bombers; four squadrons of Hurricanes; and two of Gloster Gladiators, an obsolete biplane.

Five army divisions, commanded by Field Marshall Lord Gort, started to arrive in France on 10 September. This was pretty much the total strength of the regular British army. But it was clear that the French, whose conscript army numbered eighty-eight divisions, expected a greater contribution. This meant that the Territorials, reserve part-time soldiers, were also needed.

Among these Territorials was Lance Bombadier Peter Lambert. A twenty-two-year-old insurance clerk, Lambert 'couldn't imagine using a bayonet or that sort of thing'. But he had seen the war and conscription looming, and in order to be able to have a choice of unit, in April 1939 he joined the Territorial Army (TA) in a Royal Artillery regiment based in Leith. 'Conditions in the Territorial Army were chaotic,' he remembers. 'Because of the threatened war, there was an immense drive for recruits and the administration was very stretched. Like many others, I joined knowing nothing about the army.' Twice a week, and at weekends, there were 'drill nights' and at the second of these the Regimental Sergeant Major asked, 'All those who know algebra one pace step forward march.' Although old soldiers had taught him not to volunteer for anything, Lambert stepped forward and to his surprise was appointed a surveyor, responsible for siting and targeting the artillery.

In the summer of 1939, the regiment was sent to camp at Larkhill. Finally issued with an ill-fitting uniform, Lambert found his first proper taste of army life a terrible shock. Such was the extent of the drinking that an orderly would come around the crowded tents each morning with a bucket, asking, 'Any sick here?' Issued with knives and forks, it soon became clear that the only way to clean them was by digging them into the ground.

On 1 September the regiment was brought into the regular army and two days later war was declared. The regiment was then converted to 'heavies' and equipped with 9.2-inch howitzers, only partially mobile relics of the last war, which took about five hours to get into action, involving a great deal of digging to provide sufficient ballast, and which were intended for static, trench warfare. However, they did also have a battery of more modern and mobile six-inch guns. From Larkhill, Lambert was given five days' leave. He immediately contacted his fiancée, Mary.

> I suggested we got married on the Saturday. By a miracle
> of organisation, she and Lily May, her mother, put
> together a white wedding, got a special licence and much
> to our joy we were married on Saturday 7 October. We
> had three days' honeymoon at the Strand Palace Hotel,
> which was the only place available. I then returned to
> Larkhill, not to see Mary again until after Dunkirk in
> the following June. Returning to camp was pretty
> unpleasant . . .

Back at camp, Lambert continued to learn the surveying business, fixing gun positions on a map along with targets. Apart from that, the training was rudimentary.

> We still learned nothing about soldiering in the true
> sense. I hardly knew one end of a rifle from another
> and the Bren gun was a mystery to me. We dug a lot,
> latrines and gun pits, in that order, and we did have
> one movement exercise on the insistence of the
> second-in-command who was a First World War veteran.
> This was pretty disastrous: it was at night and many got

lost. It did not augur well for our move to France,
which came on 27 October.

In common with many of the soldiers it was the first time
Lambert had been abroad. He arrived expecting to hear
gunfire, 'but there was nothing'. Stationed at Lens, he enjoyed
travelling around the French countryside investigating potential gun positions, and if his own regiment seemed unpre-
pared, he was impressed by the efficiency of the regular army
units stationed around them. For the British army, he
believed, retreat, let alone defeat, was not considered possible.

Indeed, by the beginning of May, the German forces along
their western border were outnumbered by the troops facing
them. About 135 German divisions faced a total of 156 Allied
divisions, including those of Holland and Belgium. In tanks,
too, the French outnumbered the Germans by 4,000 to
2,800, but the French tanks were dispersed along the line, in
most cases attached to infantry or semi-motorised divisions.
The decisive advantage for the Germans in numbers was in
the air, where the battle-hardened Luftwaffe had more aircraft
than all its adversaries put together.

But apart from occasional skirmishing, nothing happened.
All along the eastern frontier of France the Allied troops
waited. The RAF flew reconnaissance missions and hastily
improved the soggy French airfields. Bombing of Germany
was forbidden for fear of reprisals. In Britain, this period,
between September 1939 and May 1940, became known as
the Phoney War; in France *la Drôle de Guerre*, the joke war; in
Germany as *Sitzkrieg*.

But across the lines, the Germans were working out their
plan of attack. Hitler had wanted to move against the West as
early as October, but bad weather and the advice of his
generals held back the German offensive. Meanwhile, their
plans evolved. There was no question of the main attack

being against the Maginot Line, but a repeat of the 1914 Schlieffen Plan, when the attack on France had come through the north of the Low Countries, seemed too predictable. Events took a hand when an aircraft carrying details of 'Case Yellow', a planned German attack through northern Belgium and Holland, crash-landed on 10 January on Belgian soil. Suddenly a new plan was needed. This opened the door to Erich von Manstein to press the case for his idea of combining an attack in the north into Holland to hold and engage the Allied forces with a strong armoured punch though southern Belgium and Luxembourg, just north of the end of the Maginot Line. In terms of terrain, this was the most difficult part of the line, particularly for tanks. Once any force had picked its way through the Ardennes forest with its narrow, boggy valleys, they would be faced by the great water obstacle of the river Meuse. Nevertheless planning on the new 'Operation Sickle Stroke' began and the German army moved quickly to concentrate their tank force opposite the forest.

While the waiting soldiers in France stagnated, the Soviet Union invaded Finland in an attempt to recover disputed territory. The Red Army suffered early setbacks, and attention in Paris, London and Berlin was focused on Scandinavia, in particular on the Swedish iron ore fields on which the Allies believed Germany's arms industry depended. A disorganised attempt by French and British forces to seize supply lines from the ore fields foundered when German forces moved to seize Denmark and Norway on 9 April. The incompetence of the operation resulted in an angry backlash against Prime Minister Neville Chamberlain. On 30 April influential Conservative MP Henry 'Chips' Channon noted in his diary 'more talk of a cabal against poor Neville. "They" are saying that it is 1915 all over again, that Winston should be Prime Minister as he has more vigour and the country behind him.'[1] During his long period in the political wilderness, Churchill had endlessly warned of the threat of another war and had urged rearmament. Few among politicians and the public had wanted to hear that in the 1930s, but now that his predictions had come true, Churchill was viewed with a new respect. In 1939 he had been made First Sea Lord, in charge of the Admiralty, and in the following months he took on more and more responsibility for the running of the war. By May 1940 he was head of the Military Co-ordination Committee. But although he was one of the few senior Conservatives not tarred by the Munich brush, he was distrusted by many in his own party and had the reputation of being unstable. Moreover, some of the blame for Norway could be laid at his door.

But crucially, Churchill was a very different creature from Chamberlain. In February 1940, both Churchill and Chamberlain had been on HMS *Boudicea* returning with the rest of the Supreme War Council after a meeting with their opposite numbers in France. First Lieutenant Hubert Fox was on the boat and wrote to his father about the distinguished guests:

We lay at the quay in Boulogne waiting to take them back. Presently the neat figure of Neville Chamberlain approached, surrounded by his retinue like a popular master at a preparatory school conducting the Sunday walk. One or two of the boys preferred to trudge along by themselves. Among these was Winston Churchill.

They came on board, most of them going up to the bridge where they watched all that happened with great animation. The Prime Minister got cold so we had some soup brought up to him. Warm in the wardroom, Churchill growled, 'Tell the Prime Minister to come and have some gin.'

Churchill sat in the wardroom at the long polished

table drinking port and sucking a cigar. He was flicking
over the pages of *Blighty*, a popular magazine with
pictures of ladies without clothes. Later we lost him
altogether for a time and eventually found him on the
stokers' mess deck, sitting on a mess table swapping
yarns.[2]

By 7 May, as the Commons met to debate the failures of the
Norway campaign, there was a feeling in the House and in
the country that Britain needed this sort of man to unite and
invigorate the nation. Even Chamberlain's long-time allies
were scathing of his leadership. MP Leo Amery, quoting
Cromwell, told Chamberlain in ringing tones, 'You have sat
too long for any good you have been doing. Depart, I say,
and let us have done with you. In the name of God, go!'[3]

As the debate continued, Churchill stood by his Prime
Minister, but the mood of the House, particularly on the
Opposition benches, had turned against the complacent and
ineffective Chamberlain. At the end of the debate was a vote
of censure. Many Conservatives abstained or voted against
Chamberlain, whose majority was slashed. As soon as the
result was announced the Opposition benches started chant-
ing at Chamberlain, 'Go! Go! Go! Go!' Chamberlain still
hoped to rescue the situation by forming a National Coali-
tion Government. The Labour leaders were happy to join
such a government, but not under Chamberlain. The Prime
Minister had two obvious successors, the Foreign Secretary
Lord Halifax and the First Lord of the Admiralty Winston
Churchill. On 9 May, both were called in to see Chamberlain, who asked them whom he should recommend that the
King request to form a new government. It was clear that
Chamberlain himself favoured Halifax. 'I have had many
important interviews in my public life,' Churchill wrote later,
'and this was certainly the most important. Usually I talk a

great deal, but on this occasion I was silent.'[4]

Eventually the silence was broken by the urbane figure of Halifax, who said that as he was not in charge of the running of the war and not, as a lord, able to lead the House of Commons, he would give way to Churchill. 'Winston did not demur,' Halifax noted at the time.[5] The next day, Churchill was summoned to the Palace and asked to form a new government. He immediately asked senior Opposition figures to join a new Cabinet and himself took on the mantle of Minister of Defence as well as Prime Minister. A new ministry for aircraft production was formed, with the controversial newspaper magnate and Churchill crony Lord Beaverbrook at its head. The task before the new government was enormous. Churchill himself, although at this stage by no means enjoying the unanimous support of Parliament, King or people, bristled with confidence, and met the challenge of leadership with relish: 'I was conscious of a profound sense of relief. At last I had the authority to give directions over the whole scene. I felt as if I were walking with destiny, and that all my past life had been but a preparation for this hour and for this trial.'[6]

The trial, though, was only just beginning. On the morning of 10 May the Germans launched Operation Sickle Stroke. Blitzkreig in the West had begun.

T he attack started, as the Allies had expected, with a move in the north against Holland and Belgium, and the Allied troops began to move up to their planned defensive lines along the river Dyle. What they had not expected, however, was the speed and effectiveness of the German armour and dive-bombers. By the end of the first day of the campaign German panzers had already penetrated deep into

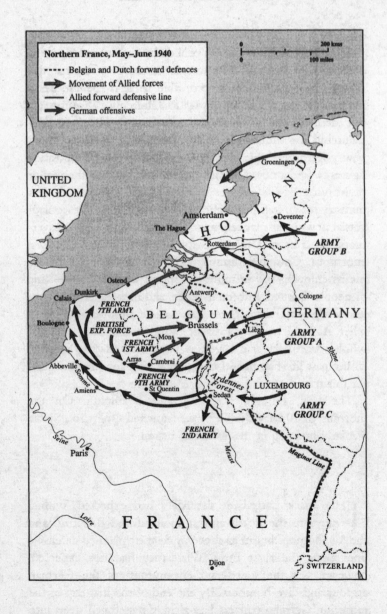

Northern France, May–June 1940

- - - - Belgian and Dutch forward defences
→ Movement of Allied forces
— Allied forward defensive line
→ German offensives

200 kms
100 miles

UNITED
KINGDOM

HOLLAND

Groeningen

Amsterdam
The Hague
Deventer

Rotterdam

ARMY
GROUP B

Ostend
Antwerp
Cologne

Calais
Dunkirk

FRENCH
7TH ARMY

BELGIUM
GERMANY

Boulogne

BRITISH
EXP. FORCE

Brussels
Liège

Dyle

FRENCH
1ST ARMY

Mons

ARMY
GROUP A

Rhine

Abbeville

Arras
Cambrai

FRENCH
9TH ARMY

St Quentin

Ardennes
Forest

LUXEMBOURG

Amiens

Somme

Sedan

Meuse

ARMY
GROUP C

FRENCH
2ND ARMY

Seine

Maginot Line

Paris

FRANCE

Loire

Dijon

SWITZERLAND

Holland. All day, paratroopers dropped from the sky to hold important bridges and disrupt Allied lines of communication.

As the BEF advanced to meet this threat, crossing the battlefields on which so many of their fathers and uncles had fallen in the previous war, the RAF contingent in France was reinforced by squadrons of Hurricane fighters from Britain, including 501 Squadron of the Auxiliary Air Force. Aged twenty-four, Peter Hairs was the old man of the squadron. Before the war he had worked in a bank and been a member of the Volunteer Reserve. When war was declared he was given the basic flying training and by December 1939 he had his wings and his commission. His next priority was to finalise the details of his forthcoming wedding to Eileen, a successful model. The banns had been read at their local church and the wedding was set for January 1940. But without warning his planned leave was cancelled. The young couple went to visit the local priest. 'Oh yes,' said the reverend. 'I can fit you in earlier. When would be suitable?'

'Oh . . . next Thursday?'

With the vicar on board, there were some quick calls to be made to friends. 'Are you doing anything next Thursday?'

'No. Why?'

'We're getting married.'

After the wedding on 21 December, Peter Hairs was sent to complete his Operations Training at St Athan in South Wales, where he learnt to fly Hurricanes. He almost did not make it after an incident in which the dangers of high-speed flying in Hurricanes were brutally brought home to him. 'There were three of us flying in formation. Flight One was leading and I was number two. We were flying in a northerly direction towards the mountains in South Wales in thick cloud when suddenly we saw the ground immediately below us, less than fifty feet away. Our leader said "Climb independently." ' Flying in formation in this situation involved following the lead plane visually. But suddenly it was gone and the two following pilots had to revert to their instruments. Even for more experienced flyers it usually took a few moments to make the transition. 'I knew I was doing all sorts of antics, the instruments were going all over the place, I must have been upside down half the time and doing steep turns and diving and climbing. At any rate, eventually I got up above the cloud and back to the aerodrome.' The third pilot was not so lucky. According to the subsequent inquiry he was doing a steep turn when he hit the ground. Peter Hairs could only console himself that the pilot would not have known much about it.

Hairs was at a posting in Chichester when the order came through that the squadron was being sent to France. Eileen Hairs remembers sitting in a coffee house in the town when another pilot came in and said simply, 'We're off to France at twelve o'clock.' Up at the aerodrome, people were dashing about as the squadron made its last-minute preparations. Peter, though, was to fly out the next day on a transport aircraft. It was to be an inauspicious arrival on the battlefield for the squadron. Hairs' transport plane landed safely but the next one in stalled about a hundred feet above the ground and crash-landed, killing a flight lieutenant and injuring several others.

Faced by the seasoned squadrons of the Luftwaffe, the British pilots had to learn quickly. In his first engagement over France, Peter Hairs was with Flight Commander Charles Griffiths and one other Hurricane as they closed on a lone enemy bomber: 'I saw this Dornier 17 and chased it and I started firing. I was concentrating on the Dornier and forgetting that I was just a few feet from my leader's plane. Out of the corner of my eye, I suddenly saw his wing tip appearing in front of me. It's rather surprising I didn't knock a bit of it off.' But in spite of this near miss, the attack hit home and the Dornier plunged earthwards, with only the rear gunner managing to bale out. When Hairs got back to the current base, the same German rear gunner was sitting on the couch in the room where the rest of the squadron were having breakfast. He was drinking a cup of coffee. After he had got over his surprise, Hairs discovered that the German had been picked up by a pilot on the way to join 501.

For the newly married Eileen, this was a period of intense worry, not helped by the lack of communication from the pilots. In the five weeks that Peter was in France, Eileen only received two postcards. These were not ordinary postcards but 'field cards' that had 'I am well/I am not well' printed on them. The pilots simply ticked the one that applied.

Other squadrons were making the day trip across the Channel to the battle. One such was 32 Squadron, also flying Hurricanes, who were based at Biggin Hill. One of the pilots was Air Commodore Peter Brothers, then a flight lieutenant.

Peter Brothers had joined the RAF in January 1936. His father had wanted him to settle down and join his company, but Peter had the flying bug, and so for his sixteenth birthday he had been allowed to learn to fly in the hope that it would get it out of his system. Instead of which, when he was seventeen and a half, he joined the RAF. During the winter period of the Phoney War, his squadron had been flying convoy patrols and occasionally scrambling for suspected hostile aircraft over the Channel. On 10 May, as the German attack began, they were ordered to strafe the airfield at the Hague, which had been captured by enemy paratroopers.

I led the squadron in. To our surprise, as we dived down
to attack we saw a mass of troop transport aircraft,
German Ju 52s, on the airfield, but they were all burnt

out in the middle, leaving only wingtips and tails undamaged. Anyhow we shot them up and then we discovered one hidden between two hangars, so we set that on fire and went home rejoicing. We discovered much later that the Dutch had recaptured the airfield about two hours before we arrived and burnt out these German aircraft. The hidden one had been kept for them to escape to England in. I don't think that we were very popular.

This incident typified the confusion and lack of communication on the ground in the Low Countries as the Germans made relentless gains and refugees blocked the roads. On one visit to 615 Squadron posted in Belgium, 32 Squadron and Peter Brothers found the airfield under artillery attack as huge numbers of refugees streamed past. What was more, there seemed to be enemies everywhere: '615 were pretty jumpy . . . one of their sergeant pilots hadn't turned up for breakfast and the early-morning call was on. When they went to his room, he was lying in bed with a knife stuck in his chest. Obviously some fifth columnist or somebody had nipped in and murdered him in bed, so they were going round looking over their shoulders all the time.'

Much of the panic was caused by the Luftwaffe. The Ju 87 'Stuka' dive-bombers in particular, with their ghastly high-pitched scream as they attacked, contributed much to the demoralisation of the defenders. Nearly 1,400 German aircraft, bombers, dive-bombers and fighters, attacked Allied air bases day and night. The small air forces of Holland and Belgium were destroyed almost straightaway and the French air force and the RAF sustained heavy losses, particularly amongst their older aircraft. Without early warning from radar, there was not always time to get airborne before bombs started falling on the runway. Peter Hairs' squadron was caught on the ground at Boos, near Rouen:

> We were just sitting around waiting for something to
> happen and suddenly on the horizon, some aircraft
> appeared, flying very low. They were Heinkel 111s,
> about a dozen of them, I think. Another dozen came
> after them and they started dropping bombs on us. I
> leapt into my Hurricane and tried to get it started but
> by this time the bombs were falling around all over the
> place. I spotted a colleague of mine nearby taking
> shelter by a little brick-built hut with oil drums around
> it. I dashed across to join him and crouched under a
> smaller oil drum. I could feel the blast of the bombs as
> they dropped. After they'd gone over we breathed a
> sigh of relief. At this moment we had a proper look at
> this building and saw a notice on it – 'Défense de
> Fumer'. I don't know what was in there but it must
> have been aviation fuel or bombs.

But the main German thrust, as planned, came through the Ardennes forest. Between the end of the Maginot Line and the advancing armies to the north, there were only nine Allied divisions, including three third-rate French divisions. By 12 May Sedan had fallen and a hole had opened up in the French lines. In London the next day, the new Prime Minister addressed the House in sombre tones:

> I would say to the House, as I said to those who have
> joined this Government: 'I have nothing to offer but
> blood, toil, tears and sweat.'
> We have before us an ordeal of the most grievous
> kind. We have before us many, many long months of
> struggle and suffering. You ask, what is our policy? I will

say: it is to wage war, by sea, land and air, with all our
might and with all the strength that God can give us.

Attacking the 'monstrous tyranny' of the Nazis, Churchill
concluded:

> But I take up my task with buoyancy and hope. I feel
> sure that our cause will not be suffered to fail among
> men. At this time I feel entitled to claim the aid of all,
> and I say, 'Come then, let us go forward together with
> our united strength.'[7]

Privately, though, Churchill knew the situation was grave. As
he was addressing the House, the Germans were crossing the
Meuse and starting to roll westwards towards the Channel
coast behind the French front, threatening to cut the Allied
forces in two. The French Prime Minister, Paul Reynaud,
reporting the German breakthrough to Churchill, pleaded for
more fighter squadrons to be sent to France. The War Cabinet
met that evening, 13 May, to consider the position. It was
still not clear which action constituted the main German
thrust and several present suggested that the German objective might be to consolidate in Holland and Belgium in
preparation for a major attack on Britain herself. In the light
of this, the Air Minster, the former Liberal leader Sir
Archibald Sinclair, argued that with home defence ever more
important, it was impossible to send large numbers of fighters
to France. Already, he pointed out, there were fewer than the
minimum agreed number of squadrons available to defend
Britain itself.

Meanwhile in the north, too, setbacks continued. As
Churchill wrote to American President Franklin Delano
Roosevelt on 15 May, 'The small countries are simply
smashed up, one by one, like matchwood.'[8] Rotterdam was

savagely bombed on 14 May and the next day the Dutch surrendered.

The Belgians for the moment held on, and the RAF pilots in the north continued to fight bravely. Gunther Büsgen, then flying the top German fighter, the Messerschmitt Bf 109, remembers meeting a British airman who had been shot down. In common with most of the Luftwaffe pilots, Büsgen, at twenty-six, was slightly older than the majority of his British counterparts. He had been in the Luftwaffe since 1937 and had already had to make one forced landing after having been shot at by a French fighter. He remembers:

> One foolhardy young English pilot was engaged with a
> German fighter right over our heads at the airfield. They
> circled round and round each other until finally the
> Englishman was shot down. Mercifully he was unhurt,
> and was greeted warmly by us all. He had a few words of
> German and made himself at home with us, looking on
> us as comrades of the air. We took care of him, gave him
> a drink and talked to him and treated him very much as
> a friend. Then our SS came and arrested him and took
> him off to prison and that's the last we saw of him.

Meanwhile Peter Brothers' squadron continued to make the day trip to the battle. But this was beginning to take its toll. The squadron left Biggin Hill by four in the morning and often would not return until ten o'clock at night. In between they had to deal not only with the German fighters but also with the confusion that reigned behind the French lines: 'We'd go to a French airfield, refuel and try and get some instructions but everything was chaotic and so we'd just go off and do a patrol around to see what we could find.'

Peter Hairs' 501 Squadron, too, found conditions in France difficult. 'Navigating over France wasn't easy. We didn't have all the facilities of Ground Control, who could tell us where we were and how to get back, so there were occasions when we got lost. In fact the whole squadron got lost on one occasion.'

But the enemy were everywhere, the skill of the battle-hardened Luftwaffe pilots in marked contrast to some of the British. Peter Brothers was an experienced pilot but, unlike most of the German pilots, had not been in actual air-to-air combat until 18 May. He remembers the shock.

The first real combat we got, we met a bunch of 109s going in the opposite direction. Our reactions were very slow, I remember seeing this thing whiz over my head going the opposite way and it was so close, I could see the oil streaks on the fuselage. I thought, Good Lord, it's the bloody enemy. I looked round to see where they'd gone and they were turning around to attack us. We got mixed up with them and I managed to shoot one of them down.

A burst of machine-gun fire from Brothers' Hurricane hit the German's cockpit and 'blew it apart'. It was the first time he had killed. 'I didn't feel great regret,' he says, 'but I did think, Oh, I didn't mean that really, I just wanted to knock a wing off.'

Returning to his French base, Brothers was annoyed to find that there were no ground crew.

We had to refill the aircraft ourselves from tins, which was a laborious business. At that time the only way to get the Hurricanes started was to have a chap each side winding the handles, so I'd get into mine and we'd start mine and then leave it ticking over. Then I'd jump out and wind somebody else's until we'd got them all going. It was pretty ghastly and the French, I'm afraid, were totally demoralised by this time.

On one of the airfields, there was a French fighter doing aerobatics over the airfield and a Dornier 17 at about four thousand feet and we thought, Oh Christ, we're going to be caught on the ground, but he [the Dornier] just flew straight past us. The French Station Commander was there and we said, 'Gosh, tell that chap doing aerobatics about the Dornier 17,' and he said, 'He's only authorised for aerobatics not combat today.' We thought, Oh my God, what have we got as allies?

Churchill had noticed a lack of morale among the French on an earlier visit to the Maginot Line, being struck 'by the air of calm aloofness, by the seemingly poor quality of the work in hand, by the lack of visible activity of any kind'.[9] Faced with the German tanks, some of the French soldiers ran away or surrendered in large numbers. A German journalist was amazed when at one point, 20,000 French soldiers, together with their officers, marched in formation into captivity. Elsewhere the French fought hard, but were hampered by a lack of communication and poor support from the air.

By the evening of 15 May, the Germans were forty miles beyond Sedan and moving rapidly westwards as the French front collapsed before them. That morning Reynaud, the French Prime Minister, had again phoned Churchill telling him all was lost, and imploring him to send more fighters. The War Cabinet met to discuss what to do. Already the British air forces had lost 206 of their original 474 planes of all types. But Churchill, confused as to the number of squadrons it had been agreed were needed for home defence, instructed that ten more squadrons be readied. This message found its way to Air Marshal Sir Hugh Dowding, the head of Fighter Command. He was incensed.

In an unprecedented move, Dowding asked the Air Minister, Sir Archibald Sinclair, whether he could present his case in person to the Cabinet. When it assembled, for the fourth time that day, there were some thirty people present, including Dowding's friend Lord Beaverbrook, the new Minister for Aircraft Production. Dowding sat on the same side of the table as the Prime Minister, about six places to his right. The atmosphere was tense, the most highly charged Dowding had known. Asked to present his case, he spoke for about ten minutes. It was soon clear that the majority of the meeting were against him and in favour of sending more aircraft. His Air Ministry colleagues showed no sign of backing him up. Then, suddenly, Dowding stood and went straight up to Churchill, pulling from his pocket a piece of paper on which he had sketched a graph in red ink showing the curve of Hurricane losses over the last few days. His message to Churchill was blunt: 'If the line goes on at the same rate for the next ten days there won't be a single Hurricane left in either France or England.'

Returning home late that night, Dowding was unsure whether his argument had hit home. 'In a mood of desperation', he wrote an official letter to the Under Secretary of State for Air, demanding that Britain should not be left defenceless in the event of France capitulating.

The next morning brought further bad news from France and a plea from Gamelin, the French commander-in-chief, for ten more squadrons to be sent straightaway. In spite of everything Dowding had said, Churchill still wanted to send another six squadrons. Sinclair protested, saying it would be against the express wishes of Dowding, and the figure was lowered to four squadrons with two more in readiness to depart.

That afternoon, Churchill, together with two military commanders, made a desperate visit to Paris to confer with Reynaud and the ageing and indecisive Gamelin. As

Churchill later recalled, 'Utter dejection was written on every face.' The requests for more fighters continued. Churchill was well aware of the pressing need for a counter-attack against the panzer thrust towards the Channel coast. 'Where is the strategic reserve?' he asked. 'General Gamelin turned to me,' wrote Churchill, 'and, with a shake of the head and shrug, said: "*Aucune* [There is none]." There was another long pause. Outside in the garden of the Quai d'Orsay clouds of smoke arose from large bonfires, and I saw from the window venerable officials pushing wheelbarrows of archives on to them. Already, therefore, the evacuation of Paris was being prepared.'[10]

Churchill returned that night to the British Embassy in Paris and telegraphed to the War Cabinet to send six more squadrons of fighters. Although the first response was a yes, in the end a plan was worked out whereby the six squadrons would be 'available for operations in France' but remain based in England. Apart from anything else, the facilities in France were inadequate to base so many squadrons there.

Furthermore, British confidence in the French forces' ability to continue fighting had been badly damaged by the breakthrough at Sedan and by the mood of defeatism Churchill had encountered in his meeting. On his return to England on the morning of 17 May, Churchill instructed Chamberlain to start drawing up a contingency plan for the withdrawal of the BEF and RAF from France altogether. Churchill's private secretary, 'Jock' Colville, noted in his diary, 'Winston is depressed. He says the French are crumpling up as completely as did the Poles and that our forces in Belgium will inevitably have to withdraw in order to maintain contact with the French. There is, of course, a risk that the BEF may be cut off if the French do not rally in time.'[11]

The BEF had itself begun to retreat from the river Dyle on 16 May. Desperately short of armoured vehicles, the British army, like the French, had been poorly equipped to deal with the tanks and dive-bombers of the Wehrmacht. The RAF, too, struggling with the chaotic facilities in France, found itself outnumbered and outgunned. On 21 May, a young pilot from Macclesfield, Eric Bann, managed to get a letter off to his parents.

> . . . Have been having a real rough time, lost nearly all my clothes and have been sleeping in any old place, plus getting into some real hot places. We have bagged about forty German planes in the last four days but their numbers are terrific. Have been going in for about six of us to forty and fifty of theirs, the air was thick. I think we lost the Flight Commander yesterday, what a nice chap, they said he was engaged by about ten fighters and went down fighting madly.
>
> Our squadron have been flying every day and we are very tired . . . Believe me, to see the German dive-bombers in their hundreds cutting at our poor troops makes you only too glad to help – it's terrible.

Bann ends the letter hoping 'with God's good grace' that he might see his parents again. Just before, though, he cannot resist a note of pride: 'Been flying Hurricanes and Spitfires – what about that, Father?'

Down on the ground, for Territorial regiments such as Peter Lambert's, much of the new equipment they did have was still unfamiliar to them and the start of combat came as a great shock: 'When the balloon went up, we were pretty bewildered, not to say scared. We hadn't got the sort of discipline needed to cope with such a situation.'

As the Germans pressed the retreating armies in the north, the southern part of the 'sickle stroke' was advancing rapidly. It was now clear that the French Ninth Army, originally positioned opposite the southern thrust from the Ardennes, had suffered a serious defeat. As the German panzers raced towards the Channel, they now encountered virtually no resistance. On some days they were able to cover up to forty miles, an unheard-of rate of movement for an army. On 18 May the leading tanks reached Cambrai, and two days later Amiens fell and the Allied armies were effectively cut in two when German panzer commander Guderian's divisions reached Abbeville on the coast.

The next day Churchill broadcast to the nation. 'I speak to you,' he said in grave tones, 'for the first time as Prime Minister, in a solemn hour for the life of our country, of our Empire, of our Allies, and, above all, of the cause of Freedom.' Although, he said, it was foolish to 'disguise the gravity of the hour', he urged ever greater effort for victory and vowed 'never to surrender ourselves to servitude or shame'. Already he spoke of what was to come: 'the battle for our Island – for all that Britain is, and Britain means'. The tone and determination of the speech enthused friends and foes alike. Colville, who had been highly sceptical of Churchill when he first took over, wrote in his diary, 'Whatever Winston's shortcomings, he seems to be the man for the occasion. His spirit is indomitable and even if France and England should be lost, I feel he would carry on the crusade himself with a band of privateers.'[12] There is no doubt the morale of the country was lifted, just as the situation in France deteriorated further.

On 20 May, the ineffectual French commander-in-chief Gamelin was replaced by Weygand, who immediately ordered a counterattack against the German armoured column. The next day, in the north, BEF commander Lord Gort launched a limited offensive on Arras, which rattled the Germans briefly before Rommel's 7th Panzer Division, along with two other tank divisions, contained the attack. A planned French offensive south of the corridor failed to materialise amongst growing panic and confusion, caused largely by a breakdown in communications between the Allied armies. Unlike the Germans, the Allies relied on landlines rather than radios, and most had been disrupted. Soon they were reduced to using motorcycle couriers and runners. On 22 May the Germans reached the outskirts of Calais and Boulogne, cutting off supply routes to the BEF. The next day, Gort was forced to put his army on half rations. The British field marshal, having lost confidence in the French and threatened with the capture or destruction of his entire army, now had no option but to retreat to the coast. As the scale of the disaster filtered down the ranks, there was disbelief and anger. Peter Lambert, who had remained in France with the immobile heavy artillery batteries of his regiment, was aghast.

> The very thought of the British army being in retreat to the extent that we had to abandon everything was unbelievable. Despite all the meandering around northern France one felt that, sooner or later, things would stabilise and we would get into action.
>
> Then came the night when we were told by our sergeant that the British army was to retreat to the coast around Dunkirk where we were to be taken off by the Royal Navy. Not one of the gun positions we had so diligently surveyed during the Phoney War was used. Instead we had trundled these large things around the northern French countryside, preparing for action only once, but not firing a single shot. We were told to leave our vehicles having made them as useless as possible. The guns were to be damaged and dumped in the La Bassee canal and we were to make our way on foot to Dunkirk.
>
> So began our trek to the coast. We moved at night to avoid the bombing, accompanied everywhere by the

barking of dogs whose owners had fled, leaving them to fend for themselves. Everyone was afraid of becoming detached from their comrades and lost. We had no sense of order. Morale was low. We could hardly be described as a military unit and on several occasions I remember hearing tanks all around us not knowing whether they were friend or foe.

In such chaos, lack of experience was quickly exposed. The commanding officer of Lambert's regiment was weak, and when things got rough he broke down completely and started drinking heavily. At one time, when the Germans were very close, he had wanted to surrender the regiment to them, and had to be restrained by the other officers. Other units, both French and British, reported men's nerves shattered by the confusion and the relentless dive-bombing attacks by the screaming Stukas.

Gort had little confidence that with German panzers only a few miles down the coast at Calais he could save any of his army or their equipment. Alan Brooke, commanding Gort's II Corps, wrote on 23 May, 'Nothing but a miracle can save the BEF now.'[13]

CHAPTER TWO

Dunkirk

I T HAD NOT ONLY BEEN THE ALLIES WHO HAD BEEN SURPRISED by the speed of the panzer advance. The German high command, too, could scarcely believe it. Concerned that the tank crews might be exhausted and vulnerable to counter-attack, such as had occurred in a limited way at Arras on 21 May, Hitler gave the order for the tanks to halt on 24 May in order to consolidate and allow the infantry support to catch up. With hindsight, it was one of the most strategically inept decisions Hitler was to make during the entire war. He had been concerned about his panzers becoming bogged down amongst the canals and waterways surrounding Dunkirk, but in fact it took another two days for the Allied forces to cross into comparative safety behind the 'Canal Line' – a natural defensive line consisting of the Aa and Colme canals.

By this time the hastily put-together plan for the evacuation of Dunkirk – Operation Dynamo – was nearly ready. On 20 May there had been a high-level meeting in Dover Castle to plan for an evacuation across the Channel. At that stage it had been hoped that the BEF would still be able to counter-attack successfully and hold on on the continent. But at Dover Castle planning on the operation started straightaway under the stewardship of Vice-Admiral Bertram Ramsay, who in the First World War had commanded a destroyer of the Dover Patrol and thus knew the Straits as well as anyone. In the tunnels and caverns below the castle, built by French prisoners during the Napoleonic Wars, naval officers worked night and day, phoning ports, dockyards and marinas all along the south coast of England as far west as Plymouth. Initially there had been only forty destroyers and thirty-five transport ships available for the evacuation. But within just a few days of Ramsay's team's efforts the fleet stood at 848 ships, including barges, lifeboats, ferries, fishing boats, motorboats and yachts. Many even smaller vessels remain uncounted.

Having been given a breathing space by the halt of the German panzers, from 24 May British troops poured into Dunkirk. Already German bombers were attacking the dock installations, quickly setting fire to the oil depot. Much of the port was by the end of 26 May unusable, and it seemed as if most of the soldiers would have to embark direct from the beaches, whose difficult sandy shallows were notorious all along the coast. Initially discipline almost broke down completely and order had to be kept by armed navy personnel.

In the absence of a killer blow from the encircling German armour, the task of preventing the embarkation had been given to the Luftwaffe. Hermann Göring, Reichmarschall, leader of the Luftwaffe, was confident that his dive-bombers could wipe out the BEF on the beaches. 'Only fishing boats can get across now,' he declared on 26 May. 'I hope the Tommies are good swimmers.' Vainly did his subordinates point out that the speed of the German advance had left much of the Luftwaffe far behind, so that together with the casualties inflicted in the campaign, there were insufficient machines near enough to finish the job. Nevertheless, crack Stuka squadrons relentlessly attacked the port and on 27 May the town of Dunkirk was firebombed.

While Stukas attacked the beaches, town and shipping, Messerschmitt Bf 109 fighters circled far above, waiting for the inevitable response from the RAF. Even if aircraft were not going to be risked for the sake of France, Göring knew that Churchill could not leave his own army trapped and defenceless. The Air Ministry ordered Dowding to provide air support over the evacuation. The effort was hampered from the start in that the British fighters operating from the south of England could only spend minimal time over the target area. Insufficient consideration was given to staggering take-off times, so there would often be periods in which no fighters were over the beaches which could be exploited by the German bombers. Squadrons patrolling further inland would often stray out of range of radar and radio, and anyone shot down would be hard pressed to make it back to England, let alone to their squadron the next day. In short, the RAF fighters suffered from all the disadvantages that the German fighter pilots would later experience over southern England. In addition, they were heavily outnumbered.

Amongst the RAF squadrons was 609 'West Riding', an auxiliary squadron that had been brought south from Scotland to try to help defend the evacuating troops. There was a pause while the Spitfires were fitted with armour plating to protect the back and head of the pilot, and then the squadron was ordered into battle. For many of the pilots it was their first taste of action. Tall and blond, John Bisdee had joined the RAF Volunteer Reserve in 1937. As a Marlborough-and-Cambridge-educated man, he was more typical of one of the smarter Auxiliary or University squadrons. On 1 September he was called up, joining 609 Squadron on 26 December, together with another young pilot called James Buchanan. The two became firm friends. At this stage, only five months before Dunkirk, Bisdee was still yet to fly a monoplane. On arriving at the squadron his flight commander took him up in a Harvard monoplane for about an hour and a half, and then he progressed straight on to the Spitfire 'and never looked back'.

But arriving over the smoky misery of Dunkirk was a shock. Although they had been in action in Scotland, this was the first time 609 had really encountered the war. The then youngest pilot recalled later, 'From being a small, semi-isolated unit, we suddenly found ourselves part of a big and often baffling circus.' It was a baptism of fire. As the squadron intelligence officer Frank Ziegler wrote after the war, 'It was a bit like sending a football eleven, whose members had never played together before, against a crack team that had never tasted defeat.' Of the eighteen pilots from 609 who fought over Dunkirk, five were killed and one seriously wounded. The squadron claimed seven German planes, but only one of these was 'definite'. One of the surviving young officers wrote home, 'We appear to be losing the war, though eventually, of course, we shan't.'[1]

Most worryingly, it appeared that the training-book tactics were at least partly to blame for the losses. Before the war, the authorities had expected their defensive fighters to be attacking unescorted bomber formations flying from Germany to England. No fighters could have the range to fly that distance and back. So no one had planned for fighters to be around as well. John Bisdee is scathing about the official policy:

> The Air Ministry or the RAF had started the war with the most ridiculous ideas about how a modern fighter should be used. They tried to pretend that the dog fight as it were from World War I had ceased and they produced a series of what they called Fighter Attack No. 1, 2, 3, 4. All of which consisted of surprising the enemy from about five miles away so that they would get a good view of you and pursuing him from behind and thus exposing yourself to all possible defensive fire and so on. Anyway, thank goodness Dunkirk put an end to that.

Also unsuccessful was the tactic of sending over the fighters in 'wings' of three squadrons. Many of the pilots found the formation flying strenuous enough even before the enemy was encountered. In addition the squadrons, each on a different radio wavelength, were unable to communicate with each other.

19 Squadron, equipped with Spitfires, was moved from Duxford in Cambridgeshire to Hornchurch, north-east of London, to help cover the beaches and harbour as well. For George Unwin, it was his first taste of combat. The son of a coal miner, he had been a sergeant when war was declared and by May 1940 was a flight sergeant. He had joined the RAF in 1929 as an apprentice clerk at the RAF records office, but applied to become a pilot, and having started flying in 1935, he was one of the most experienced pilots in the squadron.

On the squadron's first mission, there were thirteen pilots and only twelve planes. Much to his fury, Unwin drew the short straw and was left behind. It turned out to be a fortunate escape.

Actually I was lucky. The squadron that day – it will show you just how old-fashioned we were – ran straight into trouble. They saw a squadron of Stukas attacking the troops on the beaches and they went in under Fighter Command Attack No. 3. Well, the Stuka is not very fast, so they went up behind them nice and gently, as you were taught to, gradually overtaking, and of course down came the Messerschmitts. The first three Spitfires – the CO and the two wingmen – were shot down straightaway. The CO was taken prisoner, one of the wingmen had a bullet in his knee and went down near Deal, and the other fellow was killed. This was the very first time we'd gone into action against more than one German.

Amongst all the carnage, the pilots were learning fast and observing the tactics of the enemy, who flew in widely spaced twos or fours, a strategy learnt during the Spanish Civil War. When Bf 109 pilot Gunther Büsgen first saw a British squadron in flight, he assumed it was a flying school. 'We thought it was a frightful nonsense to send such inexperienced pilots against the French front,' he remembers. For George Unwin, who with 19 Squadron flew forty hours over Dunkirk in ten days, it was clear that the RAF were approaching fighter combat in the wrong way. Like Bisdee, he is scathing of the established attack plans.

Flying in threes turned out to be crazy. If you're flying in threes and you want to turn quickly you can't without running into the other fellow. The Germans knew all this and they flew in twos. We had to pick all this up and reorganise our tactics accordingly. The most dangerous period, certainly in my life and in many, many others, was my first fight, because despite all my experience, I admit I was in trouble. I was in a turn and I saw this Messerschmitt coming up and I could see sparks coming out of the guns. I thought, Look at that. I fancy they're shooting at me . . . God, yes he is. Luckily for me I was in a turn and although he did hit me most of it went behind me. If you live through the first one I reckon you'll be good for a long time. It's not fright, it's sheer fascination. For a moment I froze, thinking, God!, then I moved.

In fact, George Unwin was beginning to forge a reputation for himself. Over Dunkirk he shot down a Messerschmitt Bf 109 and a Henschel Hs 126. Although he had mixed feelings about his first 'kill', he was quick to notice a weakness in the 109 fighter. 'You were there to destroy the aeroplane, that was the target, you never thought of the bloke in it. Actually the poor Messerschmitt pilot, if ever a man had a hot seat it was him, because he was sitting on his petrol tank. His aeroplane was flying perfectly all right in a turn and then suddenly it was a ball of flame.'

Overall, though, 19 Squadron took a mauling, with five aircraft lost in one day, two pilots killed, one wounded and another taken prisoner. In total over Dunkirk, sixty Fighter Command pilots were killed, fifteen injured, eight taken prisoner and a further two were missing, presumed dead.

There is still controversy over the effectiveness of the RAF's contribution to the 'miracle of Dunkirk'. About eighteen RAF fighter squadrons had taken part and flown up to 300 sorties a day in one area. It is impossible to say how much further damage the Luftwaffe could have inflicted on the BEF without the fighters from England, but it is likely that poor weather more than Fighter Command limited the amount of bombs that fell on the beaches and shipping. Certainly many of the soldiers on the beaches felt that the RAF had not done its bit. To them, when the weather was clear, it seemed that the German aircraft could attack them at will.

During the night of 26–27 May, Lance Bombardier Peter Lambert came in sight of the coast at last.

As we got nearer Dunkirk the black smoke became denser and the flames at night more awe-inspiring. With daylight came the most incredible sight: thousands of troops in long snaking queues over the sands, rather like queues for a bizarre football match. Out to sea, in the harbour, were the wrecks of ships that had been bombed.

A hospital ship, white with large red crosses, was being dive-bombed, the bombers persistently returning to the attack until it sank. We were attacked by air consistently and would bury ourselves in the sand and pray.

The evacuation from the beach was only progressing very slowly. The destroyers were having to send their dinghies to collect soldiers from the beach. By the end of the day only 8,000 had been got away. At this rate the capture of the bulk of the BEF was inevitable. To cap it all, the news came through that King Leopold of the Belgians had surrendered.

Under this relentless attack discipline and morale were at a low ebb. In the town of Dunkirk, as a huge pall of smoke from burning oil tanks hung in the air, exhausted and despondent Allied soldiers, deserted by their officers, ran amok. On the beaches, too, some men cracked under the strain of constant air attack. Many of the troops had not slept or eaten properly for the past week and had seen friends killed and helpless refugees machine-gunned from the air. Now it seemed the climax of the horror had arrived, as they sat defenceless on a beach waiting to be strafed by German aircraft. One man 'raved in circles, stripped to a loin cloth, proclaiming himself Mahatma Gandhi'. Another private, of the Lincolns, lay flat out in the sand for more than an hour, hoping that if he looked dead already he wouldn't be shot at by the attacking aircraft. Some men clutched teddy bears; officers wept compulsively or sheltered in the dunes, immobilised by fear.[2] Every time a boat appeared, panic threatened to break out, with men rushing forward and grabbing the side. A major was shot dead by another officer to prevent him capsizing an already overflowing rowing boat. A corporal of the Guards kept order in his boat, filled with fear-crazed troops, by threatening to shoot the first one that disobeyed him. Some of the men were instructed to swim out to the boats. A group reached a ship and started to climb the ropes up the side. But in heavy, sodden clothes, tired, thirsty and hungry, they found they didn't have the strength to make it on to deck. Utterly disconsolate, they were forced to swim back to the beach.

The next morning dawned grey and overcast. Heavy cloud and the mass of smoke from the burning town prevented the Luftwaffe from making accurate attacks. Piers were constructed using lorries and other vehicles connected by planks, and on 28 May the mass of smaller craft began to appear, which made ferrying from the beach to the waiting ships quicker. Furthermore, it had been discovered that troops could be directly embarked on to larger ships by using one of the 'moles' – long breakwaters in the harbour – as a jetty. These moles had not been built with the intention of being used in this way; tides and currents would make mooring extremely difficult. Nevertheless, over half of the troops that escaped used this route, which is a testimony to the superb seamanship of the Royal Navy. The 1,400-yard-long, five-foot-wide pier was continually attacked by German bombers, but they were unable to hit it. Had they done so, the story of the evacuation would have been very different.

Getting on board a ship, however, was not necessarily the end of the nightmare. Most of the Luftwaffe attacks were directed against the boats in the harbour, over a hundred of which were sunk, many crammed with evacuees. When the old Thames paddle-steamer *Crested Eagle* was hit, onlookers saw 'men on fire from head to toe, dancing like dervishes, their faces contorted, leap screaming into the sea'.[3] Some unfortunates had ships sunk from under them two or three times. The ships also had to contend with German E-boats, small torpedo-launching motorboats. During the night of 28–29 May the destroyers *Wakeful* and *Grafton* were sunk following torpedo attacks, both very heavily laden with troops. The *Wakeful* went down in fifteen seconds and only 150 of the 600 soldiers packed on board were rescued. Nevertheless, by the next day, another 47,000 men had been evacuated in spite of renewed Luftwaffe attacks, and on 30 June French troops, too, started arriving in Dover.

The British government had been keen to keep news of the BEF's retreat and evacuation from the people at home. Major-General Mason-MacFarlane, Director of Military Intelligence, called together journalists at a London hotel on 28 May and told them, 'I am sure there is going to be a considerable shock for the British public. It is your duty to act as shock absorbers, so I have prepared, with my counterpart in the War Office, a statement which can be published, subject to censorship.'[4] Churchill, acutely aware of the importance of morale, sent a secret message the next day to his ministers and senior civil servants:

In these dark days the Prime Minister would be grateful if all his colleagues in the Government, as well as high officials, would maintain a high morale in their circles; not minimising the gravity of events, but showing confidence in our ability and inflexible resolve . . . No tolerance is to be given to the idea that France will make a separate peace.[5]

In spite of the tens of thousands of soldiers by now being carried on trains all over southern England, the press and radio patriotically declined to report the evacuation, even if hints were let out and the ground was prepared. Finally an announcement was made on BBC Radio at six p.m. on

30 May, by which time nearly three-quarters of the BEF was already back in England. Its tone might have surprised the exhausted BEF listeners:

> All night and all day men of the undefeated British
> Expeditionary Force have been coming home. From the
> many reports of their arrival and of interviews with the
> men, it is clear that if they have not come back in
> triumph they have come back in glory; that their morale
> is as high as ever; that they know they did not meet their
> masters; and that they are anxious only to be back again
> soon – as they put it – 'to have a real crack at Jerry'.

Many of the returning soldiers, shattered after a nightmare week of confused retreat, hunger, thirst and sleeplessness, would not have recognised this upbeat picture. To them, they were a defeated army, let down by their equipment, tactics and, above all, leadership. Large numbers had not even fired a shot. All along the south coast the pubs seethed with discontented men, cursing their superiors, their allies and the 'Brylcreem Boys' of the RAF. Some soldiers on the trains away from the coast were reported to be so demoralised that they threw their rifles out of the window. Others changed into civilian clothes and simply went home.

The broadcast on the BBC was also listened to by Mary Lambert, who had not heard from her husband, Peter. To her it sounded from the BBC as if the evacuation was complete, and she feared the worst. Unlike many, she had heard of the retreat the previous Monday from a comrade of her husband who had returned safely. He told her that he had seen Peter on the way to the beaches.

By now Lambert had been on the beach for nearly four days. He remembers having a terrible thirst, and the German planes 'coming back and back and bombing and bombing and bombing'. All the time the German army was closing in on the perimeter. Things became even more unpleasant when artillery fire started to hit the beaches. To some, it seemed that later arrivals were getting off the beaches before those who had been waiting for days.

On 31 May, fog descended, preventing the Luftwaffe from attacking in force. On this day 68,014 soldiers were evacuated. Among them, at last, was Lance-Bombardier Lambert.

Finally on the Friday, a positive order came through for the regiment to make for the mole, which was by now being dive-bombed regularly as well as coming under artillery fire.

So, heart in mouth, and hoping that this really was our opportunity after so many false alarms, we made for it. A destroyer, the *Express*, had hove to alongside, not secured in any way, to enable a quick getaway. We ran along the mole and jumped down on to the deck about ten feet below. Despite the large influx of passengers, we left chaos to find calm efficiency and I shall never forget the cool, calm atmosphere the Royal Navy exuded. Very shortly after boarding we took off with considerable relief all round. We continued to be blessed because there was a thick mist that protected us from air attack, and we arrived safely in Dover.

Peter Lambert was amazed at the reception back in England. Expecting to 'slink back, a defeated army', instead, 'there were cups of tea, food, waving flags. There were cheers, even.' The organisation on their return, also, seemed in marked contrast to the chaos on the other side of the Channel. Trains had been collected to disperse and ferry the army away from the coast as quickly as possible. During the nine days of evacuation, eighty-two troop trains left Ramsgate alone; from Folkestone sixty-two trains carried inland some 35,000 soldiers.

Peter Lambert's regiment landed up in Stockbridge, just north of Bournemouth. At last he was able to contact Mary's family. 'The next day Mary came down for a wonderful reunion. This was the first time we had seen one another since our very short honeymoon some eight months before.'

For others, the good news did not arrive. By 2 June, when the last British units in Dunkirk embarked, there were 30,000 officers and men missing who had fallen, been wounded or captured by the Germans. Young Macclesfield-born pilot Eric Bann, safely back in England, wrote to his parents of what he had seen after Dunkirk: 'All the boys were arriving in London on Saturday night still wet, after swimming to the rescue boats. Mothers, fathers, wives, sweethearts were all waiting there. Some poor devils just stood looking dazed when they realised that their man had paid the price, their faces almost haunted.' In Etchingham in East Sussex, a young woman, having left her baby boy with a neighbour, drowned herself in the church pond. It emerged that her husband, a member of the regular army, had disappeared during the retreat to Dunkirk. Two soldiers manning a nearby gun site by the railway station saw her taking off her coat and shoes, but were not in time to save her.

But in total 338,000 Allied troops had been evacuated, some ten times what had been estimated to be possible. This included 110,000 French soldiers, the majority of whom were straightaway shipped to the Normandy ports to rejoin the fight. Calm waters in the Channel and overcast skies had no doubt helped, but the contribution of the Royal Navy was also decisive.

Everyone expected an immediate invasion. The RAF had lost 509 fighters in the war so far and home defence was limited to 331 Spitfires and Hurricanes, supported by 150 'second division' fighters – Defiants, Gladiators and Blenheims. The home fleet was reeling from the effort of the evacuation: when the minesweeper *Hebe* was bombed on 1 June, no one on board had slept for five days and nights. Of the fifty precious destroyers taking part in the evacuation at Dunkirk, nine had been sunk and twenty-three damaged.

The BEF was more than exhausted; it was defeated and demoralised. Even more seriously, it had left behind in France nearly 2,500 guns, some 400 tanks and over 60,000 other vehicles of all kinds, as well as huge amounts of ammunition and stores. Everyone understood that if the Germans arrived now, there would be precious little to stop them.

The government faced a desperate situation. No one had any confidence in the French surviving for long, and all the plans for the conduct of the war, such as they were, had been blown away by events. The initial idea to take up defensive positions and use sea power to blockade Germany into submission was in tatters now that Hitler had access to the natural resources and productive capacity of virtually the whole of Europe. Having expected France to be able to hold Germany's armies as they had done in the First World War, the British army had been left woefully outnumbered and outgunned by the speed of the French collapse. But there were deeper, more entrenched problems as well.

The British had entered the war in a very poor state strategically and financially. The empire was at its greatest extent, but rather than being a net contributor to the UK, it was a huge drain on resources and manpower. Defence spending between 1920 and 1938 had been slashed to meet the growing social security bill, swollen by mass unemployment. Rearmament after Munich and the declaration of war had worsened the financial situation. The weakness of Britain's industrial base meant that much war equipment had to be imported from the United States. At the beginning of 1940, Britain's gold and dollar reserves, together with saleable investments in the US, had stood at a paltry £775 million. This was very rapidly being eroded. It was now estimated that the reserves would be gone by the end of 1940.

Planning for what might happen would require new thinking and hard decisions. No course of action, however odious, could be written off. It seemed that there were two choices: to come to terms with Germany, or to wait for some miraculous intervention from the United States. For the latter, the omens did not look good. Joe Kennedy, father of the future President, was Roosevelt's envoy in London. An admirer of the Nazis, Kennedy had been reporting back to Washington that America was in danger of backing the wrong side. Churchill had been pleading for the loan of fifty obsolete US destroyers to help in home waters and convoy patrols, but had had no success. The timing of the presidential election was also against him. Roosevelt, judging that the mood of the American electorate was still in favour of continuing isolationism, was unwilling to be seen to be helping Britain at any time before the polls in early November. By 27 May Churchill was fed up with the lack of response, commenting bitterly that 'it would be very nice of him [Roosevelt] to pick up the bits of the British Empire if this country was overrun'.[6] In fact the Americans were divided about the war, with the traditionally more Europe-centred east coast most in favour of helping Britain. Elsewhere there was considerable opinion against interfering, with Charles Lindbergh, the famous aviator, touring the Midwest campaigning against getting involved with war in Europe. In the meantime, the worries of the American High Command were centred on the British fleet, which would, if delivered intact to Hitler, present a serious intercontinental threat to the US, particularly if combined with the Japanese and French fleets. Another worry centred on the enormous military orders coming in from the UK. No one wanted to give credit to a country about to surrender or be overrun.

The other option – of coming to terms with Germany – had been pursued by the British to an extent since the beginning of the war. Informal channels were kept open through Sweden and there were several bungled attempts to make contact with a German opposition to Hitler. Well into 1940, Goebbels' propaganda ministry in Berlin continued to press for peace with Britain: 'Sooner or later the racially Germanic element in Britain would have to be brought in to join Germany in the future secular struggles of the white race against the yellow race, or the Germanic race against Bolshevism.'[7] In a highly charged Cabinet meeting on 27 May, as the fall of France accelerated over the Channel and most of the BEF were still being bombed at Dunkirk, Lord Halifax pressed for a deal to be negotiated through the then neutral Mussolini of Italy. Supported by Attlee and Sinclair, for the moment Churchill rejected the move, saying:

> At the moment our prestige in Europe is very low. The only way we could get it back was by showing the world that Germany had not beaten us. If, after two or three months, we could show that we were still unbeaten, our prestige would return. Even if we were beaten, we should be no worse off than we should be if we were now to abandon the struggle. Let us therefore avoid being dragged down the slippery slope with France.[8]

By 'showing the world', Churchill primarily meant the United States. As Air Minister Sir Archibald Sinclair added, 'It was important to get it realised in the United States that we meant to fight on.'[9]

The mood of the public also had to be considered. Two days later, in another Cabinet meeting, the Labour leaders Attlee and Greenwood stressed the dangers to morale that any public negotiations would entail and assured Churchill that the industrial centres of Britain 'would regard anything like weakening on the part of the Government as a disaster'.[10] The historian Eric Hobsbawm, no friend of the establishment line, has commented that historians who try to find support for peace moves among the common people in May 1940 are simply chasing shadows. His memory of the time is clear: there was strong and growing determination in the country to resist Hitler at all costs. Churchill at any rate, while keeping the door slightly ajar on a compromise peace, was sure what the public line should be. Collecting together his junior ministers, he gave them an emotional speech that promised, 'If this long island story of ours is to end at last, let it end only when each one of us lies choking in his own blood upon the ground.' The assembled ministers cried out, 'Well done, Prime Minister.' Some burst into tears, others rushed forward to slap Churchill on the back. The enthusiastic reaction surprised even Churchill. Writing after the war, he commented, 'I was sure that every Minister was ready to be killed quite soon, and have all his family and possessions destroyed, rather than give in. In this they represented the House of Commons and almost all the people.'[11]

Swelled by this support, Churchill's own determination grew, and plans – endorsed by the Prime Minister himself – to offer Mussolini Mediterranean bases and even parts of Africa as an inducement to make the peace receded into the background. On 4 June came the welcome news that efforts to increase fighter production now meant that the losses of the campaign in France had more than been made up. At the same time the final figures for the miraculous evacuation from Dunkirk were delivered to the Prime Minister. He also heard a report that a law was about to be submitted to Congress in Washington that would amend the rules that forbade the US government from delivering war material from US army stocks to Europe. These snippets of information, received that morning, helped shape the speech that Churchill was to deliver in the House of Commons in the afternoon.

Churchill's first task on taking the floor of the Commons was to explain events in France. Stressing that no one had hoped to evacuate more than 20–30,000 men, he declared that instead the 'root and core and brain' of the army had been preserved 'on which and around which' could be built 'great British Armies'. Although he conceded that 'wars are not won by evacuations' and that there had been 'a colossal military disaster', Churchill was careful to direct the blame away from the BEF. An attack on the capitulation of the Belgians was then followed by a defence of the RAF, who had come under fire for their lack of effectiveness in France, particularly over Dunkirk. Here Churchill's rhetoric becomes, for once, clumsy: 'Very large formations of German aeroplanes – and we know they are a brave race – have turned on several occasions from the attack of one quarter of their number of the Royal Air Force.' Unfortunately Churchill singled out the Defiant fighter as having been 'vindicated as superior to what they have at present to face'. Events would show that the reverse was the case. The few thousand airmen of the RAF, he went on, would now alone be the defenders of civilisation. 'There has never been, I suppose, in all the world, in all the history of war, such an opportunity for youth. The Knights of the Round Table, the Crusaders, all fall back into a prosaic past' compared with 'these young men, going forth every morn to guard their native land and all we stand for, holding in their hands these instruments of colossal and shattering power'.

Having warned of possible invasion, Churchill called up the example of Napoleon, another 'continental tyrant' who had failed to cross the Channel. The speech ended after half an hour with a stirring message:

I have, myself, full confidence that if all do their duty, if nothing is neglected, and if the best arrangements are made, as they are being made, we shall prove ourselves once again able to defend our island home, to ride out the storm of war, and to outlive the menace of tyranny, if necessary for years, if necessary alone. At any rate, that is what we are going to try to do. That is the resolve of His Majesty's government – every man of them. That is the will of Parliament and the nation. The British Empire and the French Republic, linked together in their cause and in their need, will defend to the death their native soil, aiding each other like good comrades to the utmost of their strength.

Even though large tracts of Europe and many old and famous States have fallen or may fall into the grip of the Gestapo and all the odious apparatus of Nazi rule, we shall not flag or fail. We shall go on to the end. We shall fight in France, we shall fight on the seas and oceans, we shall fight with growing confidence and growing strength in the air, we shall defend our island, whatever the cost may be. We shall fight on the beaches, we shall fight on the landing grounds, we shall fight in the fields and in the streets, we shall fight in the hills; we shall never surrender, and even if, which I do not for a moment believe, this island or a large part of it were subjugated and starving, then our Empire beyond the sea, armed and guarded by the British Fleet, would carry on the struggle, until, in God's good time, the new world, with all its power and might, steps forth to the rescue and liberation of the old.[12]

It is a fascinating and brilliant speech. The past is recreated as a terrible triumph; virtue is made of the harsh necessity of Britain's imminent international isolation; support for the Royal Air Force is stoked up and the interpretation of the coming air battle is there to take home off the peg. Finally, and crucially, the tactic – or more exactly at this stage, the hope – of waiting for American support is laid out in heroic form for all to see. How much a speech like this moulds rather than follows public opinion is impossible to say. What is without doubt is the electrifying effect it had throughout the country. A Labour MP wrote to Churchill: 'That was worth 1,000 guns.'[13] Vita Sackville-West wrote to her husband, Harold Nicolson, 'it sent shivers (not of fear) down my back'.[14]

Just as importantly, everyone now knew the plan, and the language in which the conflict would be described when it came (and ever since). The press, reporting the next day the final moments of Dunkirk, happily followed Churchill's line. The *Mirror*'s editorial headline was 'Bloody Marvellous'. For the *Daily Mail* the evacuation had been 'terrible yet glorious' and the BEF's survival was in spite of the 'trap left for them by the treachery of Leopold'.

In another, smaller piece, though, the *Mail* mentions the 'criticisms boiling up in the country'. These criticisms, however, ended up at Chamberlain's rather than Churchill's door. The former Prime Minister, seen as the arch-appeaser, was considered responsible for the poor state of preparedness of the BEF. Jock Colville wrote in his diary on 13 June 'there is great rancour against Chamberlain and his colleagues because of the lack of equipment'.[15]

Churchill himself was ashamed of the contribution of the

BEF. He wrote later that at his last meeting with Reynaud, he had felt 'grief that Britain had not been able to make a greater contribution to the land war against Germany, and that so far a nineteenth of the slaughter and ninety-nine-hundredths of the suffering had fallen on France and France alone'. In a letter he compared Britain's contribution in the first year of World War I – forty-seven divisions brought into action compared with the nine of the BEF.[16]

Nevertheless, the country as a whole wanted to believe Churchill's description of the Dunkirk battle, in which, he said, 'valour, perseverance, perfect discipline' had been so crucial. In many ways it had reflected what they were already thinking, shown in the welcome given to the stunned returning BEF men. The more the part played by the small civilian craft at Dunkirk was stressed or even overstated in the press, the more the ordinary people of Britain felt part of the war effort. Everyone, it seemed, had a role to play; it was a people's war. The papers, for their part, then as now, found it easy writing and selling a patriotic, defiant line. Following a discreet lead from the military, France as well as Belgium was blamed in the press for the disaster, in spite of the fact that both had sustained far higher casualty levels than the BEF.

The drama of Dunkirk was widely reported in the United States and many papers there were sympathetic and impressed by the achievement, whatever the circumstances. Like the British approach, some ignored the horror and waste on the beaches in favour of the relative good fortune and miraculous performance of the Royal Navy and Operation Dynamo. The *New York Times* of 1 June, appealing to Anglo-Saxon solidarities, proclaimed, 'As long as the English tongue survives, the word Dunkerque will be spoken with reverence.'[17] Two days later General Marshall fixed authorisation for half a million First World War American rifles to be sent to Britain. Although requiring non-standard ammunition, they were cheap and they were better than nothing.

To the French, all Churchill's talk of 'alone if necessary' made it look as though their ally had deserted them. With the completion of the evacuation from Dunkirk, there were now fifty-one Allied divisions, of which only two were British, left to face 104 German, and fewer than two hundred fighter aircraft. The German army attacked southwards on 5 June and made rapid progress. On 10 June Paris was abandoned, and Mussolini, scenting spoils from a German victory, declared war and invaded from the south-east.

In many places there was now fierce resistance. The garrison of the Maginot Line – 400,000 strong – refused to surrender, and isolated pockets of French infantry fought hard. On the new Italian front four French divisions faced twenty-eight Italian, but nowhere did the invaders get more than two kilometres into France. In the attack the Italians lost 5,000 men, while on the French side only eight men were killed. When the armistice was declared, the Italian High Command had to ask the Germans to airlift some of their troops behind the French lines in order to pretend to the world they had made an advance.[18]

On 11 June Churchill flew to Briare in the Loire valley to meet the French leaders, escorted by an aerial bodyguard of Spitfires from 609 'West Riding' squadron. Churchill was particularly concerned about the fate of the large and powerful French fleet, but could promise little in terms of material support for the French effort. In spite of the frequent requests for fighters, the government heeded Dowding's pleas that the whole strength should not be thrown into the battle for France.

Already Dowding was warning of a lack of properly trained pilots, much to Churchill's fury. It added to the Prime Minister's despair when on 12 June the elite 51st Division, isolated and outgunned, was forced to surrender north-west of Paris. It was, said Churchill, the 'most brutal disaster we had yet suffered'.[19] In a desperate effort to prevent the French from making peace, Churchill flew to France again, accompanied by Lord Halifax, Beaverbrook and General Ismay, who was Churchill's liaison man with the military and frequent companion. As before, 609 Squadron of Spitfires performed the escort duty. Once landed at Tours they were to keep at constant readiness in case of air attack on the government figures, British and French.

As 609 Squadron waited, ready to be airborne in minutes, Churchill was offering Reynaud a union between Britain and France that might keep the fight against Hitler going. By this stage, though, a desire for peace was crystallising around the increasingly influential figure of Pétain, the hero of France in the First World War, and Reynaud was aware of power slipping away from him. On the evening of 16 June, Pétain was asked by President Lebrun to form a new government, and the next day, as the last British troops left France, he went on the radio to announce that he was ending the fight. On 22 June, an armistice was signed that signalled the humiliation of France: the industrial north-east was to be directly ruled from Berlin; the French economy was to be systematically and ruthlessly exploited; and the huge army, a quarter of France's men of working age, was to go into captivity. Compared with this, the hated Treaty of Versailles, forced on Germany by France in 1919, now seemed lenient. To rub salt into the wounds, Hitler insisted that the French sign the armistice in the same train carriage in which Germany had surrendered in 1918.[20]

On 18 June, when it was clear that the fighting was coming to an end in France, Churchill spoke again in the House of Commons. In his speech he warned of the coming dangers for all citizens from air attacks. Everyone would now be on the front line: 'I do not underestimate the severity of the ordeal which lies before us . . . every man and every woman will have the chance to show the finest qualities of their race and to render the highest service to their cause.' Conceding perhaps that his earlier description of the RAF's battle in France had been overgenerous, he added, 'we had no right to assume at the beginning . . . the individual superiority of our aircraft and pilots'. The rousing ending contained, as usual, a desperate plea to the United States:

> What General Weygand called the Battle of France is over. I expect that the Battle of Britain is about to begin. Upon this battle depends the survival of Christian civilisations. Upon it depends our own British life and the long continuity of our institutions and our Empire. The whole fury and might of the enemy must very soon be turned on us. Hitler knows that he will have to break us in this island or lose the war. If we can stand up to him, all Europe will be free, and the life of the world may move forward into broad, sunlit uplands; but if we fail, then the whole world, including the United States, and all that we have known and cared for, will sink into the abyss of a new dark age made more sinister, and perhaps more protracted, by the lights of a perverted science.
>
> Let us therefore brace ourselves to our duty and so bear ourselves that if the British Empire and its Commonwealth lasts for a thousand years men will still say, 'This was their finest hour.'[21]

When Eileen Hairs heard the broadcast she was staying with her parents. 'I couldn't bear listening to the radio with them in the room. I just used to get up and make an excuse and say I was going to the bathroom or something, but meanwhile I stood outside the door and listened.' Eileen, who was waiting to tell her husband that he was going to be a father for the first time, now knew he would be with her soon. 'I heard them say that all the Advanced Striking Force were back. But I hadn't heard from Peter and had no idea where he was. Suddenly the phone went and my mother said, "That's Peter, he's at Croydon aerodrome." My brother drove me to the aerodrome and we stood in the bar waiting. Suddenly Peter arrived. He looked absolutely exhausted. He literally swayed.'

Peter Hairs' 501 Spitfire squadron had taken a circuitous route back home. With him was John Gibson, who became a firm friend. Although born in Brighton, Gibson had grown up in New Zealand. He sailed to England to join the RAF in 1938, having recently married Ethel Formby, sister of the famous comedian George Formby. He arrived in France having never flown a Hurricane, and remembers reporting for the first time to his flight commander, Charlie Griffiths:

Griffiths said, 'Where's your log book?' I showed him and he said, 'You've never flown a Hurricane?' and I had to say no. So he detailed me to go and fly for, I think, forty minutes in one. I was instructed to do two or three circuits. On my return, Griffiths asked, 'Are you happy with it?'

'Yes.'

'Fine.'

I'd never fired eight guns before either, until the moment that I first fired on an enemy aircraft. I didn't know what to expect.

But Gibson had hit the aircraft – a Heinkel 111 – and had a half-share of the kill with another pilot. He was to go on to get a Messerschmitt Bf 109 and another Heinkel 111 bomber while in France, and was also shot down twice but escaped both times uninjured.

When France capitulated, 501 were in Dinar and we didn't fly out, we came out by boat, from St Moreaux, and we went to Jersey first. We operated from Jersey for a couple of days, and then the Germans gave us an ultimatum to get out. Otherwise they would bomb the place. So we came back and we re-formed at Croydon.

By this stage 501 were exhausted. Morale, according to John Gibson, was only 'a little above average'. Flying to France very early in the morning, and working with the French air force, had frayed tempers. The short rest they had at Croydon would, however, be the last break for many months. For others, too, it seemed a relief. Peter Brothers' 32 Squadron had taken a mauling on 8 June, when it had lost three aircraft and two pilots. He was pleased that the fighting would now be over England. 'If your aircraft was battle damaged you could bale out and could jump into another one, rather than becoming a prisoner of war, which is what the Germans were now facing.' Back at Biggin Hill, too, it was almost as if normality had resumed. 'Quite frankly, we were terribly cheered,' remembers Brothers. 'We said, "Thank God, now we're on our own we can cope and it's up to us now" because there'd been so much disorder and chaos beforehand. We thought, now we're settled, we're back at home and everything is organised here and we can just get on with it without any nonsense and interference from the French or Belgians or whoever.'

This view was widely shared. Colville handed Churchill a quotation he had found in Shakespeare's *Henry VI Part III*: ''Tis better using France than trusting France. Let us be back'd with God, and with the seas, Which He hath giv'n for fence impregnable, And with their helps only defend our-selves. In them and in ourselves our safety lies.'[22] King George VI wrote in a private letter to his mother on 27 June:

'Personally I feel happier now that we have no more allies to be polite to & to pamper.' A war in which Britain stood alone had a much simpler, cleaner, nationalistic feel, whatever the practical strategic considerations might be. Like an international sporting event, it was now one against one. A newspaper vendor's sign in London read: 'French sign peace treaty: we're in the finals.' From this view emerged a curious mixture of alarm and fearlessness, a very real dread of sharing the fate of the continental countries under Nazi occupation and a steadfast belief that if everyone worked together, Britain could take on anyone.

In *Put Out More Flags*, written by Evelyn Waugh almost contemporaneously, the ridiculous figure of Sir Joseph comments on the new situation immediately after the fall of France:

> Finally when it was plain, even to Sir Joseph, that in the space of a few days England had lost both the entire stores and equipment of her regular army and her only ally; that the enemy were less than twenty-five miles from her shores; that there were only a few battalions of fully armed, fully trained troops in the country; that she was committed to a war in the Mediterranean with a numerically superior enemy; that her cities lay open to air attack from fields closer to home than the extremities of her own islands; that her sea-routes were threatened from a dozen new bases, Sir Joseph said: 'Seen in the proper perspective I regard this as a great and tangible success . . . The war has entered into a new and glorious phase.'

But in spite of the satire, Sir Joseph is given the last word in the novel. ' "There's a new spirit abroad," he said. "I see it on every side." And, poor booby, he was right.'

George Orwell, who had fought fascism in Spain and, declared unfit for service, had joined the Home Guard, shared this strange mixture of despair and defiance. Remembering the moment just before Dunkirk, he wrote a year later, 'The whole nation suddenly swings together and does the same thing, like a herd of cattle facing a wolf . . . After eight months of vaguely wondering what the war was about, the people suddenly knew what they had got to do . . . it was like the awakening of a giant.'[23] His contemporary diary, though, had him writing on 6 June 1940, 'Everything is disintegrating.'[24]

Thus, amongst the flag-waving welcome for the returning BEF, the enjoyment of Churchill's defiant speeches and the renewed hope and energy, Britain, expecting to be overrun at any moment, prepared for Nazi invasion.

CHAPTER THREE

Britain Alone

L ONDON HAD HAD ITS FIRST TASTE OF AERIAL BOMBING during the First World War. On 31 May 1915, a German Zeppelin airship dropped a ton of bombs, killing seven people and wounding a further thirty-five. Attacks continued until the middle of 1918. In total 670 civilians were killed by the end of the war, but the psychological effect was far greater than this number suggests. During the interwar years, as aircraft and bomb technology moved forward, experts calculated the potential damage that bombing attacks would have in any future war. A 1924 committee, headed by Sir John Anderson, postulated that every ton of bombs dropped on London would result in fifty casualties, a third of which would be fatal. They also assumed that the first day of war in which the enemy had bomber airfields close to the Channel would see 2,000 tons of bombs dropped in twenty-four hours. In the late 1930s, as the Luftwaffe was built up and war seemed more and more likely, this was later amended to 3,500 tons, which, with the earlier formula still in place, would means that 58,000 Londoners would die on the first day of any future war. Just to provide coffins for such casualties would require, it was calculated, twenty million square feet of timber. Secret plans were made for mass lime-filled graves.

It was assumed that the civilian population, particularly in poorer parts of the country, would suffer a mass nervous breakdown under such an assault. Bertrand Russell predicted that London would be 'one vast raving bedlam, the hospitals will be stormed, traffic will cease, the homeless will shriek for peace, the city will be a pandemonium'.[1] Bombing, it was feared, would be followed by widespread rioting and a collapse of order. Large numbers of troops would be needed to prevent total civil breakdown. This idea was not confined to Britain, but was also widespread in Germany. Eminent psychiatrists privately warned in 1938 that for every physical casualty there would be three psychological ones. On the basis of the casualty calculations, this would mean that three to four million cases of acute panic and other neuroses would break out in the first six months of the war. Plans were made for huge hospital wards on the outskirts of cities to deal with this mass hysteria.

It was also felt that a city such as London would be powerless to prevent such attacks. 'The bomber will always get through,' Stanley Baldwin warned the House of Commons in 1932. These doom-laded scenarios were not confined to the government and planners. In the public domain the power of the bomber assumed even greater proportions, particularly if the bombs might contain poison gas. During the famous debate at the Oxford Union in 1933 – 'This house refuses in any circumstances to fight for King and Country' – a speaker warned the audience, 'Bombers would be over Britain within twenty minutes of the declaration of war with a western European power. And a single bomb can poison every living thing in an area of three-quarters of a square mile.'[2]

The Spanish Civil War did nothing to dispel these theories; it was the horror of Guernica rather than the disciplined response of the people of Madrid and Barcelona that stuck in the public mind. When the Munich crisis brought war closer, the Air Raid Precaution (ARP) budget was tripled. Zigzag trenches started to be dug in parks and open spaces. On 9 August there was a trial run in London for a 'blackout' – the plan to avoid helping enemy bombers locate targets by night. By September 1938 over a million feet of trenches had been dug in the city. Most were soon waterlogged and crumbling at the edges. By the same time more than 90 per cent of the population of London had been issued with a gas mask and the first barrage balloons had appeared over the skyline.

Plans for fire-fighting and for public shelters lagged behind, however. Most people were expected to make their own arrangements. The Anderson shelter, named after the head of the 1924 committee but owing nothing to his inspiration, was a suggested template for a garden shelter. Very cheap and easy to construct, it consisted of two curved sections of corrugated steel fastened together at the top and sunk three feet into the ground. It was recommended that at least eighteen inches of soil be piled on top, and it was promised that it would protect up to six adults against anything but a direct hit. Unhappily the issue of drainage was not addressed and many quickly filled up with water, demanding constant bailing. They also required the householder to have a garden, of course, which was not that common amongst the cramped terraces of the East End. Nevertheless, by September 1939 nearly one and a half million shelters had been distributed to families with incomes of less than £250 per year.

Other preparations began to be made as war loomed closer through the summer of 1939. Sandbags were filled and stacked against windows and doors as blast-proofing, and public shelters and rest centres were earmarked. Least popular of the new restrictions on major cities were the blackout rules – many people got lost in the dark and road accidents were common, as was petty crime. The rigidly enforced regulations were based on a gross overestimate of what strength of light would be visible from a bomber far above.

In one incident a German-Swiss resident of Kensington was accused of trying to provide a light for the enemy by puffing too hard on his cigar.

During the First World War a bomb had fallen on a school in Poplar, killing fourteen children. This grisly incident more than any other fed fear of bombing and led directly to a policy of removing children and other defenceless members of the community from areas at risk. Before the war a list was drawn up of children, the blind, mothers and the handicapped, who, it was felt, should be evacuated. But this was neither systematic nor obligatory. It was left to parents whether or not they wanted their children listed, or whether they wanted to make their own arrangements. Three days before the declaration of war, the authorities began the removal of more than 39,000 people from towns in southeast England considered to be on the bombers' path to London, and from London itself about half of the children were evacuated. In all, about a million and a half people travelled under the government scheme and a further two million made their own arrangements, mostly journeying to hotels in the north. But as the Phoney War dragged on, over a million returned home, and when efforts were made to produce new lists in February 1940, only 2.6 per cent of parents registered their children.

But with the start of Blitzkrieg in the West, public apathy disappeared overnight and evacuation started again on a large scale. Children from the East End of London had many difficulties adjusting to life in the country. For one thing the food was utterly unfamiliar. Accustomed to a diet of bread, margarine, fish and chips and sweets, they viewed the country fare of fresh fruit and vegetables with horror. One five-year-old demanded of his foster parents 'beer and cheese' for supper. In turn, the country people were revolted by the verminous state of the city-dwellers. Many of the children were bitterly homesick; some started wetting their beds, to the further disgust of their hosts; others simply set off walking home.

Since 1933, when Hitler took power in Germany, there had been a steady flow of refugees from his regime. Later they were joined by those fleeing Austria and Czechoslovakia. On the whole they were made welcome, but as their numbers increased along with the fear of Germany, wild stories started to appear. In February 1939, the *Evening Standard* led with a story headlined 'Hitler's Gestapo employing Jews for spying in England'. By this stage there were some 74,000 'enemy aliens' in the country. At the beginning of the war a handful of obvious Nazi sympathisers from amongst these had been interned, but as the military situation worsened, public and political worries grew about the potential of this population to act as fifth columnists, that is, as spies, saboteurs, defeatists and the like. On 11 May all enemy aliens, with the exception of those women in MI5's 'least suspect' category, were rounded up. Twenty transit camps were established, often with miserably poor conditions. At one camp, 2,000 internees were held in a rat-infested disused factory with totally inadequate sanitary arrangements. When the deputy-general of the Ministry of Information, Sir Walter Monckton, investigated the conditions at another camp, he reported back, 'The two men who succeeded in committing suicide had already been in Hitler's concentration camps. Against these they held out, but this camp has broken their spirit.'[3] When Italy entered the war on 10 June, cafés and restaurants in Soho were attacked and one long-assimilated restaurateur had to put a notice in his window saying that all four of his sons were in the British army. Soon 1,687 Italians had been rounded up and put in the camps. These now contained a large number of engineers, physicists, chemists and university professors. In one camp, 82 per cent of the inmates were

Jewish. In June compulsory deportation was introduced and people were chosen at random to travel to Canada. When the *Arandora Star* was torpedoed in the Atlantic, 1,300 of them died, and it emerged that many of them were ardently anti-Nazi. As well as the Italian ex-chefs of the Savoy and the Ritz in London, prominent anti-Nazi German and Austrian politicians and labour leaders had been on board. When the immediate danger of invasion receded, many of the internees still in Britain were quietly released.

British subjects were interned also. In total 1,769 were arrested, of whom 763 had been members of the British Union of Fascists. The fascist leader Sir Oswald Mosley and his wife were amongst those interned. Many of these, including the Mosleys, were also later released.

Other measures also show the levels of panic running in the country and the political leadership. On 24 August 1939 the House of Commons had hurriedly passed the Emergency Powers (Defence) Act, by which they were empowered to do pretty much whatever they deemed necessary for the defence of the country and the efficient prosecution of the war. New government powers included detention without trial and the suppression of opinion. Public meetings were strictly controlled and individual movement was restricted. With the disaster unfolding in France, the War Cabinet met on 18 May to discuss even more measures. Conservative agents up and down the country had been reporting back that the war was not popular with the lowest sections of the community and that there was a suspicion that it was being fought in the interests of the rich. Chamberlain took the lead in demanding an end to the 'present rather easy-going methods' and the adoption of a form of government 'which would approach the totalitarian'.[4] New rules governing labour and property were rushed through the House on 22 May, and the opening of letters and the interception of telegrams was extended.

This was deemed useful not just for identifying troublemakers but also for the authorities to judge morale levels amongst the population. Some of what was read was alarming, and on 11 June it was made a criminal offence 'to make or report any statement likely to cause alarm and despondency'. A spate of prosecutions followed. A man who had told two New Zealanders, 'You don't want to fight in this bloody war' was imprisoned for three months, and another who had supported Indian independence received two months. Although the number of prosecutions led to the government advising magistrates only to imprison the most serious offenders, as late as 1941 a woman who was heard saying, 'Hitler is a good ruler, a better man than Churchill' received no less than five years' imprisonment.

At the outset of the war it had been suggested that the Germans might initiate an attack against England rather than take on the supposed might of the Maginot Line, but it was not until the following spring that invasion fears became widespread. The German invasion of Norway, where the superior Royal Navy had been unable to prevent the landing of troops, had sent a frisson of fear through the British. On 7 May Clement Wedgwood, MP, had said in the House of Commons: 'While the British Navy is capable of holding open the sea lanes to the West and thereby protecting Britain from starvation, it does not appear to be capable of cutting off the German occupation forces in Norway. It is therefore conceivable that in the event, it will not be able to oppose a landing by the Germans in Lincolnshire or the Wash.'[5]

As more of the northern European coast fell to the Blitzkrieg, so the invasion options for the Germans seemed to multiply and the amount of British coastline to be defended grew. One of the first priorities was to increase the number of trained soldiers Britain could call on. Between May and August, 425,000 men were recruited, and by 1 July the services had absorbed more than half of British males aged between twenty and twenty-five. These troops were deliberately kept very busy. It was widely believed that the French army had stagnated during the Phoney War, and there was a determination that the same fate should not befall the British troops. Four days a week the soldiers worked on defences, tactical exercises took a further day and on the sixth day they would typically do a twenty-mile march.

Initially, some of the new recruits were forced to drill with broomsticks, such was the shortage of modern weapons. In particularly short supply were modern artillery and anti-tank weapons. Factories throughout the country worked hard to make up the shortfall. Holidays were cancelled and workshops ran twenty-four hours a day, seven days a week. Some factories doubled their output straightaway, and overall production rose by a quarter in the week after Dunkirk. In armaments works, normal working hours were set from eight a.m. to seven p.m., and many employees kept going long after that, collapsing exhausted after midnight to sleep on sacks in quiet corners. As had been found during the First World War, much of this effort was counterproductive, since after a time people actually produced less the longer they worked. Nevertheless, there was no doubting the commitment of working people to overcoming the crisis.

The overriding fears in the days after Dunkirk were of paratroopers and airborne troops. On 21 May the Dutch Foreign Minister had blamed the fall of his country on parachutists supposedly dropped in a variety of disguises: as Allied soldiers, nurses, bus conductors, even nuns. There were lurid rumours of poisoned chocolate and cigarettes being distributed. In Britain, talk in pubs and clubs and in the letter pages of the newspapers was dominated by the possibility of a mass landing from the air and what steps could be taken to thwart it. In fact, the Germans only had around 7,000 trained parachute troops, but Britain was seized by a fear that they could drop anywhere at any time. Every citizen, it appeared once more, was in the front line.

Immediate steps were taken to try to foil glider and troop-carrier landings. As early as 12 May, Professor Frederick Lindemann, Churchill's scientific adviser, had recommended that holes be dug in all flat areas more than 400 yards long that were within five miles of any vulnerable or strategically important area. Churchill approved the idea and even insisted that fields planted with crops should not be excepted from this rule and that the distance away from a vulnerable site should be extended to ten miles. Soon open spaces all over southern and eastern England were dug up or crowded with obstacles to prevent a landing. Where possible, strong stakes were put into the ground; elsewhere fields, parks and commons were littered with rusting farm machinery and other improvised obstacles.

Most significantly, this fear of paratroopers and glider landings led to the setting up of a militia to be ready to deal with them wherever they might land. On 14 May, Anthony Eden, the War Minister, had gone on radio to call for 'large numbers of men ... between the ages of seventeen and sixty-five to come forward now and offer their services' as Local Defence Volunteers. Before the broadcast had even finished, queues were forming at police stations all over the country. Nobody had managed to pre-warn the police about this scheme, but they kept their composure and continued taking names and addresses until well after midnight. Within twenty-four hours a quarter of a million men had come forward, and by the end of the month, as the weary BEF was returning from France, there were 400,000 volunteers against an expected total of 150,000. By the end of the following month there were over 1,456,000 men ready to fight off the invader. Over a third of them were First World War veterans, and the age limits were not strictly applied. For some, old memories were revived:

> I think that none of us will forget our first LDV route march. On it a quarter of a century slipped away in a flash. There came memories of the Menin Road . . . of the smell of cordite and the scream of shrapnel, of the mud and stench and misery of Flanders, of hopes and fears in battles long ago . . . There were few youngsters in that first platoon of ours.[6]

Many organisations and groups formed their own units. Both Houses of Parliament had their own battalions, as did the BBC. The court at Buckingham Palace formed a battalion and the printers and typesetters of Fleet Street joined together. There was a dustmen battalion and one made up of London taxi drivers. To the horror of Ambassador Kennedy, an American battalion was formed by the expatriate community in London, called the American Squadron. In Lewes in East Sussex a group was formed complete with horses, and soon a fifty-two-strong cavalry unit, known as the Lewes Cossacks, was patrolling the South Downs. All were unpaid and had to supply their own food. They had to commit to ten hours a week and would be given twenty rounds of ammunition (when available), tea, a straw mattress and three blankets. Initially there were no weapons to distribute and the volunteers had to make do with what they could find. Within days LDV troops bearing pitchforks, shotguns or home-made clubs were a common sight all over the country. On Churchill's suggestion, their name was changed to the Home Guard.

The initial German reaction, transmitted through their leading English-language broadcaster, the renegade Irishman William Joyce, was to condemn the arming of civilians as against the Geneva Convention, calling it an irresponsible move by Eden and Churchill. The British response was to issue armbands and to equip as many volunteers as possible with some form of uniform. As the only uniforms the regular army could spare were the very small or very large sizes, the effect was not always flattering. Soon, though, Joyce – universally known as Lord Haw-Haw – turned to ridicule, sending up a suggestion in the *Daily Mirror* that miniature sewing machines be attached under the seats of bicycles left temptingly standing about. The theory was that when the invading German paratrooper tried to ride off on it, it would automatically sew his trousers to the seat.

The British laughed at this too, and were not slow to notice how many of the Home Guard units had headquarters in pubs or golf clubhouses. But at the same time the volunteers, freeing up many regular soldiers for badly needed training, worked hard to man road-blocks, guard important factories, set up observation posts on high ground and patrol the countryside in search of paratroopers or enemy agents and fifth columnists. Everywhere they checked papers, often to the annoyance of the public. On many occasions bird-watchers, walkers or young courting couples would find themselves suddenly surrounded and threatened with a motley assortment of weapons. One zealous Home Guarder even stopped the King's car on a visit to an ordinance factory and demanded to see his papers. Once he was shown the occupant of the vehicle, he saluted and the King was allowed to proceed. More seriously, on several occasions Home Guarders opened fire on those who did not stop – on one night alone there were four such instances – and some came to consider the volunteers a dangerous menace. There were also numerous false alarms when the noise of cattle moving about or wayward pieces of barrage balloons would lead to massive search operations being launched. Moreover, with censorship firmly in place, rumours flourished, turning false alarms into firm sightings which became in turn whole German army groups moving up from the coast. Even senior commanders such as Field Marshal Ironside, the commander-in-chief of Home Defence, and Admiral Ramsay, the creator of Operation Dynamo, said they were convinced that fifth-columnist activity was rife in the country, though there is no evidence for this at all. Everyone was infected. A pilot flying over Cardiff noticed a wood in the shape of an arrow pointing directly at the centre of the town. Although the wood had been there for hundreds of years, he still reported it as suspected enemy bomber-guiding activity.

Once France had fallen, the emphasis altered to cope with an expected invasion from the sea, rather than the air. Around the coast 400 fishing vessels and 700 other patrol boats of all kinds were deployed to watch for an approaching armada. On 13 June it was ordered that the church bells should not be rung again except to announce an invasion. Should a German force establish itself, it was vital that it should not be helped in any way. The removal of all signposts was ordered, together with the blacking-out of all place names, be they on shops, station platforms or even war memorials. There were strict rules that cars should be locked or immobilised and bicycles not left lying around for the use of invading troops. Petrol stations near the coast were closed or mined. After the stunning successes of the German panzers in France, the new focus of defence efforts was to stop, or at least delay, the fast-moving tanks. It was clear that in this respect the defences were still woefully inadequate. Anthony Eden, after a visit on 23 June to the army corps covering the defence of inland Kent, Sussex and Surrey, wrote to Churchill, 'There is no anti-tank regiment nor anti-tank gun in the whole of this Corps area.'[7] On the same day Churchill was at the coast, inspecting the defences at St Margaret's Bay, near Dover. Churchill's own account captures the tone of mingled desperation and defiance:

> The Brigadier informed me that he had only three
> anti-tank guns in his brigade, covering four or five miles
> of this highly menaced coastline. He declared that he had
> only six rounds of ammunition for each gun, and he
> asked me with a slight air of challenge whether he was
> justified in letting his men fire one single round for
> practice in order that they might at least know how the
> weapon worked. I replied that we could not afford
> practice rounds, and that fire should be held for the last
> moment at the closest range.[8]

Should landings be successful, the front to be held at all costs was the 'GHQ Line', a 400-mile defensive system running roughly from Maidstone to Bristol, designed to protect London and the industrial Midlands. In the absence of weapons, improvisation and sheer hard work had to step in. Extensive use was made of natural obstacles such as rivers and canals, and between these, anti-tank ditches were dug. Where the ground made this impossible, other obstacles were erected. The GHQ Line also incorporated a large number of pillboxes made of reinforced concrete, the biggest of which could fit an anti-tank two-pounder gun. Along the coast, barbed wire was spread on the beaches and pillboxes were built to provide fire on to any landing, which would also have to cope with mines and further anti-tank obstacles. There was also a government-driven mass evacuation of the coastal areas. Seaside resorts, used to bustling trade, particularly in the fine weather, were boarded up and deserted. In Margate the population fell from 40,000 to 10,000, and in Dover only 16,000 out of an original 36,000 stayed behind. Inland, people started erecting their own barricades by pulling farm machinery, tar barrels, water tanks and sandbags into roads and lanes.

As the weeks went past and the work continued, more and more strategic points in the south-east were covered by gun emplacements. Some pillboxes were disguised as cafés, toilets or haystacks. Fake advertisement hoardings, which could be any size required, were also used. (One, at Woodbridge in Suffolk, proclaimed the attractions of 'Hotel Continental', which guaranteed a 'warm reception for visiting troops'.) By late July, 8,000 pillboxes had been finished and a further 17,000 were under construction, and many roads near the coast had had explosives laid in pipes under them. The Home Guard, too, trained to knock out tanks, mainly through the use of Molotov cocktails, a weapon used during the Spanish Civil War, consisting simply of a bottle of petrol with a wick, designed to be lit and thrown at an approaching tank. In all sectors bottles were collected and practice in throwing them was initiated. In the absence of modern anti-tank weapons, desperate measures were called for. One plan involved lobbing explosives on to the roofs of enemy tanks with the help of a modified trout-fishing rod. Even the regular army had to resort to some improvised anti-tank tactics. One young soldier was instructed to lay soup plates in the path of advancing German tanks in the hope that they would think they were mines and get out of the tank to remove them, thus making themselves vulnerable to small-arms fire.

It is perhaps fortunate that the Home Guard was not put to the test by an invasion. The regular army was woefully ill-equipped to deal with German panzers; the Home Guard, however hard it trained at throwing bottles, was virtually defenceless. There is no doubt that many would have fought bravely, but it is also inevitable that there would have been terrible carnage. Once the German advance had passed through, other, far more secret plans would have come into effect. At Coleshill House, near Swindon, 3,524 men and women picked from Home Guard units were trained by a veteran of the Spanish Civil War in sabotage, explosives and ambushes. During the early summer, around twenty-five hideouts were built in Kent in caves, woods and even badger setts, designed to shelter at least six men for a minimum of two weeks. From these they could emerge at night behind the enemy lines to harass and disrupt the enemy advance. As the summer progressed, more and more of these hide-outs were constructed all over the country and were increasingly well-stocked with explosives, weapons, food and ammunition. Judging by what happened in German-occupied Europe, the cost to the civilian population of this sort of resistance could have been very high. The Germans had no qualms about carrying out abductions and shootings as reprisals for guerrilla activity.

It is easy to mock the Home Guard, but the reaction that met Eden's broadcast is not only testament to fear of the Germans and a wish to defend home and family, it is also evidence of a great loyalty to the country, King and government that contrasts sharply with the attitude of many Frenchmen to the divided and unpopular Third Republic. Some influential French writers even welcomed German rule as an alternative to French misgovernment; others preferred anything, even fascism, to war. Disillusionment, anti-semitism and fatalism about German invasion had made France a far more fertile ground for capitulation and collaboration than Britain. Many leading French thinkers, seeing the choice as between communism or fascism, came firmly down in favour of the latter. In Britain the same sort of establishment figures were preparing suicide pills and other extreme measures in the event of a Nazi conquest. 'I am not in the least afraid of a sudden and honourable death,' wrote Harold Nicolson to his wife.[9] Everyone made their own preparations. A grandmother kept an old sword by her chair, ready to swipe at any Germans entering her living room. When a woman in Buckinghamshire was asked how she would react if she came across some invading Germans, she replied that she would invite them all in for a glass of champagne. After a dramatic pause, she added dryly, 'Poisoned, of course.'[10] Elsewhere people constructed booby traps with dynamite or petrol.

Where there was defeatism, it was usually amongst those with nothing positive to do. But by June 1940, with millions in uniform, be it Home Guard or other civil defence units, this was an increasingly small number of people. Not only was the manpower (if not the equipment) ready for air raids, paratroopers and invasion, most felt that they had a part to play, and morale was enormously helped by this. Churchill was acutely aware that in the absence of modern equipment and in the face of such an overwhelming threat, improvisation and morale was pretty much all Britain had left. Broadcasting to the country in July, he lamented that France had been 'rotted from within before they were smitten from without'. In Britain there should be 'no placid lying down of the people in submission . . . as we have seen, alas, in other countries'. What was needed was unity: 'This is not a war of chieftains or of princes, of dynasties or national ambition; it is a war of peoples and of causes.'

The most serious threat to the country, Churchill therefore believed, was to its morale. Although he did not take the threat of fifth columnists seriously and had great faith in the defensive capabilities of the navy and the Channel to scupper German invasion plans, he feared greatly that the same defeatism that had ruined France would cause the British people to wish to sue for peace with Hitler. The new technique of war, he argued, was an offensive against morale. To counter this, the 'great invasion scare' must be maintained, as it was 'serving a very useful purpose . . . it is keeping every man and woman tuned to a high pitch of readiness'. The offensive against morale might well include the bombing of civilians, and frightening reports were coming out of Germany about new, enormously destructive bombs. 'Then the real test will begin,' Colville noted, 'have we or the Germans the sterner civilian morale?'[11] After the aerial assault would come not invasion, Churchill believed, but another peace offensive.

If the tactics of keeping everyone busy and morale high were working in the country at large, the Prime Minister was also inspiring those in government and in his immediate circle. The first British Prime Minister to have worn a uniform while in office, as Minister of Defence he was also far more closely involved with the running of the war than Lloyd George had been in the Great War, and his office emitted a never-ending flow of memoranda. Rarely over-ruled by the War Cabinet, he did not discuss issues so much as exhort and harangue his colleagues. On top of this he concerned himself with settling disputes in home policy, and in a turmoil of activity, he would get involved with every issue down to the spelling of foreign names and the jam ration. He frequently spent part of the day working from his bed, with his black cat Nelson nestling at his feet; by his side lay a huge chromium-plated spittoon in which to throw his cigars.

While looking into all possibilities for the defence of the island in this critical time, Churchill also kept thinking about offensives against German units and about the years ahead. On 5 June, only just after the last of the BEF had made their bedraggled way from Dunkirk, Churchill was 'full of offensive zeal' planning small forays against the enemy-held coastline. Specially trained commandos should, he suggested, 'crawl ashore, do a deep raid inland cutting a vital communication, and then back leaving a trail of German corpses behind them'.[12] The purpose of these attacks, he argued, would be less military than political. 'An effort must be made to shake off the mental and moral prostration to the will and initiative of the enemy from which we suffer,' he said. To this end he was keen for bombing to be stepped up against the enemy. 'We will make Germany a desert, yes a desert,' he said to his commanders on 13 July.[13]

The real strategic tactic remained, however, to hold out and wait for the American cavalry, or more exactly the results of the elections in November. Nevertheless, Churchill did everything he could to keep up the pressure on Roosevelt in the meantime. In telegrams to Mackenzie King, the Canadian prime minister, he warned that he could not take responsibility for what might happen should Britain be overpowered and a pro-German administration installed. Churchill was well aware that concern was still growing in Washington that the Royal Navy might end up in German hands. 'It would help,' he wrote to the King, 'if you would impress this danger upon the President.' To Lord Lothian, the British Ambassador in Washington, Churchill was even more explicitly trying to play on the American fears:

> If Great Britain broke under an invasion, a pro-German government might obtain far easier terms from Germany by surrendering the Fleet, thus making Germany and Japan masters of the New World. This dastard deed would not be done by His Majesty's present advisers, but, if Mosley were Prime Minister . . . it is exactly what [he] would do, and perhaps the only thing [he] could do, and the President should bear this very clearly in mind. You should talk to him in this sense . . .[14]

To Roosevelt himself, Churchill kept up the request for destroyers and for more war materials to be quickly dispatched. But by the end of June, the situation had actually deteriorated. Attacks in Congress had led the President to block shipment of twenty torpedo boats. An old law had been invoked that disallowed the sale of an armed vessel to a belligerent nation. The destroyers looked further away than ever. On 26 June Arthur Purvis, the man in the US responsible for placing orders on behalf of the British government, reported back to London, saying, 'for the moment I feel nothing will be gained by pressing for reconsideration. When the British ability to resist has become more evident, the attack can be renewed.' In short, many in Washington remained unwilling to send war materials to a country that seemed to be on its last legs. Churchill complained to Lord Lothian, 'Up till April [the United States] were so sure the Allies would win that they did not think help necessary. Now they are so sure we shall lose that they do not think it possible.' All that seemed to matter to Washington was what would happen after the inevitable defeat, in particular to the Royal Navy.

Churchill himself was fearful about the large French fleet. During the frantic few days before the fall of France, he had repeatedly stressed to his French opposite numbers the importance of keeping the warships out of German hands. Combined with the Italian fleet, enemy control of the French warships would drastically change the naval balance of power, and make an invasion more possible and a German blockade more effective. Amid the confusion, though, he had received contradictory signals from the French, and after Pétain's appointment, trust between the erstwhile allies was at a very low ebb. Churchill had been promised before the surrender that the 400 German pilots in French captivity would be handed over to the British. This had not happened, and the pilots were now back with their units and preparing for the attack on Britain.

France's armistice with Germany had stated that the French ships were to be disarmed under German and Italian control and would not be used by the Germans during the war. Many French warships, some still under construction, had already slipped away to British ports, where they continued to proudly fly the French flag even after the surrender. These included two battleships, four light cruisers, several submarines, including the large *Surcouf*, and up to a hundred smaller vessels. But other units awaited orders which did not come, Pétain believing that if the French fleet sailed to British or American waters, reprisals and the total occupation of France by the Germans would follow. Instead, unknown to Churchill, the French naval commanders had received secret orders to sink their ships 'so that neither the enemy nor any foreigner may take the ship by force in order to employ it'.[15]

Churchill did not trust the German promise not to use the French fleet against Britain, nor did he have any faith that the Vichy government, whom he had branded as collaborators, would act to prevent it falling into German hands. Moreover, the units in British ports, mainly Portsmouth and Plymouth, were professing their allegiance to the Vichy government. There seemed to be only one option. On 3 July British marines with fixed bayonets stormed aboard the French ships anchored in British ports. Only on the *Surcouf* was there brief resistance, in which one French sailor and three British were killed. But this part of the fleet, at least, was now in British hands. The main force, however, was in the Mediterranean. Part of it, under the command of Admiral Godefroy, came over to the British, but there still remained a sizeable flotilla at the French naval base at Oran in North Africa, which included two modern battle cruisers and three older battleships. Here the proud French admiral refused to surrender, and British ships from Gibraltar reluctantly opened fire. The French vessels were defenceless. Within moments much of the fleet had been destroyed and 1,200 officers and men had been killed.

For the French it was a bitter blow, but for Churchill, in spite of his great sadness at having to order an attack on an ally he had fought so hard to keep in the war, the action not only neutralised the perceived threat of the French fleet joining the Kriegsmarine (the German navy), it was also a vital show of determination at a time when the will to fight, let alone to win the war, was of enormous importance. In Churchill's words, it 'demonstrated that the British War Cabinet fears nought and will not baulk at anything'. To the watching Americans, it was just the sign of an 'ability to resist' that Purvis had demanded. Harold Ickes, Roosevelt's Interior Secretary, was impressed, and in New York Ralph Ingersoll, editor of *PM* magazine, wrote: 'When an allied officer gives an ultimatum . . . and it isn't a bluff, that's news,' concluding, 'I am for sending supplies to England as long as it's governed by a Churchill who will fight.' Harry Hopkins, who was in the Roosevelt circle, disclosed on a visit to Chequers seven months later that it had been the action at Oran that had convinced the American President that Britain would go on fighting. Whatever the defeatist ambassador Joe Kennedy had been reporting back to Washington, it now seemed that Churchill's rhetoric was being backed up by actions.

Raymond Lee was an American general who served as military attaché in London during the Battle of Britain. He lived in the West End and his frequent letters home record his meetings with British officials all the way up to Churchill himself, and also provide an interesting commentary on events as they unfolded. Although an Anglophile, Lee knew that his loyalties were to Washington and his job was to provide a clear-headed appraisal of how the war was developing. His reaction to the action at Oran would have pleased

Churchill: 'What a dashing, old-fashioned, Nelsonian cutting-out expedition this was. It has a fine spirited bravado about it which shows that the British are not going to sit quietly and watch Hitler's plans mature.'

British opinion and Parliament were delighted as well. Lee, sitting in the Distinguished Strangers Gallery, watched Churchill explain the action to the House of Commons, and noted: 'Cheers from every corner of the chamber greeted his every point . . . and when he finished the decorum of Parliament vanished. All were on their feet, shouting, cheering and waving order papers and handkerchiefs like mad.'[16] Churchill himself, though cheered by the reaction, had tears in his eyes as he sat down after his speech. A great Francophile, it had been one of the hardest decisions he had had to make so far.

If the naval situation had brightened, the need for more fighter aircraft to defend Britain against the Luftwaffe bomber threat was as serious as ever. Germany and Britain were described by Colville respectively as the elephant and the whale – Germany was as undisputed on land as Britain was at sea. The elephant and the whale, it seemed, could never bring their strength to bear on each other, but the unknown quantity was the air theatre. The task of building up the fighter force had fallen to Lord Beaverbrook, Minister for Aircraft Production. One of Churchill's first appointments, he had a gift for rubbing people up the wrong way and had soon made many enemies in the Air Ministry and the Civil Service. The languid and aristocratic Colville described Beaverbrook as 'twenty-five per cent thug, fifteen per cent crook and the remainder a combination of genius and real goodness of heart', while Raymond Lee found him 'dwarfish and prickly'. Nevertheless, it turned out to be an inspired choice. The newspaper magnate had straightaway set about wresting as much control as he could from the moribund Air Ministry. In this he had the full backing of the Prime Minister, who himself described the ministry as 'a most cumbrous and ill-working administrative machine'.[17] Beaverbrook appointed new men from business to key positions, and kept in constant touch with progress personally, pleading, threatening and begging for more and more effort. Red tape was slashed, labour regulations were ignored and aircraft factories were persuaded to work ten hours a day, seven days a week. Despite the resistance of the Air Ministry, top priority was given to producing Hurricane and Spitfire fighters.

The civilian population was called in to help once more when an appeal was launched for scrap metal. All over the country, garden and park railings were taken away and aluminium pots and pans collected. Appeals were started to pay for extra aeroplanes, and communities grouped together to provide funds. In all, Beaverbrook's unorthodox methods worked. Production was increased and aircraft were issued speedily to the squadrons, rather than sitting around interminably in storage units. Beaverbrook proudly noted to the Prime Minister on 30 June that there were now 1,040 operational aircraft of all types ready for service. 'I would remind you,' he went on, 'that there were 45 aircraft ready for service when your Administration began.'[18]

But there was precious little other good news. The most recent secret estimate of German air strength conceded that the enemy had overwhelming numerical superiority. On 28 June Churchill received the news that German anti-aircraft crews were being sent maps of England. This intelligence came from the team at the Bletchley cryptographic centre, who had been decoding intercepted German radio messages since 22 May. As the summer progressed Churchill was to receive more and more intelligence from this source. As soon as a message was deciphered, it was sent to the headquarters of MI6, at Broadway in London. From there a selection was made and sent by courier on the five-minute journey to Downing Street, where it was locked in a special buff-coloured box to which only the Prime Minister himself had a key.

Later in the war, this was to provide an invaluable resource for knowing the intentions of the Germans. Churchill was to call the deciphering staff at Bletchley 'the geese who laid the golden eggs and never cackled'.[19] In 1940 success was still limited and most communications between German commanders and their units travelled on secure landlines. Nevertheless, it was a considerable coup for the British. But this message about the anti-aircraft crews seemed to confirm that invasion plans were well underway. The next day a message was deciphered that stated that Germany's long-range bombers would have completed their refitting and be ready to attack by 8 July.

As these warnings reached a climax, Churchill summoned to Chequers, the Prime Minister's country residence, Major-General Thorne, who was commanding the defences in the vital sector on the southern side of the Thames estuary. Thorne was not optimistic. His divisions were 'scarcely equipped and only partly trained'. He thought he might be able to hold down the German left wing in Ashdown Forest but 'did not see what could prevent the right wing advancing through Canterbury to London'.[20] Meanwhile, in desperation, Churchill was making plans to drench an invasion force on the beaches with mustard gas.

On 30 June and 1 July the undefended Channel Islands were occupied, meaning that the German army was now on British soil for the first time. From northern France came stories of barges being prepared and paratroops being assembled. In Berlin rumours abounded that the invasion of Britain was already in motion, and in southern England an armada from the sea or the sky was expected at any time. On Tuesday 9 July, Colville wrote in his diary, 'The invasion and great attack is now said to be due on Thursday.'[21] Everywhere people were waiting, asking, 'Why doesn't he come?'

CHAPTER FOUR

Operation Sealion

HITLER WAS BESIDE HIMSELF WITH HAPPINESS AFTER THE fall of France. To the astonishment of his entourage he performed a little dance for joy. Chief of Staff of the Armed Forces Wilhelm Keitel chose the moment to proclaim his Führer 'the greatest military commander of all time'. For Hitler it was a moment of sweet triumph; at last the hated Versailles Treaty had been well and truly avenged. Making the humbled French leaders sign the surrender in the same railway carriage had been the icing on the cake. Straight after the armistice came into force, Hitler went off to visit First World War battlefields with two old comrades. On 28 June he made a sightseeing trip to Paris, which had been undamaged by the campaign. Posing in front of the Eiffel Tower, the former corporal had achieved what the Imperial German High Command had failed to do in four years of bitter conflict in the First World War. While in the French capital, Hitler spent a long time looking at the tomb of Napoleon.

But what of Britain, who had expected an invasion to follow hot on the heels of the evacuating BEF at the beginning of June? That fear, at least, was unfounded. Part of the reason for the infamous decision to halt the panzers on 24 May, when the trapped armies in the Dunkirk pocket lay defenceless before them, had been to save the men and machines for what was clearly Hitler's primary objective, the defeat of France. As with the speed of the advance to the coast, the collapse of French power during June had surprised the German High Command, who were expecting a hard battle. With the surrender, as the British busied themselves with defensive measures along the coast, an air of relative calm descended on the German army in France, who started to make preparations to send up to forty divisions home. At a meeting between Mussolini and Hitler on 18 June it seemed to some that peace was in the air. The Italian foreign minister, Count Ciano, wrote at the time, 'Hitler is now the gambler who had made a big scoop and would like to get up from the table risking nothing more.'[1]

Hitler expected the British to come to terms. How could they do otherwise? Their tiny army had been hustled ignominiously from the continent and had left their equipment behind. Their air force had been badly mauled in France and over the Dunkirk beaches. They were isolated and friendless. Hitler was not alone in this assessment. Opinion from Cape Town to Moscow expected the British to sue for peace.

Hitler's aim had been to knock out France so that he had a free hand to build a continental empire to the east. He strongly believed a French defeat would bring the British to the negotiating table. Indeed, after the cave-in at Munich, he had believed Britain would stay out of the war altogether. Hitler repeatedly insisted that he had no quarrel with the 'great British people', so close in racial background to the Germans. He saw little to be gained from defeating Britain anyway, as he predicted that the Empire would consequently fall into the hands of the Japanese, the Americans or even the Soviets.

Hitler's primary hope, and belief, was that Britain could come to some agreement that would preserve the Empire and concede German dominance of Europe. For the moment, then, he was happy to wait and see. These hopes were boosted when he heard that a senior Foreign Office politician had been talking to a Swedish envoy. R.A. Butler was a pragmatic politician and a follower of Lord Halifax. On 17 June he told the Swedish envoy, Byorn Prytz, that his 'official attitude will for the present be that the war should continue, but he must be certain that no opportunity should be missed of compromise if reasonable conditions could be agreed and no diehards would be allowed to stand in the way'.[2] He went on to add that 'common sense and not bravado' must govern the actions of the government in its dealings with Germany.

Hitler was unable to know to what extent this feeler represented the will or mood of the country and its leadership. He knew that Churchill was full of fighting talk but, naturally, there would be some changes at the top of British politics if peace was to be made, just as there were when the Phoney War ended and in France after the collapse. So great was Hitler's desire to avoid continuing the war with Britain that he almost persuaded himself to believe Butler's approach had more official sanction than was actually the case.

Ten months earlier, when Hitler had assembled his generals to tell them of his plan to invade Poland, he was already confidently predicting the conquest of France and the Low Countries. But for Britain, in the unlikely event of it holding out, the intention was to use control of the northern French coastline for a blockade of shipping by the Luftwaffe, while U-boats patrolled further out into the Atlantic. Hitler was well aware that Britain was heavily dependent on imports for food, and also for weapons and raw materials, and saw blockade as the obvious weapon. Thus in the weeks after the fall of France, he made no mention of a possible invasion of Britain. Some of his commanders, however, fearing that he might at any moment order preparations to be made, had been investigating the possibilities since the previous year.

Chief among them was Grand-Admiral Raeder, the head of the Kriegsmarine, who in the Royal Navy faced the most formidable of the British armed forces.

The German navy was never designed to go up against the Royal Navy in the open seas. At a meeting with Hitler on 23 September 1939, it had been confirmed that for this war the sole purpose of the Kriegsmarine was to act against shipping; in short, to carry out the role it had played in the First World War. Since the beginning of the war, however, the small German navy had been further weakened by the loss of the 'pocket battleship' the *Graf Spee*, which was cornered by three British cruisers off the coast of Uruguay. By the beginning of 1940, Neville Chamberlain could confidently, if a little prematurely, declare, 'The Oceans of the world have been swept clear of German shipping.' On British propaganda films much was made of Britain retaining the 'Freedom of the Seas'.

In this situation, Raeder was under no illusions about what his forces could achieve and was content to limit his surface and underwater craft to the blockade only. To a great extent Hitler understood this fundamental problem. He once told Raeder, 'On land I am a hero, at sea I am a coward.' Nevertheless, the admiral wanted to cover his back, and was keen to have some sort of plan in place should Hitler ask him to take part in an invasion of Britain. So, on 15 November 1939 he set up a small team to study the possibilities. Five days later he was presented with 'Study Red', which, as expected, concentrated on the difficulties an invasion would face from the Royal Navy and the Royal Air Force. In the Kriegsmarine, the report was quietly filed away, although copies were sent to the heads of the army and to the OKW, the body run by General Alfred Jodl to co-ordinate the three services.

In the OKW the report was also filed away, but the army

initiated their own study on 13 December called 'Study Northwest'. The navy plan had been to land on the south coast between Portland and the Isle of Wight. Hoping to avoid some of the problems they had identified, the army moved the potential landing north to between the Thames and the Wash. In no time, detailed invasion plans were assembled. In an airborne operation the ports of Lowestoft and Yarmouth were to be seized and an infantry division and a brigade of cyclists were to be landed from the sea. South of the ports a further infantry division was to land on the coast near Dunwich and one near Ipswich. A second wave was to consist of two panzer divisions, a motorised infantry division and further infantry reinforcements. A third wave of six panzer and infantry divisions was to be carried in once the transports had returned to Belgian and Dutch ports, which the plan assumed (correctly as it turned out) would be in German hands. There was also to be a diversionary action north at the mouth of the Humber river. The objective was to get forces north of London to cut off the capital from the industrial heartlands of the Midlands and north-east.

The report was sent by the army to the Luftwaffe and the Kriegsmarine with the demands of them that the plan required. The Luftwaffe were to make the airborne landings, command the air over the operation and provide support as the army drove inland. The navy were to close the Straits of Dover against the Royal Navy from the south, provide and protect the landing craft and carry out the diversion in the north.

The reply came back from the Luftwaffe on 30 December. It was brief and to the point: 'The planned deployment is only possible under a condition of total air superiority and even then only if total surprise is guaranteed.' Even the weakest air defences, they pointed out, could wreak havoc with the landing craft. The landing, they concluded, 'could only be the final act in an already victorious war against England, otherwise the conditions for the success of such a combined operation would not exist'.[3]

The Kriegsmarine liked the plan even less. Entering the narrow ports would require slow manoeuvring of ships, and there could be no question of them taking on the British home fleet, which would doubtless make haste to intercept the landing force. Also, the scale of the invasion far outstripped anything they had planned for in Study Red. To collect and prepare the necessary craft to ship over 100,000 men together with machines and equipment would, they said, take at least a year. Furthermore, support from the air would be contingent not only on the prior destruction of the RAF, but also on the weather and other unreliable factors. In fact, all that the three arms of the forces could agree on was that total air superiority was a prior requisite of any landing. Through the early months of 1940, no further action was taken to move the plan forward.

The successful German invasion of Norway in April 1940 may have raised hopes that such an attack might succeed against Britain as well. The operation had seen the first major naval engagement of the war. The Royal Navy had lost an aircraft carrier, two cruisers, nine destroyers and six submarines. The Kriegsmarine had lost four cruisers, two destroyers, three U-boats and one torpedo boat. But unlike the Royal Navy, the Kriegsmarine could not afford the losses, which amounted to almost half of its available units. The campaign left the Germans with only four destroyers. Even with the Royal Navy's substantial commitments around the world, particularly in the Mediterranean and the Atlantic, the home fleet was now even more superior to the Kriegsmarine. Furthermore, as Grand-Admiral Raeder pointed out to Hitler on 21 May, both the defences and the sea conditions were markedly different. Against Norway, soldiers and their weapons were brought to Norwegian ports and simply unloaded; although the Channel was a shorter stretch of water, it was one of the most treacherous in the world, and the British coastline was protected by reefs, shallows and difficult currents and tides.

Although Hitler still showed no sign of interest in an invasion of Britain, and insisted that no preparations be made for the time being, Raeder was keen to stay one step ahead. New plans were drafted and on 31 May preparations were even started for the assembly of an invasion fleet. Some elements within the army high command, too, began to rethink an invasion in the light of their stunning success against France. Units were moved to the coast and new plans drawn up for a landing between Margate and the Isle of Wight. Previous objections by the Kriegsmarine were ignored or brushed aside. The army even set a date of 15 August. The Luftwaffe, keen not to fall behind in the Führer's estimation, started preparing airborne forces and began to reconsider their previous objections to their part in the invasion plan. Raeder's wish to cover himself, combined with confusion and rivalry between the three German services, seems to have set the ball rolling. As momentum grew, the army collected thirteen divisions on the Channel coast, split into two waves. The first contained some 90,000 men, the second comprised 170,000 men with heavy weapons, 34,200 vehicles and 57,550 horses. Also on hand were 26,000 bicycles.

Nevertheless, there was still no word from Hitler about an invasion. Officially the policy remained to starve Britain out with a blockade and to hope and press for peace. But by 30 June, when the defiant noises from Churchill and the British people were reaching a climax, it at last sunk in that there was going to be no immediate capitulation. It was decided, then, that one last great show of force was needed to bring the British to the negotiating table. The situation was complicated by Hitler, who, never enthusiastic about pursuing the war against Britain to its bitter end, was by now concentrating on other conquests, namely to rid the world 'once and for all' of Bolshevism. From his earliest political days Hitler had been anticipating a showdown in the east and, with his dreams of Lebensraum ('living room') in the rich cornfields of the Ukraine, had set the German people on a collision course with Russia. At that time the Soviets and the Nazis were allies and the German war effort was receiving vital raw materials from the Russians. But neither Hitler nor Stalin was under any illusions that this was a lasting settlement. With the stunning effectiveness of the campaign in France, and morale in the German army sky high, Hitler was keen to sustain the momentum of success. At the same time, though, he had also vowed never to take Germany into a war on two fronts; thus the desire to neutralise Britain took on a new urgency. The original plan for a blockade was now considered too long-term.

On 2 July Hitler authorised the three services to start making formal plans for an invasion, but only along the lines suggested by Chief of Staff Alfred Jodl, who saw an invasion only as a *coup de grâce* once the British were on the verge of collapse. First, Jodl suggested, the Luftwaffe must use their superiority to eliminate the RAF and its maintenance organisation. Next there should be co-ordinated sea and air attacks against the import routes and stocks of vital supplies for the British Isles; these should be combined with occasional terror attacks against centres of population. Only once this had brought civil strife and economic and political meltdown to Britain would an invasion be able to proceed.

Raeder was still far from keen on the idea of crossing the Channel and made his feelings known to Hitler on 11 July at a meeting in the Führer's alpine refuge, the Berghof. To succeed, Raeder argued, the landings would have to take place in a narrow sea lane between Calais and Dover, which could be protected by Germany's limited naval resources together with minefields. Two days later, however, army commander-in-chief General von Brauchitsch and his chief of staff, Colonel-General Franz Halder, arrived, full of confidence, and presented their plans, which included landings all along the south coast. Hitler listened carefully and to their great surprise agreed to the plan in its entirety. This was wholly out of character – previous military plans had been heavily scrutinised, and detailed questions asked – and reflects again Hitler's lack of real enthusiasm for the invasion. Nevertheless the order was given to proceed with the plans, and with the Führer's blessing, to the army everything now seemed possible.

Jodl, previously a sceptic, was swayed by the confidence of the army commanders, itself based on a misunderstanding of what the Kriegsmarine had said was possible. In his *First Thoughts on a Landing in England,* the objections of the navy have been brushed aside, and the invasion, instead of being a threat or a mopping-up operation, begins to take on the character of a decisive action in its own right.

> In the Channel we can substitute command of the air for the naval supremacy we do not possess and the sea crossing is short there . . . The landing must therefore take place in the form of a river crossing in force on a broad front. The role of the artillery will fall to the Luftwaffe; the first wave of landing troops must be very strong; and, in place of bridging operations, a sea lane completely secure from naval attacks must be established in the Dover Straits.[4]

Nevertheless, it was still agreed that the first step would have to be a Luftwaffe assault. In fact with his powerful army the wrong side of the Channel and his navy weak, this was the only immediate option open to Hitler.

On the morning of 16 July, Major Josef Schmid, a senior intelligence officer, submitted a document to Hitler called 'A Comparative Appreciation of the Striking Power of the RAF and the Luftwaffe'.[5] In the report he guessed that the British had 900 first-line fighters, of which 675 were fully serviceable. At this stage of the conflict, the German intelligence was not far off. In fact the RAF had 587 available on a good day. Schmid also reported back that the Luftwaffe had found the Messerschmitt Bf 109 superior, particularly in firepower, to the British Hurricane and Spitfire, but admitted that the Bf 110 was inferior to the Spitfire.

Heartened by this, the same day Hitler issued his Directive 16, 'On the preparation of a Landing Operation against England':

> Since England, despite its militarily hopeless situation, still
> has not shown any signs of being prepared to negotiate, I
> have decided to prepare a landing operation against
> England and, if necessary, carry it out. The aim of this
> operation is to eliminate Great Britain as a base from
> which war against Germany can be continued, and, if it
> should be necessary, to occupy the island completely.[6]

The ambivalence about the operation is there for all to see. It is obvious that Hitler was still hoping that the invasion would be unnecessary and that Britain would be forced to come to terms purely through attack by air and the *threat* of invasion. Nevertheless, he instructed that all preparations for what was now known as 'Operation Sealion' should be ready by the middle of August.

All that remained was a final appeal to the British people to capitulate or come to terms. On 19 July Hitler made a speech in the Reichstag which has come to be known as 'The Last Appeal to Reason':

> Mr Churchill ought perhaps, for once, to believe me when I prophesy that a great empire will be destroyed – an empire which it was never my intention to destroy or even to harm . . . In this hour I feel it to be my duty before my own conscience to appeal once more to reason and common sense in Great Britain . . . I can see no reason why this war must go on.

In Britain this appeal was rejected by the BBC and the press on their own initiative. Some even saw it as a sign of weakness. Three days later the previous arch-appeaser Lord Halifax was given by Churchill the task of officially brushing it aside on the radio. But Hitler, angered, disappointed and even surprised by the initial reaction, had on 21 July already summoned his military commanders, even though further doomed peace initiatives were instigated through Sweden, the Vatican and the United States. His words to Grand-Admiral Raeder made it clear that he was still less than keen on the invasion plan:

> The invasion of Britain is an exceptionally daring undertaking, because even if the way is short this is not just a river crossing, but the crossing of sea which is dominated by the enemy . . . Operational surprise cannot be expected; a defensively prepared and utterly determined enemy face us and dominate the sea area which we must use . . . The prerequisites are complete mastery of the air, the operational use of powerful artillery in the Straits of Dover and protection by minefields. The time of year is an important factor,

too . . . If it is not certain that preparations can be
completed by the beginning of September, other plans
must be considered.[7]

Even as he set in train the aerial onslaught by the Luftwaffe
and the planning machinery of the army, Hitler's own
concentration was moving inexorably eastwards. A new argument emerged that only by destroying Russia would Britain
be brought to the negotiating table. Churchill had written to
Stalin at the beginning of July urging him to abandon his
agreement with Hitler and to act against Germany. This letter
had been passed by Stalin to the Germans. If Churchill was
relying on the Russians then perhaps it would be easier to
knock them out first, before gratefully receiving the British
surrender. Priorities and the justifications for them shifted
and slipped about. At the very highest level, there was a fog of
muddled thinking. The attack east, General Jodl confided on
29 July to his deputy Walter Warlimont, should begin at the
earliest possible moment, namely May 1941. Ironically this
announcement gave added impetus to Operation Sealion.
Only by pressing forward with the attack on Britain could
the Führer be dissuaded from launching what many in the
German High Command thought, quite rightly, would be a
disastrous attack on Russia.

At a command conference on 31 July Raeder accepted that
the transport could be ready by mid-September, but made it
clear he preferred a delay until the following spring. The tides
in the Channel would be favourable in late August and in the
third week of September, but he confessed that he was unable
to have the necessary barges ready by the first date and
warned that the second could encounter bad weather and
heavy seas. That his protests were ignored may point to
Hitler's lack of real intention to order the invasion as much as
the determination of the army to go ahead. Walter Warlimont

complained later of the 'morass of uncertainty in which German strategy was labouring during this period'.[8]

As early as the end of June, when Hitler had at least come round to contemplating invasion, a high-ranking Nazi intelligence officer, Walter Schellenberg, was charged with preparing 'a small handbook for the invading troops and the political and administrative units accompanying them'.

Organisations considered particularly hostile to Germany were identified. These included trade unions, public schools and even Boy Scout groups, which the handbook branded 'a disguised instrument of power for British cultural propaganda'. Freemasonry, too, was 'a dangerous weapon in the hands of Britain's plutocrats against National Socialist Germany', and was considered to be part of a general Jewish conspiracy. Of the universities, Oxford, London and Bristol were singled out as 'active in political propaganda'. A section on 'Important Museums in England' contained an accurate checklist of art works and documents to look out for. There was also a long and largely accurate chapter on the workings of the British Secret Service. Even the head of the organisation was named, something not known to the British people themselves until 1966.[9]

Others were labelled for immediate arrest as enemies of Nazidom. For this purpose a list was drawn up containing 2,820 names and addresses of both Britons and émigrés. On it were political figures such as Churchill and de Gaulle and also names from the literary and cultural worlds, including Virginia Woolf, H.G. Wells, Stephen Spender and left-wing publisher Victor Gollancz. When Rebecca West discovered that she and Noël Coward were on the list, she famously telegraphed him saying, 'My dear, the people we would have been seen dead with!'

This list was primarily for the use of the Einsatzgruppen, who would follow up behind the invading front-line troops.

These 'search and destroy' units were designed to eliminate anti-Nazi elements or racial or political enemies. They were to be based in London, Bristol, Birmingham, Liverpool, Manchester and Edinburgh. In overall charge would have been the notorious Dr Frank Six, who later in the war was responsible for brutal massacres in the occupied Soviet Union.

Although what was intended was a comprehensive purging of the upper echelons of British life, there were some notable omissions, including Lloyd George and George Bernard Shaw (although the former's daughter was on the list). Much to the subsequent embarrassment of these absentees, it was clear that the Nazis had listened out carefully for any comments sympathetic to Germany or against the war. It is likely as well that approaches would have been made to the Duke of Windsor, who as Edward VIII had abdicated rather than give up his liaison with the divorcee Wallis Simpson. He had opposed the war and was telling American journalists off the record that Britain should make peace with Germany in order to prevent the spread of Bolshevism.

Further plans were also discussed for occupied Britain. One pound sterling was to be worth 9.6 marks, a rate designed to ensure that much of British wealth flowed to Berlin, as occurred in France and elsewhere. All radio sets and firearms were to be handed in, with stiff penalties for those who disobeyed. Raw materials and industrial equipment were to be removed to Germany. Perhaps harshest of all was the plan for all males between the ages of seventeen and forty-five to be exiled to the continent immediately, there to work in the German arms industry and on Hitler's grandiose construction projects. This would have removed eleven million Britons from the country and brought any semblance of normal life to a standstill.

There were also 430,000 Jews living in Britain. Stories had

already started filtering back about the treatment of Jews in lands controlled by the Nazi party. Events in Germany were well known. In November 1938 had come Kristallnacht ('crystal night'), named after the glass wreckage that littered Jewish areas after Nazi thugs had gone about smashing the windows and contents of Jewish homes and businesses. Stories had also come from émigrés who had left Austria after the Anschluss ('attachment') with Germany in May 1938. In June of that year Harold Nicolson had written to his wife: 'Yesterday I chanced upon an Austrian who had just escaped from Vienna. What he told me made me sick . . . Last Sunday they arrested all the people out for a walk in the Prater [park] and separated the Jews from the rest. The Jewish men were made to take off all their clothes and crawl around in the grass on all fours. They made old Jewesses climb into the trees on ladders and perch there. They then told them to chirp like birds.' But such things could not be true, surely? Nicolson went on, 'I had my doubts that even the Germans could act in such as manner. However I had dinner with Count Bernstoff, who said, when I repeated the stories to him: "Yes, they are true." '[10]

Many of the 430,000 British Jews would, like those in France, have been transported east, for 'resettlement'. It has been argued, however, that the relative lack of anti-semitism in Britain would have meant fewer denunciations, and therefore many may have been hidden or helped to escape overseas.

For the moment, though, all this was in a possible future. First, as everyone had agreed, the Luftwaffe had to achieve air superiority over the Channel and southern England. But from the very start, the role of the Luftwaffe was confused. It was far from clear whether its attack would be merely the first phase in an operation culminating in an invasion – the view of the army, who were keen to have their service perform the feat of destroying Germany's last enemy – or whether it was planned that the Luftwaffe alone could bring Britain to its knees, destabilise Churchill's warlike administration, and therefore render the invasion nothing more than the *coup de grâce* initially suggested by Jodl. Certainly the latter was still the preferred option of Hitler, who valued the army's earnest preparations as a threat designed to back up the Luftwaffe campaign. In the event the Luftwaffe was given both tasks simultaneously. It was to destroy the RAF and coastal defences, engage 'approaching naval vessels' and also carry out attacks against infrastructure and blockade targets.

I n June 1940 the Luftwaffe was unquestionably the strongest air force in the world. Blooded during the Spanish Civil War, it had been conspicuously successful in the three campaigns of the conflict so far. In France and the Low Countries it had shot down or destroyed on the ground over 3,000 enemy aircraft. Furthermore it now had control of airfields all along the North Sea and Channel coasts. Engineers had been working round the clock to repair and adapt the French, Norwegian, Belgian and Dutch aerodromes.

The Luftwaffe had been forced to grow fast. The Treaty of Versailles had forbidden the Germans any air force. But straight after the First World War, German warplane manufacturers had set up commercial arms and airlines, amongst them the company of Hugo Junkers, who pioneered metal aircraft. Lufthansa was by 1930 larger than the British and French airlines combined, and flying was enormously popular in Germany, which led the development of stronger and faster civil aircraft. In 1920 state-sponsored gliding clubs had been set up to train new pilots. By 1929 these had over 50,000 members. Adolf Galland, aged nineteen in 1933, was typical of the glider pilots selected to convert to powered flight in Lufthansa. From there he was sent to Lipesk, a secret installation south-east of Moscow, where the Russians had allowed Germany to discreetly train pilots and ground crew. Afterwards he did further training in Italy, including the firing of live ammunition, before returning to Lufthansa, where navigational skills were taught. When Hitler came to power in 1933, an order went out almost immediately for as many combat aircraft as possible to be built. Lufthansa was taken over, all Lufthansa pilots were made Luftwaffe reservists, and the civil aircraft designers and manufacturers were set to work. Thus many of the German warplanes that fought the Battle of Britain evolved from civilian designs that were already world-beaters. In 1937 the Messerschmitt-designed Bf 109 held the world speed record for single-engined aircraft, and the following year the Junkers Ju 88 broke the speed record for twin-engined flight.

The new Luftwaffe was the most Nazi-dominated of the three German services, partly because it was so new and partly because of its leadership and structure. In overall charge was Hermann Göring. He had started as an infantry officer in 1914, but got into the air service through a friend. He became one of the best known German pilots of the First World War and in 1917 took over Baron von Richthofen's famous 'flying circus'. So when he joined the Nazi party in 1922, it was a move that boosted the party's respectability considerably. He remained central to the party after it came to power in 1935, holding a variety of high state positions, and was in charge of the 'Four Year' economic plan. Along the way he amassed considerable wealth in jewels, property and art. The most extravagant of his many castles and residencies was Karinhall, named after his first wife. There, amid splendid gardens and lakes, he was waited on by servants dressed in richly trimmed knee-length coats. Here also was kept much of his art collection in a grand hall. In the basement a model beer hall had been installed. Albert Speer, a senior Nazi, visiting later in the war, commented, 'He even had a life-size nude statue representing Europa mounted above the canopy of his magnificent bed.' At dinner later Speer noticed that 'an ordinary brandy was poured for us, while Göring's servant poured his, with a certain solemnity, from a dusty old bottle. "This is reserved for me alone," he commented without embarrassment to his guests.'[11]

In hindsight, seen in photographs bulging out of his ridiculously ornate uniforms, Göring seems a comic-opera figure, a mixture of South American dictator and music-hall turn. But at the beginning of 1940 he was the second most powerful man in German-dominated Europe and his Luftwaffe was the most feared engine of war anywhere. The named successor to Hitler, he was not a man to be trifled with; many of the senior officers had difficulty standing up to him, even when they knew he was making mistakes.

Early in the development of the Luftwaffe a tactical confusion had arisen. Göring's only qualification for running the German air force was his World War I fighter experience, when chivalric duels had alternated with attacking troops on the ground and dropping bombs, often by hand. As Göring appointed to high positions cronies from those days, this approach to air power permeated planning and construction. Thus the priority in aircraft development was given to fighters and dive-bombers, ideally suited for close support of army operations on the ground. At the same time, however, Göring was influenced by the interwar theories of the overwhelming power of strategic air attacks on the economy and civilian population of an enemy. Air power alone, Göring believed, could be decisive. Thus ambitions were developed that, as we shall see, were at odds with the capabilities of the Luftwaffe aircraft.

With the limited resources initially available, the Luftwaffe had opted to discontinue development of heavy four-engined bombers in favour of lighter but much faster aircraft such as the Ju 88. In addition pressure was put on the designers to allow these light bombers to dive-attack as well as drop their bombs from a horizontal position. In 1937 this policy had seemed justified. With a maximum speed of 286 m.p.h., the Ju 88 was faster than any fighter in the RAF at that time. It seemed that it would always 'get through', and with a maximum bomb load of 2,200 pounds, it seemed it could do considerable damage. During the later stages of the Battle of Britain, however, the Ju 88 would turn out to be as ill-equipped for its task as any of the other German bombers.

In the Bf 109, however, with a top speed of 357 m.p.h. and a very fast rate of climb, the Luftwaffe was confident it had the best fighter in the world. Unlike the Spitfire and the Hurricane, it was equipped with fuel injection, which prevented it from stalling when in a fast dive. Above 20,000 feet it was demonstrably the better aircraft, but its light construction, particularly in the wings, made it less sturdy than its British counterparts.

Although these two were to be the most effective German planes in the Battle of Britain, for Luftwaffe pilots the real prestige lay in flying a Destroyer or a Stuka. The Messerschmitt Bf 110, known as the Destroyer, was a twin-engined fighter with a maximum speed of 336 m.p.h. With a crew of two, it was armed with two forward-facing cannon and four machine-guns. For defence there was a single machine-gun facing backwards. Designed as a long-range fighter, it carried three times the fuel of a Bf 109 and had a range of 350 miles, which meant that it could operate almost anywhere in southern England from its bases in France. Its front-firing weapons produced the most devastating effect of any fighter in the battle, but because of its weight it was difficult to manoeuvre into a firing position.

The Junkers 87, or Stuka, a twin-engined two-seater with a fixed undercarriage and distinctive cranked wings, had already become famous during the campaigns in Poland, the Low Countries and France. For attacks on the ground it was unrivalled in accuracy, diving at about seventy-five degrees from the horizontal, its fixed air brakes used to control its speed. Its pilot could hold the target in sight until it reached its bombing altitude of about 2,300 feet and then strike with great accuracy. In air-to-air combat, however, it soon proved itself vulnerable. Slow and unmanoeuvrable, it was particularly easy to hit as it came out of its dive.

Although by the summer of 1940 it was being phased out in favour of the Ju 88, the Dornier 17 – known as the Flying Pencil – was still a mainstay of the German bomber force. Like the Ju 88, the Do 17 had a crew of four, two engines, and was defended by four hand-held machine-guns. Slower than the Ju 88, it also had a smaller bomb-carrying capacity. Nevertheless, like the other German bombers it could take a lot of damage. Its air-cooled engines were far less vulnerable to enemy fire than those liquid-cooled engines – like the Spitfire and the Hurricane – that needed a system of radiators and coolant pipes.

The third major component of the bomber force assembling to attack Britain was the twin-engined Heinkel 111, which had a crew of five and flew at similar speeds to the Dornier 17. Its bomb load was greater, though, and the He 111 also carried over 600 pounds of armour plating, through which few RAF bullets would be able to penetrate. All the German bombers also had self-sealing fuel tanks, which worked by having layers of rubber around them. The bullet would pass straight through the side of the tank, but when the leaking petrol came into contact with the rubber it would cause it to swell up, sealing the hole.

Thus in many cases dangerous fires were avoided.

Erhard Milch, head of the German Air Ministry, complained that 'the Luftwaffe was not ready for a major war in 1939 . . . the plans envisaged were scheduled for completion in six or eight years . . . about 1944–6'[12] But whatever the reservations, the Luftwaffe had so far seemed unstoppable. The set-back over Dunkirk, when in spite of Göring's promises to the contrary the BEF had escaped, was ignored. Instead the focus was on the ships sunk and the many British fighters shot down. By the end of June, the two strongest of the five German Luftflotten (air fleets) were stationed on the Channel coast: Luftflotte 2 under Field Marshal Kesselring in the area between Rotterdam and Amiens, and Luftflotte 3 under Field Marshal Sperrle to the west in the Cherbourg area. Between them they had a formidable quantity of fully operational aircraft – 656 Bf 109 fighters, 246 Bf 110s, 769 Dornier 17, Ju 88 and Heinkel 111 bombers and 248 Ju 87 (Stuka) dive-bombers.

Albert Kesselring, the forty-five-year-old commander of Luftflotte 2, had become Chief of the Luftwaffe General Staff in 1936, but his original background was in the army, and he acquired a reputation for having a scanty technical knowledge of aircraft. Nevertheless he was an able administrator much respected by his men. Later in the war he would return to the army and distinguish himself during the defence of Italy. Hugo Sperrle was older at fifty-five and, like Göring, had served in the Imperial Flying Service during the First World War. Transferring to the Luftwaffe in 1935 after a spell in the army, he had risen rapidly. In 1936 he had commanded the German squadrons in the Spanish Civil War, and was therefore one of the most experienced officers on either side. Humourless, monocled, obese and stern, he was almost a British caricature of a German high-ranking officer. Hitler called him one of his 'most brutal-looking generals'.

In the middle of July, Sperrle and Kesselring were summoned to Karinhall and ordered by Göring to start making plans for the demolition of the RAF. But over the Channel, on the south coast of England, the battle had already begun.

—CHAPTER FIVE—

The Royal Air Force

FOR MOST OF THE FIRST WORLD WAR, THERE HAD BEEN only navy and army airmen, until on 1 April 1918, in response to German bombing of south-east England, the Royal Air Force had come into existence as the world's first independent air arm. After the war, its commander-in-chief, Sir Hugh Trenchard, had to fight for its existence. Like the army, the RAF had suffered between the wars from the fact that the country could afford only a very small defence budget. At the end of the First World War, the number of squadrons had been reduced from 188 to twenty-five and the annual budget to £11m. It was to remain under £20m until 1935. Moreover, unlike in Germany, flying remained a luxury pursuit, dominated by smart and exclusive flying clubs.

Under pressure for its very existence, it is not surprising that the RAF took up interwar ideas of the enormous independent power of air attack. Only by stressing that aircraft alone could be a war-winning weapon, rather than merely a support for ground troops, could the RAF leadership prevent their fledgling outfit being taken over by the army. It is important to remember that air power between the wars, with a background of very fast technical change, was militarily something of an unknown quantity. No one was quite sure how this new technology could be used most effectively. In the RAF a preference for bombers developed. These, it was argued, could help enforce a blockade against an enemy, a tactic Britain preferred to the costly and bloody business of putting an army in the field in Europe. Furthermore, the threat of the terror-bombing of civilians, the effects of which, as we have seen, were much exaggerated, would surely act as a deterrent to Britain's enemies. Even if there was a general reluctance to attack civilian targets (that lasted well into 1940) it was hoped that the threat alone would deter aggressors. Bombers were thus to an extent the nuclear weapons of the 1930s, with gruesome outcomes envisaged should they ever be actually used. Stanley Baldwin summed up this nightmare scenario: 'you have to kill more women and children more quickly than the enemy if you want to save yourselves.'

For Hitler's birthday on 20 April 1935, a huge air parade was held in Berlin. Britain's representatives there were horrified. Immediately air defence became a key component of overall home defence. It was clear that the 'island fortress' of Britain, if invulnerable from the seas, could now be attacked from the air, perhaps decisively. In 1925 steps had been taken to expand the tiny number of trained pilots in case of an emergency, and the Auxiliary Air Force had been formed along with the Oxford and Cambridge university air squadrons and another at London University. By 1926 the first four Auxiliary squadrons were in existence, 600 to 603. But in 1935 this expansion was given new impetus when the RAF Volunteer Reserve was formed, which aimed to train 800 pilots a year. For the majority who would never have normally been able to afford to fly it was a great opportunity. All volunteers were made sergeants and trained at the weekends in armaments, signals and navigation as well as flying. The following year, further Auxiliary squadrons were formed, including 609 'West Riding', and the RAF was split into Bomber Command, Coastal Defence and Air Defence. The man appointed to take over Air Defence, including

Fighter Command, was Sir Hugh Dowding, who had been passed over for a more senior position at the Air Ministry because he was considered too defensively minded and did not subscribe to the current orthodoxy about the primacy of the offensive bomber.

The son of a schoolmaster, Dowding had left Winchester school at seventeen and was accepted into the Royal Military Academy at Woolwich. Returning to England after a spell abroad as an army officer, Dowding became fascinated with flying, a highly glamorous and fast-changing field. He soon learnt to fly and was accepted into the Royal Flying Corps just as the First World War was starting. In only a year he was commanding a squadron and by 1918 he was a brigadier general. Tragically, his wife died in the 1920s after only two years of marriage and from that moment on Dowding's social life ended and he threw himself into his work, rising steadily through the ranks. His previous job before taking over Fighter Command had been a position on the Air Council as Member for Research and Development, giving him an excellent grasp of, amongst other innovations, radar.

Dowding was a complex figure, largely devoid of charm, but with immense strength of mind and character, unafraid to stick to his guns. Known as 'Stuffy', he was aloof and tactless, but his formidable gifts as an organiser, combined with his knowledge of the latest technical developments, were to be of crucial importance to the Battle of Britain. Sir Frederick Pile, who commanded the anti-aircraft batteries arm of Dowding's patch, called him a 'difficult man, a self-opinionated man, and a man who knew more than anybody about all aspects of aerial warfare'. Much of the vital work he did occurred before the war actually broke out. The changes he oversaw in air defence and aircraft development from 1936 onwards would prove to be the building blocks of success in the battle ahead.

When Dowding took over Air Defence, there were only 356 outdated fighter aircraft at his disposal, the most modern being the Gloster Gladiator, a biplane, and only 2,000 anti-aircraft guns. From the moment he arrived at Bentley Priory, the gloomy residence outside London where Fighter Command was based, he worked hard to push for more resources for his role, however many backs were put up by this at the Air Ministry. Along the way he made plenty of enemies, but also managed to significantly improve the air defences. By the beginning of the war, Anti-Aircraft Command controlled 2,232 heavy and 1,860 light guns as well as 4,128 searchlights, even though siting the guns had provoked complaints from local residents. Even if people wanted defence from the threat of bombing, few wanted anti-aircraft guns situated in their particular back yards.

Anti-aircraft balloons, too, were deployed in increasing numbers from 1938. These were usually positioned no higher than 5,000 feet, and were moored to the ground by steel cables with a view to preventing low-level attack. The suspended steel cable would simply cut through an enemy aircraft's wing like a cheese wire. Public confidence in these preventing the feared bombing attack was high.

But by 1936 the primacy of the bomber had at last begun to be challenged. Two new developments seemed to suggest that the bomber might not always get through after all. One was the emergence of early-warning systems; the other the technical leaps and bounds occurring in the design of fighter aircraft, particularly in terms of speed. One of Dowding's first orders on taking on the research and development job had been that new aircraft should no longer be designed around a wooden frame. He was also in favour of monoplanes, much to the dismay of biplane purists. From these dicta were to emerge the two principal British weapons of the Battle of Britain, the Hawker Hurricane and the Supermarine Spitfire.

Design of the Hurricane began in 1934 under Sydney Camm, chief designer at Hawker's. Incorporating advances such as an enclosed cockpit and a retractable undercarriage, the plane was built with traditional methods of construction, using a tubular metal structure and fabric covering. Such simplicity made the plane relatively cheap and easy to build without wholesale changes to existing factories. (In 1939 it took less than half the time to build a Hurricane than it took to construct a Spitfire.) Convinced that demand from the Air Ministry would follow, the Hawker company started plans for large-scale manufacture of the Hurricane in March 1936. Three months later the gamble paid off when the Air Ministry confirmed that the Hurricane would feature in their plans. The Mark 1 Hurricane came into service in December 1937 and further improvements followed to the defensive armament, the engine – a Rolls-Royce Merlin – and the propeller mechanism, before eventually, in August 1940, the fabric covering on the wings was replaced with metal sheeting. Although the Bf 109 was faster and out-performed the Hurricane at high altitude and in diving and climbing, the Hurricane had a smaller turning circle and could take much more punishment than either the Bf 109 or the Spitfire.

The Hurricane might have been numerically superior during the Battle of Britain, but it was the Supermarine Spitfire that caught the public imagination. Equipped with the same engine, but with less weight, the Spitfire climbed faster and at 20,000 feet had a maximum speed of 362 m.p.h., some 50 m.p.h. quicker than the Hurricane. The Spitfire owed its inspiration to R.J. Mitchell at Supermarine Aviation, a subsidiary of Vickers, and emerged from the competition for high-speed flight. With an all-metal stressed skin, it was not an easy aircraft to build, and the first operational models were not delivered until August 1938. The lucky squadron was 19 at Duxford, who began intensive flying trials straightaway. Again, as with the Hurricane, improvements followed to the propeller, the cramped canopy over the cockpit and the defensive armour around the pilot, including the introduction of supposedly bullet-proof glass. At low and medium altitudes it was highly manoeuvrable and it could climb to 20,000 feet in a little under eight minutes. It was a good match for the Bf 109 – victory in a dogfight would not be decided by the machine but by the prowess of the pilot.

The other factor that challenged the idea that the bomber would always get through was the development of early-warning systems. After experiments in the First World War, the Air Ministry initiated a variety of schemes, including looking into ways that the heat from a hostile bomber's engines could be detected from afar. Sound detection was given more attention as well, and huge curved mirrors were built to act as amplifiers. One, at Hythe in Kent, was 200 feet long. On Romney Marsh a curved eight-metre-high and seventy-metre-long concrete wall was erected, equipped with microphones to pick up the approach of enemy formations from across the Channel. But soon it was decided that there was too much interference from shipping and the sea itself for this to be effective.

As these experiments continued, great leaps in aircraft design and flying technology were leading towards faster and faster potentially hostile bombers. The task of discovering an effective early-warning system became all the more pressing and urgent. At the end of 1934 H.E. Wimperis, Director of Scientific Research at the Air Ministry, suggested that a committee be set up under the chairmanship of H.T. Tizard, chairman of the Aeronautical Research Committee, to review all possibilities, however unlikely. It first met in January 1935.

One of the early ideas now seems both far-fetched and dated, like something out of an H.G. Wells novel, but it was to lead indirectly to the great breakthrough. Wimperis asked Robert Watson-Watt of the National Physical Laboratory at Teddington whether there was any chance that an electro-magnetic 'death ray' could be used to destroy hostile aircraft or their crews in the air. Understandably, Watson-Watt was highly sceptical and pointed out that the aircraft would first have to be located. Watson-Watt had spent many years detecting approaching thunderstorms using equipment largely of his own creation. He found that some atmospheric conditions caused radio waves to be bounced back to earth. Perhaps they might also bounce back off aircraft? With two transmitting and receiving stations, maybe the distance of the incoming objects could then be calculated?

On 26 February 1935 Watson-Watt gave a demonstration using the BBC's transmitter at Daventry. To the delight of all present a test aircraft was followed on a screen for a distance of twelve kilometres. What particularly impressed the Air Defence team was that the system would work just as well at night. Straightaway Watson-Watt was given a large amount of money to continue development. Everyone was sworn to the utmost secrecy, and the device was christened Radio Detection Finding (RDF), considered a vague enough description in case word got out about the project. Work proceeded rapidly. Soon a prototype was up and working in Suffolk at Orfordness. This time the range was twenty-three kilometres. By now Watson-Watt had met Dowding and suggested to him the advantages that such a system might offer to Air Defence. Dowding was impressed and gave Watson-Watt his full support. The project also had official approval from elsewhere, including a visit from the King, and by the time war broke out there were seventeen radar stations, each with a transmitting tower 100 metres high. Range had grown to a maximum of 165 kilometres, which meant that from Dover, much of the airspace over northern France was mapped out on screens in England. Initially, the original chain of stations had only been able to pick up incoming aircraft at over 300 metres, but by November 1939 there was a secondary system, called Chain Home Low, which covered this area on a different frequency. Mobile units were also constructed. To determine whether the blip on the radar screen was hostile, British aircraft were fitted with a device called IFF (Identification Friend or Foe).

To back up this system and to track aircraft once they had crossed the coastline, the Royal Observer Corps was expanded, its members recruited from the local population to man posts on high ground from where they could telephone position, number and approximate height of incoming aircraft back up the chain. Although sometimes hampered by low cloud, the lookouts performed a valuable role, particularly in identifying the type and approximate numbers and height of hostile aircraft. By the summer of 1940 there were 30,000 observers manning more than 1,000 posts.

Obviously detecting the aircraft was only the first stage of defence. With the bombers flying faster and faster, it was necessary to get the information on the radar screens to Fighter Command and the anti-aircraft defences as quickly as possible. A system of reporting to a central location had been put in place at the end of World War One by Major General E.B. Ashmore, head of the London Air Defence Area. Coloured counters on a huge map were used to indicate the latest positions of hostile formations. This system was updated by Dowding, who was proving himself an excellent organiser. As radio messages were not immune to interception, one of the first steps was to ensure that the radar stations were connected by landlines to Fighter Command. Throughout the late 1930s, Post Office engineers worked hard to overhaul the landline system and to install back-up lines between command positions.

As war approached, the system was tested again and again. Once a radar signal had been picked up, the information would travel by landline to Bentley Priory, Dowding's headquarters north-east of London. Far beneath the old house a huge subterranean operations headquarters had been built. Here the information would be filtered – checked against RAF units known to be in the air, and compared with other reports, including those from the Observer Corps. Next the information would be passed to subordinate, or group, commands. Initially there were two of these, for northern and southern England, each with sub-commands covering geographical areas known as 'sectors'. At both levels the aircraft positions – friendly and hostile – relevant to their areas would also be plotted on giant maps. The arrangement was that the group headquarters would order aircraft up, and then tactical control would pass to the sector stations, who were in contact with the actual pilots through radio. After much practice, the whole process from detection to the sector stations ordering up aircraft took just six minutes.

Thus while minute-by-minute tactical control was decentralised, the collection and processing of information was based on Bentley Priory. If the fighter squadrons were the arms of the system, the RDF stations the eyes and the landlines the nerves, then Bentley Priory was the brain. Raymond Lee, the American military attaché, visited the house at the beginning of August 1940. He was highly impressed.

We went down, down, down into great subterranean chambers where in two great rooms, two of the most intricate and modern organisations of the world are housed. In one room is the huge map on which moment by moment the reports of enemy location are plotted and enemy air and sea movement exposed, in another an even greater chart where actions are followed [second] by

> second. The great rooms are almost silent – only a soft
> murmur of voices as messages come and go over headsets,
> and only a little movement as operators move counters
> and markers from point to point and others tend electric
> bulletins and switchboards . . . I had no idea the British
> could evolve and operate so intricate, so scientific and
> rapid an organisation . . .[1]

But in June 1940, although the preparations seem to have
been in place, there was great anxiety in high circles. Like air
power itself, the technology was in its infancy. No one knew
if it would work against the Luftwaffe, who, it was widely
feared, might have some terrible new air weapon anyway.
Meanwhile, round the clock, the system was manned, ready
and waiting.

During the First World War, as the huge drain on
manpower worsened, many women left their homes
for the first time and took up work usually done by men. In
the Second World War, in Britain at least, this was accepted
from the start. Many of the personnel employed in radio,
radar, filtering and plotting operations at sector, group and
Fighter Command headquarters were women. Felicity Peake,
who had joined the Women's Auxiliary Air Force (WAAF) in
1938, was involved in the recruitment process: 'People
swarmed to get in, coming from miles away. I couldn't
believe that so many people could get into a queue and stay
there all day and all night. There was never a shortage of
recruits at any time in any branch.' Hazel Gregory had been
in Paris at the outbreak of the war. She was studying modern
languages at the Sorbonne and staying with a Jewish family,
teaching their four children English in return for her keep

(after the war she tried to trace the family, but they had disappeared). She returned to England at Easter 1940 because her mother was ill, and by that stage a return to France was clearly no longer feasible. Instead, in June 1940, she volunteered for the WAAF. After fourteen days of training she was posted to Uxbridge, West London, headquarters of 11 Group. There, her task was to plot the filtered information that came from teleprinters stationed around the operations room. Originally sent from the RDF stations and the Observer Corps to Bentley Priory, the information they received had already been filtered at the main headquarters, so that they only received reliable information relevant to their sector. This was then plotted on to the main operations map. The clock was divided into coloured sections, and as each plot went on the map it would be coded to the time it was placed, so that the commanders looking down from the balcony above could date the information they saw in an instant. Hazel Gregory's sector covered Watford down to central London.

The Women's Royal Auxiliary Airforce had been formed in June 1939. There had been no checks on age, and some girls as young as fifteen were recruited. Most, though, were eighteen or nineteen. Many of the volunteers were from well-off backgrounds, and Hazel still found the money to visit the cinema at Uxbridge or go into town to dance at the Savoy. Members of a nearby Canadian squadron were particularly popular as escorts.

With her at Uxbridge were two friends, Vera Shaw and Philippa Robertson, also from well-to-do backgrounds. Philippa had joined the WAAF seven days after the declaration of war. She married in February 1940 and her new husband immediately took off for France. She then did not see him until after Dunkirk. When he came back he was plagued with nightmares about being dive-bombed. Her friend Vera then joined, partly, she says, because of a feeling of national emergency, and partly because she didn't like the army khaki of the other women's volunteer groups. The blue uniform of the WAAFs was much more to her liking, especially once she had had a tunic with a luxurious red lining specially made in Savile Row. In the same way she managed to get away with wearing non-regulation underwear and shoes and smuggled in a feather mattress to cushion the uncomfortable straw ones with which they were issued. Officially the plotters were supposed to be trained for six weeks. When Philippa joined, this period had shrunk to three weeks. By June 1940, when Vera joined, it was six days. All were sworn to secrecy and Philippa had to tell even her mother that she was a 'clerk special duties'.

Nevertheless, the attitude to the women was often chauvinistic by modern standards. On 14 July at Kenley airfield in Surrey, the pilots were released to do recreation. The 150 WAAFs on the airfield, however, were sent to bed 'in case of any nervous reaction'. Unsurprisingly, they were not best pleased by this. Although every role apart from combat pilot was interchangeable between men and women, the latter only received two-thirds of the men's pay. Hazel Gregory remembers this as 'quite a sore point'.

Initially there was little for Hazel Gregory, Vera Shaw or Philippa Robertson to do at Uxbridge: 'You did get the odd reconnaissance plane, and we plotted the convoys through the Channel.' During the quiet periods the WAAFs would write letters, knit, sew and embroider. Hazel Gregory spent much of her time making underwear. 'It was the fashionable thing to do at the time – it was before any rationing of clothing or materials. We were all hand-stitching glamorous undies. Most of the men were very intrigued.'

After a few isolated attacks at the beginning of the war, there had been few incursions by the Luftwaffe over England.

The first civilian to die from air attack was after a raid on Scapa Flow in the Orkney Islands on 16 March 1940. On 30 April two more died and 160 were injured when a mine-laying Heinkel 111 was shot down and crashed into the town of Clacton in Essex. The first deliberate attack on the mainland came on 10 May, when a lone aircraft dropped bombs near the villages of Petham and Chilham in Kent, but no one was hurt. Thereafter, as French airfields along the north coast fell into the Luftwaffe's hands, more and more aircraft, usually flying solo, started to appear over England.

A t Tangmere, a sector station airfield near Southampton, the early months of summer were, for sisters Anne and Evelyn 'Tig' Lowe, in marked contrast to what would come later. The two young women had joined the WAAF from the Auxiliary Territorial Service (ATS), where they had found the warden and lookout work very boring. When a glamorous blue-uniformed WAAF had spoken to their group and asked for recruits, Tig had nudged her sister, whispered 'Pilots!' and thrust them both forward. Posted to Tangmere, they had volunteered as cooks, even though at home they'd always had someone employed to do that for them. Soon it became apparent that their cooking was terrible – Anne was nicknamed 'Hitler's secret weapon' – and they were transferred to radio operation.

Anne Lowe remembers her training sergeant, Warrant Officer Jock Anderson, with affection. 'A little sturdy fat Scotsman,' he used to say it was difficult to drill us because he couldn't get us all lined up properly, our bosoms were all different . . . I was flat-chested, Tig had bosoms out here!' Most of the radio training involved sitting by an operator and learning the ropes that way. Incoming radio calls would be filtered through these operators and logged by them in shorthand. 'We'd take them and then we'd call the controller and put them through. While we were waiting, we'd often ask for dates on the air!'

Swimming nude in the fire tank, repelling unwanted advances and cheerfully living in conditions indescribably worse than they had known at home, the two women were utterly determined to work hard and play hard.

Peter Brothers' 32 Squadron at Biggin Hill found it strangely quiet after the tumult of the fighting in France, in spite of the paratroop scares that caused them to go armed to the pub. Biggin Hill was a sector station in 11 Group, which had responsibility for London and south-east England. Other 11 Group sector stations were situated at Debden, North Weald, Northolt, Hornchurch, Kenley, Tangmere and, for the moment, Middle Wallop. Clearly 11 Group would be the most important, and Dowding appointed as its commander Air Vice-Marshal Keith Park, a forty-eight-year-old New Zealander who in the First World War had fought at Gallipoli and been wounded on the Somme before transferring to aircraft and shooting down twenty German planes. Park was popular with his men, and would often turn up unannounced at airfields in his Hurricane. During the air battle over Dunkirk, he had flown several sorties to find out what was going on. Over six feet tall, he was an austere-looking man and a devout Christian, taking great strength from his pre-battle prayers. The WAAF plotters at Uxbridge remember him during tense moments handing out liquorice allsorts to the women there.

At Biggin Hill the pilots waited for what seemed to be the inevitable showdown to come. Depending on their state of readiness, they would kick a football around or play mah-jong, listening to a wind-up portable gramophone playing Bing Crosby, whom one of the airmen thought he could imitate pretty well. Another, says Peter Brothers, 'had a guitar and wrote a song about the squadron. It went, "High rank, low rank, everybody come, join us in the pilots' room and make yourselves at home. Take off your gloves and overalls and light your pipes and let us introduce you to the fighting 32." And then he'd go through each chap in the squadron.'

During the war, some of the games became more violent and dangerous. Peter Brothers remembers one involving a Very pistol, designed to shoot coloured flares for recognition purposes:

> You blindfolded a chap and you all stood around in a circle. You spun him round and round and round and then he had to count to ten whilst you all scattered and then he'd fire. On one occasion one of the sergeant pilots got hit in the seat of his pants and burnt a hole in them. Fortunately it didn't hurt him. But that caused a bit of a stir because he had to go down to stores and they wanted to know why and how he had burnt a hole in the seat of his pants and needed a new issue. So that one didn't go down very well and we had to give it up after that.

On some evenings off the officers would drive down to the White Hart, where the landlady, Cathy Preston, gave them a warm welcome. The station commanding officer fixed a tannoy to the top of his car, and as he approached the pub would call out for six pints of beer and a large gin. By the time he reached the bar, they would be set out ready for him. The sergeant pilots had their own pub, the Old Jail in Biggin Hill. Few had cars to enable them to go further afield, and as elsewhere, the officers and NCOs did not drink together often.

In spite of this, the atmosphere in the squadron had changed since pre-war days. Peter Brothers, who had arrived as a pilot officer in October 1936, remembers the sharp distinctions then between the ranks.

Back then you were a 'bog rat', just a pilot officer, lowest of the low, unwanted, and underpaid. Nobody spoke to you except when a flying officer or a flight lieutenant would tell you to go and press the bell so a waiter would come in to get him a drink. I remember in the summer just before the war started sitting out on the terrace on a Sunday chatting. There was a flight lieutenant with us who was talking away. Then, saying, 'It's hot!' he took his shoes off. Chucking one away, he looked at Pat Conolley and me and said, 'Whichever is the junior of you two, go and get my shoe back.'

But after the war started, as hundreds and thousands of their friends and acquaintances joined the army, the RAF in contrast became less hierarchical, more concerned with excellence rather than status. Combat in France had taught the pilots the real value of expertise and teamwork. The army and navy may have looked down on the 'upstart' RAF, but they in turn considered themselves above the 'thickies who are prepared to worm their way through a soaking wet ditch loaded with gear on their backs clutching a rifle'.

The ground crews, too, were included in this teamwork. The taste of combat flying in France had impressed upon the pilots the importance of their aircraft and armaments not letting them down. Returning from France each day, Peter Brothers would bring his crew out a case of beer and spend some time discussing the day's action with them, even if he had been up for twenty hours. 'We wouldn't have got off the ground but for them,' he says. 'They were all super. And of course, their aircraft had to be the best in the squadron, naturally.'

During quiet moments at Biggin Hill, his crew helped Brothers personalise and improve his Hurricane. They installed a curved mirror on the inside of the cockpit, which enabled him to see all around, but avoided the drag of an external mirror. Other, smaller improvements yielded surprising results.

The Spitfire had flash riveting on the wings, beautiful smooth wings, and the Hurricane had ordinary pop rivets, so you got all these little nobbles on the wing. While we were sitting on the ground at readiness, the airframe mechanic and I used to sit on the wing filing away at these nobbles. We couldn't get down to flush riveting, obviously, or the whole thing would have come apart, but I thought if we filed some of the tops off, we'd get a bit more speed. I reckon I got about an extra five miles an hour out of that aeroplane over the others ones as a result.

Meanwhile, to 'show they were still in being', they were ordered to patrol along the French coast. Soon it became apparent that this was a disastrous policy:

We were losing people unnecessarily because the Germans would just wait and watch you fly past and wait for you to come back. By then you were coming north and you had got the sun behind you, which was just how they wanted it. They would take their time and then jump on you. So that stopped and then slowly the raids began on a fairly smallish scale to start with and then building up.

The respite had not lasted long. By 10 July, 32 Squadron were back in the thick of the fighting.

John Bisdee's 609 'West Riding' Squadron returned battered and bruised from Dunkirk. The mood among the officers and men had been utterly changed. The previous easy-going attitude had been replaced by one of grim determination. They had lost nearly half of their Auxiliary pilots in the action over France and the Channel, local West Riding men who had been friends long before joining the RAF together. John Bisdee remembers that when he joined the squadron in December 1939 with James Buchanan, 'We were conscious of being the first adopted children in a family – everyone else had known each other for years.' As the losses at Dunkirk were made up he suddenly found himself to be one of the more senior pilots. 'We took in an awful lot of extra, new pilots at that stage, and from being a very junior chap I suddenly found myself halfway up the list.'

Although still in the front line, 609 Squadron busied themselves with replacements and improvements. Seven new Spitfires were delivered, and by the end of June all the fighters had been upgraded from variable pitch to constant speed propellers, which gave better speed and control. The whole conversion was performed at lightning speed by a crew from de Havilland who turned up 'quite unheralded'. The lack of official-channel notification of the visit and the speed of the work betrays the hand of Beaverbrook. At the same time the Hurricane fleet was undergoing similar conversion.

On 28 June a new commanding officer was appointed: H. S. 'George' Darley, who was to head the squadron until after the end of the Battle of Britain. He was already familiar with leading an Auxiliary squadron, and he knew that because they had at their core a small community of personal friends who had probably grown up together, they felt losses particularly keenly. His first task was to restore morale. An experienced fighter pilot and ex-flying instructor, he immediately began training the squadron in dogfighting, as opposed to formation flying. He then taught them close-quarter attacks, with himself as the elusive target. Copying the Luftwaffe, Darley also instigated a tactic of flexible formation flying, with a section weaving about up-sun, higher and behind the main body. According to John Bisdee, the new leadership in the form of Darley 'saved the squadron, really'.

A few days after Darley's arrival, the squadron was posted to Middle Wallop, about halfway between Andover and Salisbury. As the entire north-western coast of France had fallen into German hands, the defences, originally designed to deal with attack from Germany or, at worst, the Low Countries, had to be extended. The radar chain was hastily enlarged and a new group, 10, formed, with sector stations at St Eval in Cornwall, Filton near Bristol and Pembrey in South Wales. The commander was Air Vice-Marshal Sir Quentin Brand, who had shot down a German Gotha bomber in the last raid on England of the First World War, and had been knighted after his pioneer flight from England to the Cape in 1920. At the beginning of August, responsibility for the sector station at Middle Wallop was transferred from 11 Group to 10 Group. Even with 609 at Middle Wallop there were still only four Hurricane and two Spitfire squadrons directly opposite Sperrle's powerful Luftflotte 3.

Instead of flying from Northolt direct to their new base at Middle Wallop on 4 and 5 July, the squadron received orders that it should fly to Warmwell, a forward base of Middle Wallop's, fifty miles to the south-west, near Weymouth. Portland naval base had come under attack; there were rumours that a gin factory had been hit. From then on, the

The Organisation of Fighter
Command and Luftwaffe bases,
August 1940

—— Group boundary
- - - Sector boundary
⊙ Sector station
▓ London Inner Artillery Zone

Luftwaffe bases
⊛ Bomber
⊗ Stuka (Dive-bomber)
✚ Fighter (Bf 109)
⊕ Twin-engined Fighter (Bf 110)

- - - - Luftwaffe command boundary

200 kms
100 miles

Wick

Turnhouse⊙

Acklington⊙

Usworth⊙

**No.13 GROUP
(SAUL)**

Aldergrove⊙

Catterick⊙

Church⊙
Fenton

Kirton-in-⊙
Lindsey

**No.12 GROUP
(LEIGH-MALLORY)**

Digby⊙

Wittering⊙

⊙Coltishall

Duxford⊙
⊙Debden

Pembrey⊙

LONDON ⊙North Weald **No.11 GROUP
(PARK)**

Northolt⊙ ⊙Hornchurch

⊙Filton

Kenley⊙ ⊙Biggin
Hill

**No.10 GROUP
(BRAND)**

Middle⊙
Wallop Tangmere

LUFTFLOTTE 2

(KESSELRING)

St. Eval⊙

E N G L I S H   C H A N N E L

PARIS

**LUFTFLOTTE 3
(SPERRLE)**

squadron alternated between Middle Wallop and the forward base at Warmwell. Flight Lieutenant John Dundas, who had by this time taken over the writing of the squadron diary, describes Warmwell as 'possessing the two chief characteristics of a forward station – action and discomfort'. When 609 arrived there was no water or sanitation and they were forced to sleep in the dispersal tent (the place where the pilots would wait to be scrambled to their aircraft). It was very dry and the tent would be filled with dust and stones whenever an aircraft passed nearby. Worst of all, the civilian cooks refused to serve meals outside of regular times. As Dundas commented, the Luftwaffe was no respecter of lunchtime or teatime. In the end the pilots were forced to rustle up bacon and eggs for themselves on an assortment of rickety stoves in the dispersal tent. Middle Wallop itself, although one of the key sector stations, was still under construction when 609 arrived. The squadron's dispersal hut was a cramped cottage at one end of the field. Next door, in another small house, Darley and his wife took up quarters.

The short break after the fall of France had given Fighter Command time to regroup and refresh. Amongst the new squadrons formed was 238 Squadron, which included pilots of all backgrounds.

Gordon Batt had joined the RAF in 1938 through the Volunteer Reserve, learning to fly in his spare time from his job at the Daimler engineering works in Coventry. With war approaching, he says, 'there was no way I wanted to crawl about under hedges and Christ knows what in all weather and see all the gory details of war'. By contrast, he felt, the battlefield of the sky would be 'clean'. He had completed his training at Rissington by early April and was recommended for a commission. 'It was turned down,' he says, 'because the quota had been taken by the university intake.' Then a rugby injury to his hand delayed his transfer to a squadron for six weeks. Once the injury had healed, he was posted to 153 Hurricane Squadron at Kenley. Having never flown a Hurricane, he was given an instruction manual and told to sit in the cockpit until he had worked it out. On 19 May he did his first flying in a Hurricane. At this time half of 153 Squadron was fighting in France. If it were not for his rugby injury he would almost certainly have been there as well. 'This was a turn of fate, the first one that contributed to my becoming a survivor,' he remembers. At the end of May the France contingent returned 'in dribs and drabs, very bedraggled, extremely tired and a little demoralised'. They had taken heavy losses.

A few days later a Fairy Battle light bomber arrived back at Kenley from France. Batt asked the pilot what the aircraft was like. 'Absolutely bloody useless,' came the reply. 'The Bf 109s and 110s slaughtered us. They are slow, carry a pitiful bomb load, are under-armed and not very manoeuvrable.' After the terrible mauling they had received in France, the Battles were withdrawn from the front line.

Most of the exhausted squadron was posted to Scotland to rest and regroup, but as Batt was still fresh he was sent to Tangmere to join 238 Squadron, currently being formed. Feeling green himself, Batt was alarmed to discover that none of the pilots, from the CO downwards, had any operational experience. 'So we set about training, mainly in formation flying, but it was a bit like the blind leading the blind.' They were also flying Spitfires, a new experience for Batt. Again he was issued with a training manual and pointed towards an aircraft. On 23 May, only four days after his début flight in a Hurricane, he was airborne in a Spitfire for the first time.

It was quickly decided, however, that the Spitfires would be better used in the hands of more experienced pilots, so 238 Squadron was transferred to Hurricanes, and by 13 June Batt was back where he'd started. Although he appreciated the need for Spitfires elsewhere, he was disappointed to see his 'lovely' aircraft being taken away: 'The Hurricane after the Spitfire was like a carthorse compared to a racehorse.'

On 19 June, 238 were moved to Middle Wallop and soon afterwards acquired a new squadron leader, H. A. Fenton. Also joining the squadron was Sergeant Eric Bann, the young pilot who had written to his parents from France sympathising with the poor dive-bombed soldiers. He quickly settled in with the other sergeants, and he and Gordon Batt became firm friends. Gordon learnt that Eric had recently been married, to a Birmingham girl, Agnes May Butler. Eric's brother, who was also in the RAF, had been best man.

At Middle Wallop the fledgling 238 Squadron shared the facilities with 601 Auxiliary Squadron, which had been attracting a lot of press attention. Known as 'the Millionaires' Squadron', 601 was a particularly smart outfit, even for an Auxiliary squadron. Novelist Len Deighton tells the story of how an officer of 601, sent out to do something about a petrol shortage at the base, returned having bought a filling station, 'but announced that the pumps there were only half-full. The situation was remedied when another pilot remembered that he was a director of Shell. His secretary arranged a delivery.'[2]

Gordon Batt, like many of the more middle-class Volunteer Reservists, was unimpressed by this sort of behaviour and by the 601 officers' greatcoats lined with expensive hunting-pink silk. His first impression was 'what a lot of pompous show-offs'. The posher the squadron, the less the officers seemed to deign to talk to NCOs like himself. As the battle wore on, and 601 proved their fighting spirit, his view about them would change. By the end of the year, most were dead anyway. John Bisdee took over 601 when it went to Malta in 1942: 'I can assure you that there weren't any millionaires in sight by that time.'

Officers and sergeants didn't mix, but Batt was happy in the sergeants' mess, where the food was good, 'equal in every way to that for the officer pilots, although obviously we did not enjoy the same degree of service'. He was also much happier with the new CO. In contrast to his predecessor, he was 'friendly, and talked to us more like fellow pilots, irrespective of rank'.

Two weeks after converting to Hurricanes, 238 Squadron became operational. Typically they would report to the flight hut on the airfield half an hour before dawn. 'We would be allocated an aircraft,' explains Gordon Batt. 'We had our own mostly, although servicing upset this sometimes. We would put our parachutes in the cockpit or on the wing, don our Mae Wests [lifejackets], then return to the hut, which was mainly full of beds, lie down and wait. If you had no feelings you could sleep!'

When the phone in the hut rang, it could be just someone being granted permission for a test flight; it might be a time check, a change of duties or some other trivial matter. But it could also be an order to scramble. The ground crew member operating the phone would shout, 'Squadron scramble!' and run outside and ring a bell. This was the signal for the ground crews to start the engines. 'We would dash out to our aircraft, the engines would burst into life, and as we put on our parachutes the fitter would get out of the cockpit, then stand on the wing ready to help strap us in after we had donned our helmet, which had been draped over the control column. Waving "Chocks away", we'd move off,' remembers Gordon Batt. 'Invariably we could take off straight away as the flight hut was located on the east side of the airfield; however, if the

Peter Lambert, who was amongst the thousands trapped on the beaches of Dunkirk.

The photo of Sid Wakeling that he gave to Daphne Portnall.

Hermann Göring (left) with Adolf Hitler in 1940. At the time, Göring was the second most powerful man in Nazi Germany (*Hulton Getty*).

Ju 87 'Stuka' dive-bombers in formation. Brilliantly effective in support of ground troops, their weaknesses were quickly exposed during the Battle of Britain (*Hulton Getty*).

Winston Churchill inspecting
coastal defences near Hartlepool,
31 July 1940 (*IWM*).

Sir Hugh Dowding, the architect
of Britain's Air Defence system
(*The Art Archive/IWM*).

A Bf 109 fighter pilot shot down in October 1940.

German Bf 109 fighters at a base near Calais (*TRH*).

Boulton Paul Defiant pilots play draughts as they await the order to scramble (*TRH/IWM*).

Boulton Paul Defiants: one of several aircraft on either side that proved to be terribly vulnerable during the Battle of Britain (*TRH/IWM*).

Although highly visible, radar towers were difficult to destroy as bomb blast tended to pass through the structure (*IWM*).

A Chain Home Receiver room, showing the console (right) and receiver (left) (*IWM*).

WAAFs at work in the operations room at an RAF Station, Fighter Command (*IWM*).

Ground crew hold down the tail of a Hurricane as its engine is tested (*The Art Archive/IWM*).

Hawker Hurricanes in 'vic' formations. This grouping of three fighters was called a 'bunch of bananas' by the Luftwaffe (*The Art Archive/ IWM*).

Peter Hairs with his Hurricane. Many pilots came to be grateful for the plane's robust construction.

wind was strong from the east we had to taxi to the opposite side of the airfield before taking off, a vulnerable moment.' During the climb in formation, the radios would remain silent, particularly if it was cloudy. This manoeuvre required total concentration from the pilots. As soon as the cloud cover was broken, the rear (in 238, 'yellow') section would break formation and start weaving about at the back, to keep a watch on hostile aircraft attacking from behind.

Sometimes no contact was made with the enemy. On other occasions the German planes would veer off on another course, or simply push off. Initially there were several 'nuisance' raids, designed to test the defences and keep up the pressure on the defending fighter pilots. 'But the tempo was being stepped up,' says Batt. 'Each time the numbers of the bombers was being increased.' Soon after becoming operational, the squadron had considerable successes against the vulnerable Ju 87 Stuka dive-bombers, who were attacking convoys in the Channel.

But defending convoys initially presented problems all of its own. When a convoy was approached by a friendly British aircraft, the procedure was for the pilot to fire a Very cartridge of a certain combination of colours. Initially this friend-or-foe identification was less than entirely successful, as Gordon Batt explains: 'I soon leant that one fired the correct colour on arrival, and kept very well away, out of gun range. These brave mariners took no notice of any signals; if you came within range they opened fire. This included the navy; at this stage I don't think they had any training in aircraft recognition.' Soon it became necessary for the convoys to carry a squadron leader with them to identify friendly aircraft, but still several British fighters were hit by 'friendly fire'.

Gordon Batt was part of 'yellow' section, the weaving section, universally known as 'arse-end Charlies'. In 238 this was the domain of the sergeant pilots, and later in the year, the Czech and Polish flyers. With him in this section were his good friends Sergeants Eric Bann and Henry Marsh. As they were soon to discover, it was the most dangerous place to be.

CHAPTER SIX

The Channel Battle

O N 14 July, on the chalk cliffs high above Dover harbour, excited journalists watched a convoy being attacked by dive-bombers as it passed through the Straits. Among them was Charles Gardner, who to protect himself had strapped a mattress to the roof of his car and donned a tin helmet. His famous radio commentary, which at times sounds as though it is describing a sporting event, seized the imagination of the public. It also gives a good impression of the speed and confusion of air-to-air combat.

> The Germans are dive-bombing a convoy out to sea;
> there are one, two, three, four, five, six, seven German
> dive-bombers, Junkers 87s. There's one going down on its
> target now – bomb! No, he missed the ships . . . Now
> the British fighters are coming up. Here they come . . .
> Somebody's hit a German and he's coming down with a
> long streak – coming down completely out of control – a
> long streak of smoke – and now a man's baled out by
> parachute. The pilot's baled out by parachute. He's a
> Junkers 87, and he's going slap into the sea – and there
> he goes. Smash! A terrific column of water and there was
> a Junkers 87. Only one man got out by parachute, so
> presumably there was only a crew of one in it. Now
> then, oh, there's a terrific mix-up over the Channel! It's

impossible to tell which are our machines and which are
Germans . . . there are fighters right over our heads . . .
Oh boy! I've never seen anything as good as this.

In fact the Junkers 87 he described going down was actually a
Hurricane. The British pilot who baled out was rescued by
the navy but died of his injuries the following day. After the
broadcast, which had contrasted sharply with the official
communiqué style of much of the BBC's output, there were
numerous complaints about it being undignified and sensa-
tional, and the experiment was not repeated.

The full deployment of the two Luftflotte was not completed until 24 July, but the Luftwaffe were also following
their original instructions to enforce an aerial blockade of
Britain. In addition, by attacking Channel shipping, they
hoped to test southern England's air defences and lure the
British fighters into battle as near as possible to the Luftwaffe
fighter bases. The purpose was to destroy Fighter Command
in the air. Once this had been achieved, mainland targets
could be attacked with impunity.

Initially the RAF had refused to rise to the bait, only flying
sorties against the long-range reconnaissance aircraft that were
searching out targets for bombers. But they came under
increasing pressure to defend convoys in the Channel and not
to gift the Germans air superiority over the Straits of Dover,
and on 7 July they struck back. That evening forty-five
Dornier 17s, protected by about sixty Bf 109s, attacked a
convoy near Dover. Although the shipping escaped almost
unscathed, the twelve Spitfires of 65 Squadron sent to
intercept suffered a mauling. Only managing to damage two
of the bombers, three of the British fighters were shot down
over the Channel by the Bf 109s and a further three were
downed near Manston airfield in eastern Kent. At least one
half of the German plan seemed to be working.

The other objective, to close the Straits of Dover to British shipping, initially proved more difficult. The weapon originally detailed to perform this task was the Ju 87 Stuka, which, with its dive, could land a bomb with pinpoint accuracy. On the ground, against enemy artillery or infantry positions, this was devastating, and a hail of shrapnel and flying debris would wreak havoc over a large area. But over the water, even greater accuracy was needed. Unlike an explosion on the ground, a near miss in the sea would do little other than shower a boat with water. What was more, the Stuka dive-bombers, the élite of the Luftwaffe, were proving very vulnerable to British fighters. On 10 July sixty Stukas, together with seventy-five Dornier 17s, assembled over the French coast, where they were joined by an escort of 200 Bf 109s. As the formation approached a convoy in the Channel, thirty Spitfires came hurtling in. This time they went straight for the bombers and did not allow themselves to get involved in dogfights with the Bf 109s. Hurricanes from Peter Brothers' 32 Squadron at Biggin Hill, which had transferred to forward airfields at first light, also joined the fray. The damage to the Stukas was severe and from this day on they were known in the Luftwaffe as 'the Fying Coffins'.

Nevertheless, when weather permitted, attacks continued on naval bases and convoys in the Channel, and over southern England Bf 109s made offensive sweeps, trying to draw the defending fighters into battle. Weaknesses in Britain's radar system were being noted by Dowding, increasing his reluctance to commit his fighters to the Channel battle. For fighting over the water, the German planes could mass out of range of radar. Furthermore, the equipment could not distinguish between bombers and fighters. A squadron might scramble to intercept a bombing raid and find itself facing a host of Bf 109s. Nevertheless, under pressure from the Air Ministry, Dowding continued to send up his forward squadrons. On 15 July the aircraft factory at Yeovil was attacked and the fighters in the south-west were in action.

For 609 Squadron, there had been little time for settling in at Middle Wallop. A few days after their arrival Churchill ordered that all convoys should be given a standing patrol of six aircraft. This meant long, gruelling days in the air during which the Luftwaffe could strike at leisure with superior forces. For 609 the losses started mounting again.

Pilots like John Bisdee found it hard to understand why the sacrifices were necessary.

I often wondered why these convoys were going all the way up [the Channel]; they could have stopped at Plymouth or somewhere and put all their stuff on a train. But they went on and on and on with these convoys and they were latterly a bit of an embarrassment because we had really rather more important things to do than to spend hours patrolling convoys.

In addition to the convoy duties, air defence had to be available at all times during daylight, which at this time of year lasted twenty hours out of the twenty-four. On some occasions night patrols were called for as well. But Spitfires were fairly hopeless as night fighters, as the flare from the exhaust, invisible by day, was blinding for the pilot, particularly on landing, and a beacon for any hostile aircraft while in the air.

At this time, the squadron received its first intake from one of the newly created operational training units (OTUs). These, designed to bridge the gap between flying school and a combat squadron, were not highly thought of by the more experienced pilots. John Gibson of 501 Squadron was a teacher at one later in the war: 'All we did was to teach these chaps formation, aerobatics and landing the aeroplane and take-off and things like that. Not enough time was spent on teaching the man how to fight the aircraft.' There were sighs of relief all round when it was discovered that the three new pilots for 609 Squadron had all at least done a few hours in Spitfires. One of the OTU pilots was Noel Agazarian, a great friend of Richard Hillary, author of the classic *The Last Enemy*. Noel's flying was described by Hillary as 'typical of the man: rough, slapdash and with touches of brilliance'. Neither of the friends would survive the war.

Sometimes it was immediately clear that new pilots were simply not up to the job, and that the training they had received had failed to show this up. Moreover, there was only so much time for training – many had to learn on the job. John Bisdee remembers flying with one such pilot.

We were going up in the direction of Portland in a fairly tight squadron formation of three vics [three aircraft in 'v'-shaped formation] and the aircraft on my left started edging in towards me. I thought, What can this bugger be doing? Then I realised that if I didn't get out of the way he was going to hit me. So I dived down and he sailed over the top of me and disappeared out of sight. It turned out that the pilot had something wrong with his ears that had caused him to lose consciousness. His Spitfire happily took him off into the distance before he suddenly woke up and discovered himself flying along all on his own and he recovered his bearings and flew back to Middle Wallop. As he landed he became unconscious again and his aircraft trundled across the aerodrome and ended up by the far fence luckily having come to a halt with the engine ticking over. He was found unconscious in the cockpit. So the Spitfire had really rather looked after him.

New pilots were quickly in combat. Although the Luftwaffe was still only using a fraction of its strength, the enemy planes seemed to be getting more and more numerous. On 21 July John Bisdee was scrambled from Warmwell with 609 Squadron to intercept an attack on Portland naval base.

This was the first time I'd ever seen a really large German formation. The controller on the RT said, 'One hundred-plus bandits' and then told us the direction. Moments later he said, 'Two hundred-plus bandits' and then finally he said, 'Very many bandits!' I happened to be flying L1082, which was our oldest Spitfire and slowest. I had some difficulty keeping up, however I did more or less. I remember the incredible sight of this great swarm of rotating German aircraft, each following their own tail, going round and round emitting condensation trails. The feeling I had, and a lot of us had, was, What are these buggers doing here? How dare they? It was really quite a shock to see this vast number of black crosses and swastikas in the sky over our country. Then we all plunged in.

In spite of John Bisdee being hit in the engine by anti-aircraft fire from the naval base, the squadron expended all their ammunition and did a fair amount of damage. But because they had been scrambled from so near the battle, they were at a disadvantage.

We were actually climbing up towards them all the time and we had not got into a good position to attack. After

that our controllers and ourselves, we certainly learnt a
lesson and as far as it was possible the controller used to
try and get you higher than the Germans. The bombers
were usually at about 20,000 feet and fighters above
might have gone up to 30,000. The great thing was to
get round wherever the sun was and try to attack them
from above and out of the sun. Of course there was
another factor that was that you were trying to hit them
before they did much damage with their bombs.

As the Spitfire took just under eight minutes to climb to
20,000 feet, Bisdee preferred to be scrambled from Middle
Wallop: 'One of the great advantages of Middle Wallop was
that it was about sixty miles from Portland and those sort of
places, it was about sixty miles from London, which gave you
enough time when you scrambled to climb up and attack
from the top. Whereas the poor chaps who were at that time
at places like Kenley and so on, they had to climb up
underneath the Germans.'

The timing of the scramble was of great importance. Radar
meant that enemy raids could be intercepted without having
to fly standing patrols. This would have made the pilots' and
aircrafts' time in the air terribly inefficient, and would have
prevented sector stations responding to raids with different
forces depending on the number of hostiles. On top of that,
the chances of actually making an interception would have
been slight. Quite simply, Fighter Command would not have
survived without radar. Even so, pilots frequently complained
of being scrambled too late to achieve the vital height
advantage. But it was a tricky art to get right, as Peter
Brothers explains:

We were fortunate, very fortunate in having radar.
Otherwise we would've been flying standing patrols,

which is terribly wasteful in flying hours as well as tiring, so instead we could wait. The only problem being of course that we were always scrambled, we reckoned, too late to get a height advantage on the enemy and the controllers were always blamed for this. But in fact they were being very wise, they didn't know whether it was going to be a spoof attack. Of course the Germans would launch a spoof and hope to get everybody airborne and then the spoof would go home and the real raid would arrive just when you were all on the ground refuelling. So inevitably they waited until they were certain it wasn't a spoof entirely, and then launch you off, which meant you got off rather late in the day, so you were struggling for height all the time. You try preferably to get above the Germans.

For John Bisdee, returning from combat to the serene surroundings of Middle Wallop was quite a contrast. Unlike army or navy personnel, the fighter pilots would be in the thick of the battle one minute and relaxing on deckchairs in the sun the next.

The contrast between the ground and the air was fantastic. I mean, imagine coming back from, say, Portland and being surrounded by black crosses in the sky, then you landed and everything was fairly quiet at Middle Wallop. In the evening we would go to a lovely pub, the Black Swan in Monxton that we called the Mucky Duck. There one would have a nice glass of beer with the locals, and discuss progress on the Spitfire fund that was being run by a well-known actor/comedian of that time called Gordon Harker. The landlord used to come round and say, 'Fill up when you need to and just tell me how much you have had before you leave.' So

this was absolutely wonderful. In the village the blackout
was only observed rather partially and the back garden
area of the pub was almost floodlit. If we were
night-flying we always used to go and beat up the Mucky
Duck from the air. Alternatively we went into Andover
where there was a club called the Square Club and one
was very welcome there, too. Life on the ground didn't
seem to have changed much. Generally it was very quiet
on the ground in 1940 outside of London, whereas there
was all this mayhem going on in the sky.

There was little contact with the wider war, except for some
training exercises that 609 carried out with the army on
Salisbury Plain. In order to accustom the soldiers to air attack,
the Spitfire pilots were asked to 'beat up' the men on the
ground. 'We came down so low that everybody who could
lay down.' On another occasion, Bisdee was asked to give a
talk to the local Home Guard.

Compared with the later stages of the Battle of Britain,
when 609 were posted to Biggin Hill, the time at Middle
Wallop is remembered by John Bisdee fondly. The spirit, he
says, 'was absolutely first class'. Darley, the CO, had done his
morale-boosting work. Occasionally he would organise a
dance at Middle Wallop for all ranks, and a small barrel of
bitter was always available at his and his wife's house on the
airfield perimeter if the pilots were free.

But this free time was in very short supply. For most of the
day, the pilots would be in one of three states of stand-by.
John Bisdee explains:

You might be on readiness, in which case it was a
matter of pride that you were in the air in about two
or two and a half minutes at the most from the call.
The next stage down was fifteen minutes from

readiness, and thirdly there would be 'thirty minutes available', which gave you a chance probably to dash up to the mess and have lunch or something like that. But then the tannoy in the mess would say, '609 Squadron to immediate readiness' and one would have to drop one's knife and fork and dash down to dispersal. There was constant tension; one never knew when the tannoy was going to go.

If a pilot was on readiness, he would often be already sitting in the cockpit. Alternatively he would be a short sprint away from his aircraft.

Your ground crew were sitting round your aeroplane more or less. You dashed up and put your parachute harness into your cockpit. You put on your helmet, connected up your oxygen, plugged in your radio and then you pulled the two main straps of your parachute harness across your chest. It all clipped up in the centre of your tummy and then generally your rigger put the shoulder straps in the aircraft across you. Now strapped in like a turkey, off you went. Everything would be prepared beforehand and therefore it took you almost a matter of seconds to put all these things on.

Like most pilots, John Bisdee was keenly aware of the importance of his ground crew, all of whom were volunteers from Yorkshire who had worked as mechanics in garages and been with the squadron from before the move south. For them, too, the work was around the clock.

When we came down at night or in the evening there would probably be a number of aircraft that were unserviceable and had the odd bullet hole in them or something like that. The ground crews used to work through the night to get your aircraft serviceable. I used to have a little Ford car and every Thursday it was understood that my ground crew could borrow the car and go off on a pub crawl. As a result my Ford was always very well looked after and polished and the petrol tank mysteriously was always full. I never understood why and didn't ask.

The ground crew also had their fair share of risk. In August a raid of Ju 88s and Bf 110s penetrated the defences at Middle Wallop and hit two hangars. The force of the explosion blew down two enormous steel doors directly on to eleven ground crew inside, all of whom were killed. Most of the squadron was in the air at the time, and only heard the news on their return.

Forming strong friendships in such a situation held obvious risks. On 27 July, 609 lost James Buchanan, who had joined the squadron at the same time as John Bisdee. During a convoy battle in which 609 Squadron, together with 238, were taking on Stukas and Bf 109s, he simply vanished. Two pilots searched out to sea for him, but could find no sign. Bisdee remembers his car, a little Singer sports car, rather like an MG. 'It sat forlornly outside the dispersal hut for several days until somebody could be found to take it away. The empty motor car definitely had an affect on me. I'd been in it on many occasions and known its owner well. I was quite pleased to see that little car go.'

Particularly close to John Bisdee was John Dundas, with whom he had shared quarters for many months. The two, both Oxbridge men, had taken to each other immediately. 'We had a gramophone and he used to contribute the classical records and I contributed the jazz records,' remembers Bisdee. Dundas had got a double first at Oxford and had been in Czechoslovakia when the Germans marched in. 'He had no illusions about the Germans,' Bisdee remembers. 'He knew the war was coming.' As a pilot, Dundas was totally ruthless. 'I regarded him as really indestructible,' says Bisdee. 'He flew his aircraft absolutely to the limit. I'd hate to have had his Spitfire after him at any time because in battle he had one position, which was the throttle flat out. He regarded the Spitfire as first and foremost a weapon and any idea of saving the engine or anything like that never occurred to John at all; he just banged about in his aircraft.'

Whatever the tactics, Dundas was a successful pilot, destroying at least eleven enemy aircraft and winning a DFC and bar. But his last and greatest moment was to come later in the year. 'I came back off forty-eight hours' leave and it was the evening and I thought, I'll go into the ops room and find out what is happening,' remembers John Bisdee. 'One of the girls said, "I don't suppose you have heard about John Dundas, he's missing." Generally speaking, missing meant dead. I was absolutely shattered. I went back to our room and I found all his kit had been packed up. It really struck me terribly. He was such an exceptional man.'

Dundas had succeeded in shooting down Helmut Wick, one of the Luftwaffe's top aces, with over fifty kills. Over the radio telephone (RT), the rest of 609 Squadron had heard him shout, 'Whoopee, I've got a Hun!' Moments later he was hit by Wick's wingman and killed instantly. As soon as the Germans heard about the loss of Wick, they sent out a message on the International Distress Wave, asking for information on him. When a dinghy was spotted off the Isle of Wight, the Germans sent over E-boats in the hope of picking up their star pilot. The Royal Navy responded with motor torpedo boats, and a fight developed. It came to be known as the 'Battle of the Dinghy'. When the fighting was over, it was discovered that the little craft was empty.

As replacements arrived, the original core of Yorkshiremen

amongst the flyers of 609 was rapidly being diluted. Not just other Englishmen but other nationalities were now joining the squadron. On 1 August, two Poles arrived as replacements for killed Yorkshiremen: Flying Officers Nowierski and Ostaszewski, neither of whom could speak English, but who rapidly acquired proficiency in flying their Spitfires. Both were seasoned pilots, albeit in far older planes. They had fought the Germans in September 1939 over Poland and then escaped through Romania to join the French Armée de l'Air. From France they had managed to reach Britain. Their fighting spirit instantly impressed the squadron. 'They were very bitter,' recalls John Bisdee, 'very concentrated on killing the Hun.'

Initially British pilots, who had not had first-hand experience of Nazi occupation, had a more complex attitude to killing German flyers. John Bisdee remembers the first time he hit a Bf 110: 'It had a solitary tail gunner behind the pilot in the fuselage and he was shooting at me. I let off a burst and I saw him actually collapse. I lost quite a lot of sleep that night. To see a chap die in front of you was rather unnerving. In fact it was pretty ghastly.'

In the same intake as the Poles were three very different foreigners, 'Red' Tobin, 'Shorty' Keough and 'Andy' Mamed-off, amongst the first Americans to join the RAF. Two of them, Red and Andy, had originally travelled to Europe to help the beleaguered Finns against the Red Army. Unable to get into action in time, all three joined the Armée de l'Air, but were again too late to see combat, escaping on the last boat out of France. Frank Ziegler, the squadron intelligence officer, describes them as 'a colourful, wise-cracking trio'.[1] Red had a 'delightfully casual outlook and manner', Andy was a keen gambler, and Shorty, at four foot ten, was famously the shortest pilot in the RAF, requiring several cushions to be able to see out of the cockpit of his Spitfire. But they had received only four weeks' operational training, and for the moment, Darley was keen to shield them from the worst of the fighting.

The squadron would continue to take on an increasingly cosmopolitan air as the war progressed. Two more Poles would follow, as well as a Frenchman and a 'wonderful collection of Belgians'. One of these was the aristocratic Rodolf de Grunne, who had actually flown Bf 109s on the side of Franco in the Spanish Civil War. Later in the summer, when the squadron was moved to Biggin Hill, the Belgians used to frequent the pub the Old Jail. There, the publican presented them with a goat. Soon the creature had RAF roundels on its horns and was made an honorary member of the squadron. Later in the war, 'Flying Officer William de Goat' was to take part in the liberation of Brussels.

Rather than there being a babble of languages on the RT in the cockpits, Darley insisted that there should be an English-only rule. Communication once in the air was difficult enough already. The high-frequency radio transmitters and receivers first fitted in British fighters were of a low quality and were vulnerable to all sorts of interference, including from BBC radio programmes, and their range was only about forty miles, although this extended in fine weather. Furthermore, they had only two channels, one of which was used to receive a shrill whistle, code-named 'Pipsqueak', which sounded for fourteen seconds. This enabled direction-finding (DF) stations to plot the position of a squadron or single aircraft. Once more than one of the networked DF stations had picked up linear positions, with the use of string on a map, the location of the plane could be logged at sector, group and Fighter Command headquarters. Although of immense importance to the controllers on the ground, the device further inhibited the effectiveness of the radio for the pilot, who had to be off air for the fourteen seconds. Bisdee was not alone in finding the RTs problematical: 'At the beginning of the war we had rather inefficient radio telephones in the Spitfires. They worked but they needed rather a lot of attention and tuning.' 609 were fortunate to receive some VHF sets soon after the battle started. These had a far longer range and four channels. 'Fortunately 609 had amongst its volunteers a man who'd run a radio shop in Yorkshire – Warrant Office Hartley – and he turned out to be a great expert on RT. He got us converted to these new RT sets more or less in a day and they were wonderful, the reception was as good as you get on the telephone anywhere.' As long as no one left his set on 'transmit', thereby jamming it for everybody else, the advantages were immediate. 'Ops then were able to tell you immediately what the latest news was.'

'We got a signal from Group on one occasion saying the use of bad language on the RT was bad because it shocked the girls in the ops rooms who heard all this,' says John Bisdee, 'but needless to say, they revelled in it.' The pilots and the WAAFs adored each other. Often, says Bisdee, pilots would go into the ops room ostensibly to 'find out whether anything was happening' and while there would enjoy a cup of tea and a 'jolly good chat' with the WAAFs.

Often the women radio operators would be able to piece together the action in even the largest battles. On 11 August radar picked up a large raid heading towards Portland. Five Hurricane and two Spitfire squadrons were sent up to intercept what turned out to be 150 Ju 88s, He 111s, Bf 110s and Bf 109s. Then 609 were scrambled from Warmwell and fought hard to gain height. While Hurricanes were sent against the bombers, 609 were vectored on to the enemy fighters. Squadron Leader Darley led 'B' Flight into the attack against a formation of Bf 110s. Flying straight at the circle of German fighters, Darley narrowly missed a collision. 'A'

Flight followed, and John Bisdee, who so far had only a half-share in a kill, found a target right in his sights.

> I hit one of the Messerschmitt 110s and one of its engines started pouring smoke. It turned over on its back to try to evade but I was determined not to let the bugger go. I turned over as well and shot down after him. I lost him for an instant and the next thing I saw was a pile of burning wreckage down below just near the long man, the Cerne Abbas giant, who had a very rude male organ sticking up. I remember seeing a whole lot of farm labourers dancing around it waving pitchforks and that kind of thing. So I beat the thing up and did a victory roll and at that moment I looked up in the clouds and two parachutes appeared. The crew of this thing had got out. They landed safely a long way away from the farm labourers with their pitchforks, who might have given them a rather unpleasant reception.

The squadron returned in ones and twos to Warmwell, where one of the crew who had not flown watched from the ground, noting 'to my surprise nobody was missing. After such a fierce scrap it seemed too good to be true.'[2]

In spite of their fortune or skill that day, 609 and other squadrons in the south had taken the brunt of the early phase of the Luftwaffe attack. Between 10 July and 7 August, 609 had lost nine pilots and flown 670 sorties, both figures twice the average for a single squadron. It was noted in the 609 Squadron Operation Record Book that 'The utter futility of sending very small sections of fighters to cope with the intense enemy activity in the Portland area is bitterly resented by the pilots.'[3] Furthermore, too many of the engagements were fighter-to-fighter, which Dowding had been keen to avoid.

☆ ☆ ☆

A few days after 238 Squadron had become operational, Sergeant Gordon Batt had his first encounter with the enemy at about 15,000 feet above Chesil Beach near Weymouth. 'The first thing that reacts to fear is your stomach,' he remembers. 'It's like being in a boat.'

> There were six Bf 110s. The flight commander ordered us into line astern, ready to attack. As he started to attack the rearmost aircraft in their formation, the others went into line astern. Now as I was 'arse-end Charlie' of our formation, the leader of theirs was forming the circle behind me. So I broke formation, did a very steep turn in utter panic, and managed a frontal attack on the leading aircraft.
>
> I could see my tracer bouncing off his starboard wing. By this time we were on a collision course and he chickened out and pulled up above me at the last moment. Even now, when I think about it I break into a sweat.

His plane had a bullet hole in the port wing, and another had gone between the engine and the oil tank.

Meanwhile, other novice fighter pilots in 238 Squadron were having their first taste of combat. Sergeant Pilot Eric Seabourne had joined the Auxiliary Air Force in 1935 and applied to join the Volunteer Reserves as a pilot in 1938. He was originally posted to 151 Squadron, but once they found out that he had no experience at all in a Hurricane, he was sent to Tangmere to join the newly formed 238 Squadron. After only seven hours in the fighter, and having never fired his guns, he was declared operational. On 13 July he was scrambled to intercept a raid by Bf 110s on Portland. The

German planes were in a circle, trying to protect each other. Following his squadron leader, Seabourne went in for the attack. Moments later one of the German planes swooped down just above his cockpit.

It was pale blue underneath with black crosses on the wings, so I thought, It's not one of ours, and pressed the gun button and gave it a good blast. As I did so another appeared and I did the same again. They clearly took objection to this because then large holes started appearing in my port main frame and I could feel bullets hitting the armour plating behind my seat. It was time to get out of the way, so I stuffed the nose down and achieved a magnificent speed of over 400 miles per hour going straight down. But I then couldn't get out of the dive and could see the sea directly below me. I heaved and tugged at the control column but nothing happened.

So very slowly I started winding the tail trim back, something we had been told never to do. But it worked and I came out in a beautiful, gentle curve and I was again flying straight and level. I throttled back and returned to Middle Wallop. My aircraft had rather a few holes in it and needed a complete new wing. The engineer officer said it was amazing that the wing hadn't pulled off in the dive as two armour-piercing bullets had lodged in the main spar.

Eric Seabourne wasn't the only pilot to be grateful for the Hurricane's rugged construction and ability to absorb enemy fire and stay in the air. Peter Hairs in 501 Squadron survived having part of his wing removed by a cannon shell, and another 501 pilot managed to return to base missing half of his tail fin. As Brothers explains: 'The Spitfire stood up for itself pretty well. I've had a lot of battle damage on a Spitfire.

But the Hurricane was a more rugged aeroplane. This gave you a lot of confidence.'

After his first meeting with the enemy, in which he was credited with a share in destroying one of the Bf 110s and damaging another, Eric Seabourne quickly learned the essentials of air-to-air combat: 'You daren't fly for more than a few moments looking straight ahead. You were always twisting your neck back looking behind you. If the sun was behind you, that was the most dangerous time.' He also soon learned to get as much height as possible. If the ground controller said, 'Angels twelve', meaning at 12,000 feet, the squadron would go to 14,000. 'You always wanted maximum height. Once you'd got height you were in the driving seat.'

He also had to learn the hard lesson of dealing with the loss of comrades when he witnessed the death of one of the Australian pilots in 238 who had helped in teaching him to fly. His attitude is typical of most of the RAF pilots: 'It was just hard luck. You were all right and he wasn't. There simply wasn't the time to grieve. You registered – Oh God, that's awful – but then you had to get on and do something else.' It just didn't have time to sink in.

A routine was quickly established on a four-day cycle for each pilot. Day one would be 'standby', which meant the pilot had to be on the base available to fly within an hour. The next day he would have to be available to fly within fifteen minutes. For this he would have to be in the dispersal hut or very near by. On day three, the pilot would be on 'readiness' to take off immediately, which would necessitate him being in the cockpit with his parachute ready. The final day of the cycle would be 'stand down', which meant he could leave the base if he had permission from the flight commander. Alternatively this fourth day would be used for training. However, as the German intruders overhead grew in number, this routine would often go by the board. By August and September a pilot could find himself going from 'stand down' to 'available' to airborne in half an hour. Pilots quickly wised up to this and made every effort to get away from the airfield when stood down, as Peter Brothers explains:

> To start with we didn't made an effort to leave the base, we made a mistake. We'd have a jolly in the bar at lunchtime and then suddenly the weather would clear and we were there and they'd say, 'Immediate readiness and scramble.' I remember scrambling and blinking in the sunlight full of beer, thinking, 'now where is the gun switch . . . turn that on . . . ready.' So then we learnt the lesson that if you were stood down you got the hell off the camp, went to the cinema or went into the local pub, whatever. But you didn't hang about.

But like 609 Squadron, 238 were alternating between Middle Wallop and Warmwell and there was precious little free time. Eric Bann, the sergeant pilot friend of Gordon Batt, wrote to his parents on 19 July:

> I am very sorry for not having written sooner but things have been impossible just lately . . . Have been missing for three days. Poor May's heart was in her mouth but I got 24 hours leave upon arriving back at base just to go and prove to the dear girl that I was really OK.
>
> The C/O and two of us were out on early morning patrol when along came a shower of bombers to attack our convoy. In we went, roaring all over the sky with odds of seven to one, but this time I could not dodge quick enough and I was knocked for six right into the English Channel. Gosh it was cold so early in the morning. Well I broke all swimming records and was eventually picked up by a boat and landed at Portsmouth.

There they detained me just to make sure that I was all right. However, apart from a few gallons of sea water in my stomach, I was otherwise OK and I have been doing plenty of flying since.

On the same day that Eric Bann was writing his letter, in Berlin Hitler was giving his 'Last Appeal to Reason' speech, and over the western Channel, things were going disastrously wrong for the RAF.

Formed in June, 141 Squadron was the second to be issued with Boulton Paul Defiants. The Defiant was similar to the Hurricane, except that it had a large gun turret operated by a second crew member. Taking off late morning of 19 July from Hawkinge, in Kent, they were ordered to patrol Folkestone at 5,000 feet. Squadron Leader Richardson had only selected officers for this sortie, among them the New Zealand pilot officer John Gard'ner.

North-east of Dover, well away from the Defiants, an armed trawler was under attack from Bf 110s, escorted by twenty Bf 109s led by Hauptmann (Flight Lieutenant) Hannes Trautloft. Having shepherded the fighter-bombers back to France, Trautloft decided to return to the English coast on a free hunt. Soon a call came over the radio from one of his flight. The Defiants had been spotted far below flying in tight formation. With the sun behind him, having made sure that there were no Spitfires or Hurricanes about, he dived in to attack. 'I aimed at the right Defiant ... my guns fired ... pieces of the Defiant ... broke off and came hurtling towards me ... I saw a thin trail of smoke ... then suddenly just a fiery ball.'[4] In this first attack John Gard'ner's Defiant was also hit. 'The first that I knew,' says the New

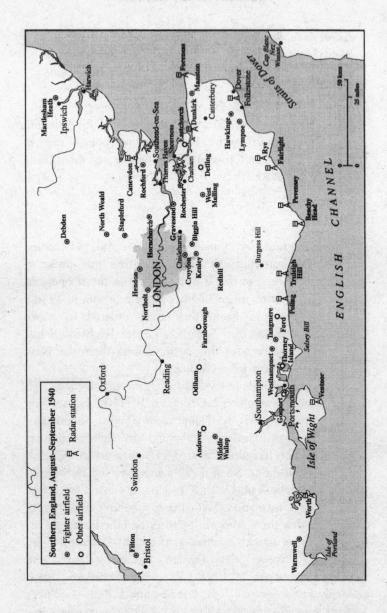

Southern England, August–September 1940

Fighter airfield   Radar station

Other airfield

Zealander, 'was suddenly I had white tracer bullets going through the cockpit and then I had a flash of airplanes right and left under fire. I thought, I'm going to get out of this. I dived down. The prop was dead in front of me. I was lucky I didn't catch fire . . . There was a dreadful smell of cordite and bluey smoke in the cockpit.'

As his Defiant was diving towards the sea, the Bf 109s reeled around for another attack on the remaining British aircraft. Another two Defiants were hit, both catching fire immediately. As the carnage continued, John Gard'ner wrestled with the controls of his stricken aircraft.

There was no engine and the rudder pedal was just loose under my foot. I don't know how I managed to keep it level. I saw this boat and I thought, I'm going to have to crash by that boat, but I was going so fast it was impossible. For some reason or other I stupidly undid my safety straps and I thought, I'm going to get into the water so I want to get out quickly, forgetting that I would hit at 100 m.p.h. I hurriedly pulled the hook back on the cockpit. At the moment of impact I was thrown forward and hit my head. I blacked out and came to deep down in blackness. But the hood was open and I could get out. There was a big flap of skin that was hanging loose from my forehead and I had been hit on the back of the head as well. We had a certain amount of armour behind us and I presume that some of the bullets hit the armour and it shattered.

Gard'ner was quickly picked up, but the squadron had been decimated. Of the nine Defiants, only three made it back to Tangmere, and one of these was forced to make a crash landing.

The Defiants had initially been mistaken by the German fighters for Hurricanes, and their performance over Dunkirk had given Fighter Command an exaggerated belief in their ability against the German fighters. Coming in on the standard attack from behind, the Bf 109s had come under fire from the four Browning machine-guns in the Defiant's rear hydraulic turret, to devastating effect. However, it did not take long for the German pilots to work out the aircraft's debilitating weakness: an attack from the front and below met no resistance, as the Defiants had no forward-facing guns. In effect, one pilot complained, you had to fly past the enemy in order to fire at him. As the Defiant's top speed of 298 m.p.h. was dwarfed by that of the Bf 109, there was little chance of that happening. After the carnage over the Channel, the Defiants were withdrawn from daytime-fighting duties.

In the afternoon of the same day, the RDF picked up a large formation massing to attack Dover. As it came within sight it was reported to contain some seventy bombers with fighter escort. The German planes were intercepted just short of Dover. For Peter Brothers, scrambled from Biggin Hill with 32 Hurricane Squadron, it was the largest raid he had seen to date. 'The German planes blackened the sky, all stacking up with fighters on top and below a vast bomber formation. You thought, where do we start on this lot?'

By now Brothers had worked out an original and highly intelligent way of avoiding being hit by German fighters on his tail. The essence of aiming during air-to-air combat was calculating where the enemy plane was going to be when the bullets reached it. By making his course as unpredictable as possible, Brothers estimated that he would be far more difficult to hit. To do this, he trimmed his rudder so that instead of flying straight ahead, he was always wobbling slightly from side to side. This trick was soon picked up by the others in 32 Squadron.

But the interception force over Dover of thirty-five Hurricanes and Spitfires was outnumbered and able to do little damage. Only two enemy planes were shot down, one of them by Peter Brothers, who got his second Bf 109. The RAF had lost ten fighters in the day's fighting. With this sort of success, Göring became understandably more and more confident of the ability of his air force to bring Britain to her knees. At a conference with the leaders of Luftflotten 2 and 3 he pronounced, 'Fighting alone all these weeks on the Channel front, Jagdgeschwader [Fighter Wing] 51 has already shot down 150 of the enemy's aircraft: quite enough to have weakened him seriously. Think now of all the bombers we can parade in the English sky. The few RAF fighters will not be able to cope.'

CHAPTER SEVEN

Dowding Holds Back

A S LOSSES CONTINUED TO MOUNT, SQUADRONS RE-EQUIPPED with new pilots and aircraft. In July alone, 145 fighters had been lost. But damage had been done to the enemy, too. In Germany air production plans had not anticipated a campaign of the nature of the Battle of Britain. Although by the summer of 1940 aircraft were being given priority, production lagged behind that in Britain. German estimates were that Britain could produce only 180–300 fighters a month and assumed that under the conditions of war this figure would have decreased. In fact, with Beaverbrook supercharging the process, the British factories had turned out 325 fighters in May, 446 in June, and had reached an all-time high of 496 in July. By contrast, Bf 109 production was 164 in June and 220 in July.[1] In addition, by this time, the Civilian Repair Organisation (CRO) was in full swing under Beaverbrook's leadership. If a RAF plane was shot down over land, it was not necessarily lost, unlike the Luftwaffe crashes and forced landings. Damaged aircraft that could not be repaired at the airfield workshops were scooped up by civilian mechanics. By mid-July they were returning 160 fighters a week to the squadrons. By August, a third of 'new' aircraft delivered to the squadrons were actually from repair units. In Oxford, No. 1 Civilian Repair Unit was working a fourteen-hour day, seven days a week, and pilots could fly there direct for repairs. Some aircraft were known to come back two or three times a week.

Those planes too damaged were stripped of parts and recycled, and downed German planes, too, were used to build new British fighters. By the beginning of August the RAF had more serviceable fighters than it had had at the beginning of the previous month.

By the same time, many more of the Poles who had escaped to Britain on the fall of France had completed their rudimentary operational training and were arriving at the squadrons depleted of pilots. Soon after three Poles had arrived at Biggin Hill, a downed German airman was brought to the base. Peter Brothers, who had lived with a 'charming' German family before the war, got talking to him.

> This particular chap, he wasn't going to give any information away on anything. Drawing his attention to the wing of a 109 we'd got propped up against the dispersal hut, we said, 'That's one of your 109s.' All he would say was, 'Maybe.' Then we took him over to the mess and gave him a drink and chatted to him and he asked for a paper and pencil.
>
> 'What do you want it for?' we asked.
>
> 'I want to write all your names down so that when the Luftwaffe blackens the sky tomorrow and you lose the war, I'd like to see that you're well looked after.' He couldn't understand why we fell about laughing, and were saying, 'Sorry, you've chosen the wrong side, chum.'

But in the corner of the mess, sitting very quietly, were the three Poles. Stony-faced amid the laughter, they were glaring at the German. 'If we don't keep an eye on them,' thought Peter Brothers, 'they'll probably knife him or something.'

'They were prepared to do virtually anything, as we would have been in the same circumstances,' says Brothers. 'After all, if you left your family behind in an occupied country and all . . . they were pretty upset.' A little later Squadron Leader Athol Forbes was leading on an exercise sortie a group of Polish pilots not considered fit for combat. Suddenly they spotted a formation of Germans. There was a jabber of Polish over the RT and then the squadron leader found himself alone. The Poles had descended on the Germans and decimated them. 'After that they were definitely placed on the combat-ready roster and the Luftwaffe suffered accordingly.'[2]

In the battle as a whole, Poles accounted for 20 per cent of all enemy aircraft destroyed. Often they would disobey direct orders in order to chase a German plane for as long as it took. Together with the Czechs, they brought a new attitude to the squadron dispersal huts across the south-east.

But the RAF, if keeping up its numbers and its morale, was losing experienced, irreplaceable pilots. By the beginning of August, Dowding had lost eighty flight commanders and squadron leaders. Now only about half of the fighter pilots available had any experience of flying against hostile aircraft. Dowding was also concerned about the wear and tear that flying so many patrols was causing to his pilots. On 27 July he ruled that pilots must have a minimum of eight hours off duty in every twenty-four, and a continuous twenty-four hours off every week. Above all, though, he and Air Vice-Marshal Park tried to hold back their strength. Wherever possible, they avoided fighter-to-fighter combat. Kesselring's 'fighter sweeps' over the southern counties were allowed to go unchallenged, even though they had a demoralising and sometimes deadly effect, strafing farmers and land-girls as they worked in the fields close to the coast.

In the same way, enemy fighters would be allowed to cross the coast unmolested. Dowding knew that the German Bf 109 could normally only carry enough fuel for eighty minutes' flying time. With the journey back and forth across the Channel accounting for sixty minutes, this left little time for escort duties over southern England and off the coast, particularly if the fighters became engaged in fuel-guzzling air-to-air combat. Accordingly, the sector controllers would attempt to time the take-off of the Hurricanes and Spitfires when they thought the Bf 109s would be starting to head for home. Just to delay them could mean a downed aircraft. The German pilots, for their part, came to hate the cold, choppy waters of the Channel. Gunther Büsgen, the Bf 109 pilot who had been so friendly with a shot-down British flyer in France, remembers how much a watery death in the Channel was feared. 'On one occasion the English drove the whole unit off course to the Isle of Wight. Six planes went down in the Channel because they had simply run out of fuel. They just fell into the sea and the pilots drowned. It's something you never forget.' Many pilots developed a gastric complaint that came to be known as 'Channel stomach'. It was thought to be caused by looking at the waves, although it might have had psychological causes as well.

Dowding was aware that time was against the Germans and that Fighter Command merely had to survive the summer to be able to threaten any invasion fleet in order to win the battle. Thus he was keen to avoid the decisive all-out combat that Kesselring was trying to tempt him into. In fights over the Channel, a bare minimum of planes was used to intercept raids, so in almost all fighter combats of this period the defenders were outnumbered, even as pilots and planes were sitting idle further north. To some in 12 Group, which covered the eastern counties and the Midlands, there was frustration at not being in the action.

At this time 19 Squadron, equipped with Spitfires, was based at Fowlmere in Cambridgeshire, an airfield controlled by the nearby sector station at Duxford, part of

12 Group. As with squadrons in the south, they spent July on convoy escort duties, but unlike hard-pressed 238, 609 and 501 over the Channel, they hardly met any hostile aircraft off the east coast. Between the fierce fighting over Dunkirk and the end of July, coal-miner's son Sergeant Pilot George Unwin did not encounter a single German plane. 'We weren't used as much as we should have been,' says Unwin now. He considers Keith Park foolish for flying his 11 Group squadrons so hard, with 'sixty serviceable aeroplanes up at Duxford, ten minutes' flying time away, and time and time again we were never used'. Unwin's 12 Group also had a far higher proportion of Spitfires compared with 11 Group, which made it all the more confusing to 19 Squadron that they were held back from the early parts of the battle. 'A Hurricane pilot will tell you that his aeroplane was the best. I'm awfully sorry but I've flown them both . . . how can you fight somebody thirty miles an hour faster than you are? It's as simple as that,' says Unwin.

The commander of 12 Group was Air Vice-Marshal Trafford Leigh-Mallory. Group HQ was at Watnall, near Nottingham, and there were sector stations at Coltishall, Wittering, Digby, Kirton-in-Lindsey and Church Fenton, as well as Duxford. Leigh-Mallory was an ambitious officer, and felt that it should have been him, rather than Park, who was in command of the vital 11 Group. The antagonism between the two men would cause serious problems at the height of the battle.

Fred Roberts was an armourer with 19 Squadron and often worked on George Unwin's Spitfire. Before the war he had been employed at the Tin Plate Rolling Mills in Neath, but, he says, 'it was a dreary job. Slave labour, really.' After the Munich crisis, when Britain and France were shocked into rapid expansion of their armed forces, the RAF had appealed for volunteers. Roberts was recruited and after training at

Uxbridge was offered the chance to choose a trade. 'For no special reason' he elected to become an armourer. After a further six months' training at Mamby in Lincolnshire, he was posted to 19 Squadron at Duxford. 'I had no idea what they were and didn't know anything about them. Lo and behold, when I got there I found out they were Spitfires. Who could want anything more than to work on Spitfires?'

Both the Spitfire and the Hurricane had eight 7.7mm-calibre Browning machine-guns. Each of the 'tanks' held 300 rounds, which meant that a fully armed plane had 2,400 rounds. There would be a mixture of ball, armour-piercing, tracer and incendiaries. The tracer was useful for the pilot to see where he was firing, and some armourers, says Roberts, would arrange for the last six rounds in the tank to be tracers so that the pilot knew when he was out of ammunition. The German pilots of the Bf 109s usually had at this time two 7.92mm machine-guns on top of the engine and two 20mm Oerlikon cannon on each wing, which fired thin-walled shells containing explosive. In general the Messerschmitts had a lower rate of fire, but delivered a bigger punch than the Hurricanes and Spitfires. More seriously, the thin design of the wings of the Messerschmitt meant that the Oerlikons only had sixty rounds per tank, so that a two-second burst consumed well over a quarter of the supply of cannon shells. By contrast the British planes could fire for up to seventeen seconds, although in combat an enemy plane would rarely be in the sights for more than two or three seconds.

In all the aircraft of the battle that carried wing arma-ment, problems were encountered when aircraft climbed through cloud to high altitudes. Condensation picked up on the climb could freeze, disabling the guns. To counter this, oil diluted with paraffin was applied to the guns, although this did cause extra work for armourers such as Fred Roberts as it did not prevent rust. The other way was to cover the gun ports with canvas and therefore seal the guns away from the condensation, as well as stop air-flow down the gun ports. Naturally, once the aircraft had fired, this was ineffective, but it did mean that it took only a very quick look for the armourers to establish whether the guns had been used and would therefore need reloading. If that were the case, a well-drilled routine would be underway in moments. At Fowlmere, where Fred Roberts worked, there would normally be an armourer and an assistant for each wing of the Spitfire:

> Charlie and his assistant would work under the one wing, I'd work under the other wing with my assistant Dag. First we'd drop the empty tanks out, and while I was pushing the full tanks back up in and pulling the belt through, my assistant would be running the cleaning rod down the barrel. This had to be done before the plane was re-armed otherwise the first round in the belt would already be in the breech. So you had to push the cleaning rod down, clean it out quick, a bit of oily four-by-two, and as soon as the assistant pushed that through, we pulled the belt through and let the breech rod go forward. Once we'd done that with each of the four guns on each side, the plane was fully loaded.

The whole process only took three to three and a half minutes.

There were other, less specialised tasks for which all the ground crew were needed. When they had arrived at Fowlmere, the first job had been to help the local farmer get in the hay so that a runway could be cleared. The grass was then kept short by flocks of sheep, specially drafted in for the purpose. Then there were slit trenches and latrines to be built and tents to be erected. Living conditions were far from luxurious. Food had to be brought from neighbouring Duxford, to where the pilots and ground crews alike had to travel for a weekly bath. The officers had two Nissen huts, but there was not room for everyone:

> The rest of us, we took our chances in tents. When the sun was shining it wasn't too bad, but Fowlmere is on top of a hill overlooking that part of Cambridgeshire and even today when you go up there on a windy day, it's really rough. When it rained, well that was it. I'd be out there one o'clock, two o'clock in the morning holding the tent down and we had to dig trenches around the tent to take the water away.

With accommodation so tight, some of the pilot officers who lived locally were allowed to sleep at home. Amongst these was James Coward, who had recently married and whose wife, Cynthia, was expecting a baby. They lived in her parents' country house in the picturesque village of Little Shelford four miles from Duxford. In the morning they had breakfast together and he would leave, giving her a farewell kiss and saying, 'See you later.' Within half an hour he could be at 25,000 feet shooting at Germans.

Some airfields were well served by local activities and diversions, but Fowlmere village had no shop and only two pubs. Going further afield was difficult for Roberts and his colleagues as transport was scarce. 'All you could do was either buy a pack of candles and sit in the tent with a book or go down to the village pub, and of course what I was getting then didn't run to going down the pub every night of the week.' Nevertheless the villagers of Fowlmere went to great lengths to welcome the men from the airfield. 'The people in Fowlmere made us very, very welcome, they were lovely people there. They opened a little canteen after we'd been there a while. Where they got the food from I'll never know but they made sausage rolls and little tarts and so forth for us. They treated us very, very well and as for the pubs, they were very, very welcoming in there.'

As ever, there was one pub for the officers and one for the men. 'The old boy who kept the Chequers, he didn't want the ground staff, he was quite satisfied with the flying staff, the sergeants and the officers, but we went to the Black Horse, when they had the beer. We used to play a lot of cards, pontoon, rummy, Napoleon, gambling games which were illegal, but they shut their eyes to it.'

George Unwin, too, remembers a strict hierarchy in operation. He remained a non-commissioned officer – a sergeant pilot – throughout the Battle of Britain, despite acting as squadron leader on many occasions. At that time taking a commission would have actually involved a cut in his salary. In fact about 42 per cent of the 'Few' were NCOs, denied the status and perks of being an officer. In spite of Unwin's experience and leadership once the squadron was airborne, down on the ground the distinction was important. 'They were still officers as far as we were concerned, there was no familiarity or anything like that. You never mixed at all, you were trained like that, the RAF built it into you.'

On the whole, ground crew had neither the money nor the time for much fun. Roberts remembers his colleagues as a sober lot; there was none of the high jinks or letting-off steam associated with the flying officers. And as the battle continued, few had any real idea what was going on in the larger picture. Roberts remembers:

We didn't know if we were winning or losing. All we knew was what the newspapers told us – that we had shot down fifty for the loss of twenty-five, that sort of thing. We knew nothing at all for ourselves. I'm sure even the pilots didn't know. All we knew was getting up in the morning, how many planes are going to take off today and how many times. We lived day to day then. We had no concept of how the war was shaping or anything at all.

There was one way that the ground crews could stay in touch with their own planes, however. 'If the squadron was in action and there was a Spitfire left on the ground, the radio mechanic or wireless mechanic then used to plug into the radio set a spare pair of earphones with a long lead.' This enabled the ground crews to listen in on a dogfight fifty miles away. But this did not happen very often and most of the information would be gleaned from the pilot on his return. A strong bond would grow between a pilot and his crew.

Of course the pilot, he became part of the team of armourer, rigger [the flight mechanic in charge of the airframe] and fitter [flight mechanic in charge of the engine]. We three and the pilot were a team of four. The radio operator, the electrician and the instrument mechanic, they probably had three or four aircraft to look after, so they weren't part of our team. But we three were always there together and usually when you had a scramble, you were there, the fitter was in the cockpit starting the engine up, the armourer was there, sometimes he would be on the starter trolley pressing the accumulator to start the engine. The airframe wallah, he was there with us ready to pull the chocks away. As soon as the engine was warmed up, the pilot came, he got into the cockpit, the rigger was on one side the fitter was the other side, I'd be there strapping him into his harness. When that was done, the other two would come back to the tail with me and all three of us lay

across the tail, to hold it down. Some of the chaps
preferred to sit on the tail facing forward, but most of us
preferred to face backwards, one on each tail plane and
one across the fuselage to hold it down while the pilot
revved. As soon as he had revved the engine up, then the
rigger, the fitter and the armourer went to each wing tip
to guide him out on to the airfield. We worked as a team
and we became close to the pilot like that.

When the Spitfire returned, the ground crew would be
needed again as it landed.

As soon as the plane came to a stop, we used to dash out
to meet him, because the Spitfire was an unsteady plane
on the ground as the legs were close together. While the
Hurricane's legs were wide apart and folded up with the
wheels under the belly of the plane, on the Spitfire the
legs were closer together and folded up into the wings.
That was all right on a concrete runway but on a grass
runway the plane used to wobble as they went over the
bumps, so we always used to dash out and one man
would grab each wing tip to steady it as it taxied in.

The ground crew were aware of the enormous importance of
doing their job properly. A small mistake could cost the life of
their pilot. On one occasion, Peter Brothers of 32 Squadron
had serious cause for complaint.

My aircraft hadn't been re-armed properly. When I
pressed the trigger nothing happened. I was pretty
upset about this and we got the armourer in. I'd got
my revolver, which was always stuck in my flying boot,
and I took it out and banged it on the desk and said,
'I've a good mind to shoot you rather than put you on

a charge.' I was very cross with him and he was very frightened. I rang up the Group headquarters and said I wanted the flight sergeant posted and replaced.

So George Unwin and 19 Squadron had a quiet July, while in the south, squadrons were being decimated and exhausted. When the time came for fighting, Unwin, together with the rest of 12 Group, would be keen to make up for lost time.

For 501 Squadron, however, there was to be no real break from the fighting from May to the end of the battle. Over France, the squadron had claimed seventy-one enemy aircraft shot down for the loss of eighteen Hurricanes and eight pilots. Having flown continuous sorties over Dunkirk they were exhausted. But their brief rest at Croydon came to an end on 4 July when the squadron was posted to Middle Wallop. During the day, like Gordon Batt's 238 Squadron, they would operate from Warmwell nearer the coast, returning to Middle Wallop just before dark. Flying over the sea was the least favourite part of the battle for Sergeant Pilot Peter Morfill, who had been with 501 Squadron since the posting to France at the beginning of May, and had been with John Gibson when they were forced to leave Jersey. 'That was the bit I didn't like, flying up and down over the sea with only one engine. It's cold and it's wet.'

Initially the Germans were better organised about rescuing their airmen out of the Channel, using float planes that could not only find but also pick up downed airmen. By contrast the RAF only had eighteen search motor boats along the whole of the south coast. To aid air-sea rescue the German airmen had been issued with self-inflating life jackets, flares, yellow skull caps and bright orange dye that could be released into the sea to give a vivid signal. (In 1940 a German plane crashed into a tennis court near Hurst Green in East Sussex. Firemen rushed to the blazing scene and ended up washing the dye from the stricken plane into a local water source. The spring flowed brilliant orange for several weeks.) This life-saving tactic was soon adopted by the RAF, although it did not work in choppy water.

The water in the Channel was rarely warmer than 14°C, and an airman in a life jacket could not expect to last more than four hours. German Bf 110 pilot Jochen Schröder was shot down by Hurricanes near Plymouth whilst protecting Ju 87 Stuka dive-bombers on a convoy attack:

> We hadn't had any practical experience of landing on water but we had been instructed in the theory. One had to put the plane down parallel to the waves, neither into them nor going with them. With luck the plane wouldn't be tossed over and you then had fourteen seconds before it would sink. I was a good pilot and I put the plane down gently. My rear-gunner was all in. I pulled him out of the cabin. He had a lot of bullet wounds in the shoulder and was crying and screaming and bleeding heavily from the neck. I ducked him in the water and got his life jacket inflated. You just pressed the 'Luft' button and the whole thing ballooned up. He went on screaming and I tried to help him start swimming.

After several hours in the water, Schröder was picked up by the Royal Navy and taken to Weymouth, where, he remembers, he collapsed asleep in the police station for six hours. His rear-gunner did not survive and was fished out of the water some time later.

Some German bombers and fighters were issued with dinghies, a practice later adopted by the RAF, but in order for them to be used, the stricken aircraft had to make a landing in the sea. This was particularly difficult in a Ju 87 Stuka, as the fixed undercarriage would often cause the plane to somersault on hitting the water. Single-engined fighters, too, of both sides, tended after a landing on the water to turn tail-up and sink.

For the British pilots, routine escorting of convoys had become increasingly dangerous. On 11 July, 501 Squadron lost a sergeant pilot who had been flying one of three Hurricanes to take on ten Dorniers and twenty Bf 109s. He managed to bale out but an extensive search by the Weymouth lifeboat failed to find him. The following day another pilot was lost in combat with an enemy bomber. RAF Command were determined to attack lone bombers that were carrying out reconnaissance. On 12 July another pilot from the squadron was lost and a second injured when low cloud and heavy rain made flying conditions highly dangerous.

On 20 July the sector controller told the squadron that a convoy was being attacked near Jersey. Racing along the coast and out into the Channel, they eventually found the ships halfway between Jersey and Portland Bill. They were under attack from Stukas while 109s circled above. The fight that followed saw the first Battle of Britain kill for 501 pilot Sergeant J.H. 'Ginger' Lacey, who had already scored five victories in France and was destined to become one of the top-scoring RAF pilots in the battle.

At this time 501 Squadron, with its experience in France, was one of the most battle-hardened in 10 Group. In spite of his hatred of flying over the sea, Peter Morfill had perfected a dangerous move which seemed to be keeping him out of trouble. If he found an enemy fighter on his tail he would cut the throttle and throw the plane into a sharp turn. To master the side-effects of the resulting G-force took courage and confidence.

You black out, your eyesight goes but you know what you are doing. Once you're round 180 degrees, you ease forward, straighten her out, and there's the 109 in front of you instead of behind you. You could control this blacking-out, you knew exactly what was going on but you couldn't see because the blood rushes from the head. I've done it many a time, you get quite used to it. You know how far you've gone round and you can straighten the wing back again, ease it straight forward, and back it comes and what was behind you is now in front. In fact you're so clued up that your fingers are on the button already, you know. In fact I think that's why I'm still here instead of making a hole in the ground somewhere.

Although the Squadron still flew in the 'vic' formation – the new pilots coming from the training schools didn't know anything else – they were by now familiar with the dogfighting that took place after the initial attack. But however practised the pilots were, dogfights were always chaotic, fragmentary and incredibly fast-moving. John Gibson, who had also been with the squadron since France, was by now an expert: 'The squadron would go in as a squadron on the first pass, but then everything broke up. I can remember the sky full of aircraft and suddenly there is nothing. Everyone seems to have disappeared. Then everyone had wheeled around and the battle continues. The fighting ended up as a sort of individual go but your number two and three kept with you for as long as they could.'

On 26 July 501 were posted to Gravesend, but most of the time they were operating out of the forward airfield at Hawkinge. It was an exhausting schedule as John Gibson remembers: 'When we got back to Gravesend and Hawkinge we had interceptions every day, two or three times a day, mostly on Ju 87 dive-bombers escorted by 109s, of course, going for the shipping.' Often, having left Gravesend at first light, they would not be back until nine or ten at night. At Hawkinge there were scant facilities, and the airfield was frequently pitted with bomb craters.

Nevertheless, there was still time for the occasional quick pint. The squadron's intelligence officer – or 'spy', as they were always known – had a connection with United Dairies and managed to get hold of a milk float. This was charged up during the day in a hangar and then at night provided the all-important transport to carry the pilots down the road to the pub. On one occasion, fellow 501 pilot Peter Hairs remembers, he was drinking there with John Gibson when an enormous explosion rang out. Both brave pilots threw themselves to the ground under a table, much to the amusement of the unperturbed locals, who knew a large anti-aircraft gun had just been set up nearby.

But there was little time for friendships to develop. Furthermore, it was at the back of everyone's mind that you might not see a friend again. New pilots would be welcomed, but everyone knew that they were the most likely to be killed quickly. Some disappeared on their very first mission. Many of the pilots who had been in France with Peter Hairs were dead by the end of August. Hairs remembers:

> The majority of us didn't form close friendships. I don't think it's because we didn't want to, but generally speaking, there wasn't all that much opportunity. You came across each other when you were waiting at readiness. There we'd be either reading, smoking, playing chess or listening to the wind-up gramophone playing 'Stardust'. In the mess in the evenings we'd probably have a few drinks together. But that was pretty much it. Maybe it was the Almighty's way of letting us get through this, I don't know.

As the losses mounted, Fighter Command was forced to throw less experienced pilots into the action. Bill Green, who cheerfully describes himself as 'probably the most inexperienced pilot to have fought in the Battle of Britain', arrived at 501 Squadron just before the move to Gravesend. Originally a ground crew fitter, Green had applied to join a new scheme in October 1938 for the Auxiliary Air Force to train its own pilots. Having completed just half of his Advanced Flying Training – something of a misnomer, according to Green – he was posted to 501 at Middle Wallop. The first thing to do was to go and meet and salute the commanding officer. 'Right, who are you?' the CO asked.

'I'm new Sergeant Green.'

'What are you looking for, what have you flown?'

'I've flown Manchesters and Tutors and Hawker Harts,' Green replied.

'Have you ever fired any guns?'

'No.'

'Used oxygen?'

'No.'

'Used the radio?'

'No.'

'Flaps?'

'No.'

'Well, you're no earthly good to me. I'm sending you to an OTU and there you'll learn to fly the Hurricane.' In fact, after a mix-up with service bureaucracy worthy of *Catch-22*, Bill Green ended up on an RT course at Uxbridge. A football field and a selection of bicycles had been commandeered for new pilots to practise radio-led interceptions, and Green found himself zigzagging across a pitch, pedalling furiously as a radio set in the bicycle basket barked instructions in code. For the moment, though, he was saved from combat action.

☆ ☆ ☆

On 24 July, a comparatively quiet day over the Channel, 17,000 tons of shipping was sunk from three convoys and more boats were badly damaged. The Admiralty were slow to pick up on the fact that the German dive-bombers seemed to be able to judge exactly where to attack the shipping. The Germans were actually ahead in radar technology, but its practical application had evolved differently. While the British had been quick to use the new technology in air defence, what military interest that had been shown in Germany had come from the navy, and the system had evolved for their use, rather than for that of the Luftwaffe. By the middle of July the Germans had radar established on the cliffs at Wissant, on the Channel coast opposite Folkestone. On 25 July this picked up a large convoy off Southend.

Early mist cleared as the ships entered the Straits of Dover, and the convoy (CW8) was attacked in force by Stukas, while forty Bf 109s kept the intercepting British fighters busy – 32 Squadron from Biggin Hill and 615 Squadron from Kenley. Fighting at full throttle, both sets of fighters were soon heading home to refuel, and the Stukas could attack at will. Thereafter, each time Park sent up Spitfires or Hurricanes to defend the convoy, there always seemed to be superior numbers of Bf 109s waiting for them. The convoy was attacked by Ju 88s in the afternoon and then strafed by Bf 109s as it passed Folkestone. More Stukas and E-boats were brought into the attack and eventually only two of the original twenty-one colliers and coasters reached their destination undamaged. On this day alone 65,000 tons of shipping was sunk and seven RAF fighters were lost. After this, daylight traffic through the Channel was restricted, and freight was moved to western ports such as Liverpool and Glasgow.

Most serious was the damage done to the precious destroyers

that guarded the convoys. Two had been damaged during the events of 25 July when they came under attack from Stukas and German E-boats. Britain could not allow her home fleet to become too depleted, any more than she could afford these heavy losses of aircraft and pilots. The day's action pointed to an early German invasion.

Attacks continued over the next week, with Dover being heavily bombed. On 27 July Bf 109 fighters were used for the first time as bombers against Channel shipping, an innovation far from welcomed by their pilots. On the same day HMS *Codrington* was sunk in Dover harbour, and the port had to be abandoned by the Royal Navy as a destroyer base. A further destroyer was sunk off Portland on 29 July by Stukas. The vulnerability of warships against attack from the air – so important a feature of the wider war to come – was being demonstrated for the first time, even if the Luftwaffe failed to understand the importance of this discovery. But control of the Straits of Dover had for the moment been lost by the British.

For Churchill, with his long view of the 'island kingdom', this was a matter of great concern. But he was less worried about the air battle, and Jock Colville reports his glee at the figures announced for enemy aircraft destroyed or damaged. Believing the claims of the RAF, he overestimated the damage that had been done to the hostile air fleets across the Channel. While much of the fighting was still over the sea, many claims could not be checked. Inevitably, with the heavily armoured German bombers often needing several attacks to be brought down, many aircraft were claimed by more than one pilot. This is no slur on the honesty of the claimants – with combat in the air happening at hundreds of miles an hour such inaccuracies were inevitable. On some days the RAF claim was actually lower than the Luftwaffe's private tally of their losses. On the whole, though, the enemy losses announced were about double the real total and an air of unreality, characterised by beautiful summer days and fantastic scores being chalked up on blackboards, permeated right through the country. On almost every day of the opening stages of the campaign, both sides celebrated their version of events.

Dowding and Park, though, kept calm and continued to avoid the big head-on battle that the Luftwaffe, and many in Britain, had been trying to push them into, refusing to subscribe to the widespread view that the Luftwaffe must be nearly finished. In fact, the Luftwaffe had not even started their offensive. The operations so far, according to Göring, were 'armed reconnaissance' only.

On 30 July Hitler ordered the Luftwaffe to speed up preparations for an all-out air attack on England, so that it could be launched within twelve hours. The following day he scheduled the invasion for 15 September. On 1 August leaflets were dropped over England printed with Hitler's 'Last Appeal to Reason' in English. The press had a field day photographing people cutting them up, threading string through them and then fastening the bundle to the privy door. More serious were the events in Berlin on the same day, when Hitler issued his Directive 17:

In order to create the conditions for the final overthrow of England, I intend to wage the air and sea war against the English homeland in a more intensified form than before.

For this I order the following:

1. The German air force is to beat down the English air force with all available forces as quickly as possible. Attacks in the first instance are to be directed against airborne formations, their ground bases, and lines of communication, furthermore against the air armaments

industry, including the industry for the production of anti-aircraft equipment.

2. After a temporary or local air superiority has been achieved, the air war is to be continued against the ports, and here particularly against installations for food supply . . . With regard of our intended operation, attacks against ports on the south coast are to be kept at the barest possible minimum.

3. Compared with this, the battle against enemy warships and merchant ships from the air can be postponed, unless it is a matter of particularly favourable targets of opportunity, or unless an additional effect can be achieved within the framework of attacks to No. 2, or unless it is necessary for training of crews for future deployment in battle.

4. The increased air war is to be conducted in such a manner that the Luftwaffe can be called in with sufficient forces at any time against favourable targets of opportunity in support of naval operations. Furthermore, it must be available in battle strength for Operation 'Sealion'.

5. I reserve the right to order terror attacks as a form of reprisal.

6. The increase in the air war may begin from 5/8 on. The Luftwaffe may set the exact date itself, depending on when preparations are completed and weather conditions permit.

Simultaneously, the Kriegsmarine will initiate the intended increase in the war at sea.

[signed] Adolf Hitler[3]

After the unfocussed bombing attacks of the previous weeks, this signalled a clear timetable of priorities for the Luftwaffe.

Hitler's message was simple: all forces in the forthcoming attack should be directed against the RAF. On 6 August Göring held a conference at his sumptuous Karinhall. Sperrle and Kesselring were there, along with Hans-Jürgen Stumpff, the commander of Luftflotte 5, based in Norway and Denmark. But in spite of Directive 17, there was still confusion and disagreement within the Luftwaffe high command and amongst the pilots themselves about their aims. Some were still wedded to the original plan of enforcing a blockade and compelling the British to capitulate through attacks on infrastructure, industry and ports. Others suggested that terror-bombing of London would do the job, although this was expressly forbidden by Hitler, who feared reprisals against Berlin. No one was quite sure whether the invasion plan was serious, or whether the Luftwaffe were expected to do the whole job of defeating Britain themselves. The result was that the Luftwaffe continued to pursue disparate aims. As Göring put together his detailed plans for the attack, he included naval and blockade targets – such as commercial docks and railways – in spite of the clear instruction from the top that the might of the Luftwaffe should be concentrated on the destruction of the RAF. Overestimating the damage that had been done by his bombers and fighters, Göring believed that the Luftwaffe could perform a number of tasks at the same time.

Radar sites were, however, included in the target list. The head of the Luftwaffe signals department had urged that something be done about these 'radio' towers, which seemed to be successfully directing British fighters on to raids. It was also decided that as many fighters as possible were to be used on sweeps to lure the British defenders into the air so that they would be back down and refuelling when the bombers arrived.

Göring expected to be able to force the British to their knees in a few days, two weeks at most. All that was needed was a short period of final preparation and then three consecutive days of good weather. Out over the Atlantic, four-engined long-range Condor aircraft took meteorological readings and radioed them back to the two Luftflotte command centres. On the airfields of France and the Low Countries, the entire strength of the huge airfleets was readied for what would be the largest air offensive in history. The start of the attack was set for 10 August.

In Britain the rumour mill, official and unofficial, had gone into overdrive. On 31 July the Prime Minister's secretary Jock Colville had heard from the head of the secret service that he had by 'now received news of imminent invasion from over 260 sources. The main attack would be in the south, with diversions against Hull, Scotland and Ireland.'[4] On 2 August, the American ambassador, Joseph Kennedy, reported to Washington that if the Germans possessed the air power everyone supposed, they would put the RAF 'out of commission', after which British surrender 'would be inevitable'.[5]

The message was heard loud and clear on the other side of the Atlantic, where observers knew something of the strength of the Luftwaffe. A few days later, arms buyer General Pakenham-Walsh, on a buying mission to America, reported 'a doubt in the capability of Britain to survive'. The United States, he said, was 'shy of starting production of weapons for a country which might "go under" at any moment'.[6]

Churchill for his part showed every sign of wanting to beat the attack off personally. A few days later Colville accompanied the Prime Minister to a shooting range. 'He fired his Mannlicher rifle at targets . . . he also fired his revolver, still smoking a cigar, with commendable accuracy . . . The whole time he talked of the best method of killing Huns. Soft-nose bullets were the thing to use and he must get some . . .'[7]

CHAPTER EIGHT

Eagle Day Begins

A S A SERVING OFFICER IN WARTIME, BEING ASKED WHAT you would like to do next is a very rare occurrence. But finishing his duties in Scapa Flow, Lieutenant Arthur Hague was given just such a choice. Twenty-six years old, he had been a merchant seaman before the war, working for the Blue Funnel Line, and had just qualified as a master mariner. As a naval reservist he had been called up at the beginning of the war. In his merchant job, he says, it would be twenty years before he became the captain of a vessel. Now, in July 1940, asked what he would like to do, unhesitatingly he replied that he wanted to command his own small ship. He wasn't to know what he was letting himself in for.

After a short spell of leave, he was summoned to Southampton. Arriving on Monday 29 July, he booked in to the Crown Hotel and then made his way to the Naval Office. There he found five other officers and an assortment of personnel from the Royal Naval Patrol Service, who had been on invasion look-out duty. Some were fresh from training; others were fishermen or merchant seamen. 'Like picking scratch football teams at school', the officers selected their crews. 'Then we all trooped down to the docks to find our ships, a miscellaneous collection of tugs and tenders.' Many of the vessels had come from abroad; one even hailed from the Great Lakes of Canada. In order of seniority, the officers chose their ships. Arthur Hague chose second and selected HMS *Borealis*. Originally an Antwerp pilot cutter, *Borealis* had been built in 1930, 'a beautiful little diesel-engined craft of 451 tons'. She had slipped away from Antwerp when the Germans arrived and had assisted in the evacuation from Dunkirk, but now she had a new purpose. All six of the vessels were to fly barrage balloons to deter dive-bombing attacks on convoys.

They were ordered to get their ships provisioned and ready within forty-eight hours. There followed a hectic two days of preparation, as the crews struggled to understand the French and Flemish boat instructions. Arthur Hague's second-in-command, Sub Lieutenant Nursey, had only just completed his apprenticeship and Midshipman Currayer had only made one previous trip to sea. The engineer had never worked with a diesel engine before. No cook had been found, so one of the seamen who had worked in a retail Co-op was given the task. Very brief gunnery lessons followed as each crew member was taught how to operate the twin Hotchkiss machine-guns mounted on the deck, which it was hoped would deter air attack. The six ships left Southampton on the morning of 4 August and met up with an eastbound convoy that had left Falmouth the previous day. Their orders were to deploy their balloons and station themselves around the edge of the convoy. The balloon on the *Borealis*, operated by three aircraftsmen volunteers, was then inflated with just under 20,000 cubic feet of hydrogen from tanks on deck. Sixty-two feet long, with a diameter of twenty feet, it could be floated up to 5,000 feet above the ship. Travelling for some of the time under thick fog, the convoy made it safely to the mouth of the Thames. Arthur Hague was relieved but exhausted – he had been on the bridge continually for thirty-six hours. But instead of standing down, the barrage-balloon ships were to meet up with a westbound convoy, CW9, at Sheerness.

Flying barrage balloons from convoy ships was one of a range of measures designed to prevent a rerun of the devastation caused to convoy CW8 on 25 July. Convoy CW9, code-named 'Peewit' by the RAF, was also to be accompanied by two destroyers and greatly improved anti-aircraft trawlers. Above all, the convoy was scheduled to pass through the dangers of the Straits of Dover during the night, when darkness would hide it from German aerial reconnaissance. Before the convoy had set sail on the first leg from Southend to Sheerness, the masters of the assorted twenty-one merchant ships, most of which were colliers, were addressed by an RN commander. Recent German radio propaganda had claimed to have closed the Channel to British shipping. 'We don't give a damn for your coal,' the RN commander told the assembled skippers. 'We'd send you through empty if we had to. It's a matter of prestige.'[1]

On the evening of 7 August, CW9 'Peewit' slipped out of the Thames on the evening tide and met up with the accompanying defence vessels. The convoy formed into two columns, each led by a balloon ship. Arthur Hague's *Borealis* took the starboard, coastward side. The balloon floated above at 3,250 feet.

Night fell as we passed Dover and in a calm sea under a moonless sky we crept past Beachy Head. Some time in the middle watch I became aware of the powerful throb of engines and assumed this to come from enemy bombers crossing the Channel on a night raid. Suddenly a loud explosion lit the sky and I saw that the coaster immediately astern of *Borealis* had fallen out of line and was listing. In a flash, it occurred to me that the throbbing I had heard was not aircraft but German E-boats, and they were on the shoreward side of us, attacking from under the cliffs.

Although the British Government had warned of the possibility, the organisers of the convoy had reckoned without the German radar at Wissant. This had duly picked up the convoy in the darkness with plenty of time to set a trap. E-boats had spent the early part of the night manoeuvring themselves into a position to attack craft moving through the narrow mine-free channel in the Straits. Arthur Hague's ship was a sitting duck.

> It immediately struck me to present as small a target
> to the E-boats as possible, so I ordered 'hard a port'
> to throw the stern towards the attackers. As the ship's
> head slowly – oh so slowly! – swung to port I saw
> the phosphorescent wake of a torpedo come out of
> the darkness and pass underneath the counter of the
> ship and come out on the other side.

Hague's prompt action had saved the ship, but by now another had been successfully torpedoed, and 'all hell broke loose'. Tracer fire from the anti-aircraft ships lit up the sky and the merchant ships themselves opened fire. In the darkness there was confusion and panic, and 'some of the coasters appeared to be firing at each other'. The E-boats continued to harry the convoy along the south coast, sinking two ships and damaging a third. In their haste to evade torpedoes, two of the merchant ships collided. Dawn saw the remaining vessels steaming close under the cliffs for safety as the Royal Navy vessels tried to shepherd them back into two columns. RAF fighters, including Hurricanes from 145 Squadron, arrived from Tangmere as escort. Formed up by 10.30, the convoy proceeded on its way, and Arthur Hague managed to snatch a couple of hours' much-needed sleep. Hurricanes from 145 still intermittently patrolled the skies above. But at 12.19, some five miles south of St Catherine's

Point on the Isle of Wight, German Bf 109 fighters appeared and headed straight for the balloons. 'Under a hail of incendiary bullets', the *Borealis'* balloon 'disintegrated in flames. Then, out of the sun, roared a flight of Ju 87 dive-bombers.' Arthur Hague was on the bridge. 'I saw this W-shaped silhouette of the dive-bomber coming zooming down towards us.' The *Borealis* opened fire with its Hotchkiss guns but they didn't seem to deter the enemy in any way. 'I saw the bomb leave the plane before it zoomed off upwards and a fraction of a second later there was a violent explosion on the foredeck. The foremast jack-knifed and everything movable on the bridge crashed around us. Then, within minutes, RAF Hurricanes fortuitously appeared overhead.'

It was 145 Squadron again. Fighter pilot Peter Parrot remembers arriving at the scene.

Our first view of the convoy near St Catherine's Point was of Ju 87s in their bombing dives. Above the Ju 87s were the escorting Bf 109s and farther to the south-east were two more large formations of enemy aircraft approaching the convoy – a formidable sight. I had already taken part in the Battle for France, and patrolled over Dunkirk during the evacuation, but I had never before seen so many aircraft in the sky at once.[2]

Already there were two or three ships stopped and on fire. The Hurricanes went straight for the bombers but were quickly intercepted by the fighter escort, and dogfights ensued in the skies above the convoy, while the Stukas continued their attacks. More British fighters were scrambled from Tangmere until there were nearly thirty Spitfires and Hurricanes engaged. At last the bombers turned for home, and Arthur Hague was able to take stock of the damage to his ship. Three crewmen were injured, the gun positions were destroyed and the steering had been demolished. The casualties were transferred to another vessel and only a skeleton crew remained on the *Borealis* as she came under tow, with another ship alongside to steer.

> We made good progress towards Portsmouth until about 1700 when a further wave of dive-bombers appeared overhead. Vulnerable and defenceless, there was little alternative but to take to the only remaining lifeboat and lie off from where we had an uninterrupted view of the action as RAF fighters swept down upon the enemy.

145 Squadron had returned, flying their fourth sortie in defence of the convoy, along with John Bisdee's 609 Squadron from Warmwell and Gordon Batt's 238 from Middle Wallop, as well as four other squadrons. Facing them were over eighty Ju 87s and eighty Bf 109s. Watched from below by anxious sailors, dogfights filled the sky. The recently formed 238 Squadron showed their inexperience when they opened fire on the enemy from far out of range. The squadron also lost two pilots into the Channel, but after about twenty minutes, the German bombers were driven off and headed for home along with their escort, one of whom was to meet Eric Seabourne from 238 Squadron, who had become separated from his fellows:

> We were given instructions then to return to base. There were no other aircraft about so I set course for home. But after a few moments I saw a speck on my port side and I thought I had better see what it was. I went to look and it was a Me 109, flying straight and level about five or six hundred feet above me. I was a bit wary about him because I was waiting for him to do a sharp turn and attack me. Anyway I slipped in behind

him and followed right below him at about two to
three hundred yards' distance. He still didn't move. He
just flew absolutely straight and level; it never varied a
bit. So I set up my gun sight and lined him up. Still
nothing happened so I got a bit closer. Still he went on
straight and level. So I just eased the nose up till he
absolutely filled the gun sight and then put my thumb
on the button and kept it there. Large pieces flew off
his aircraft, all over the place, and he went down in a
vertical dive. Usually you had to watch out for anybody
else and wouldn't stay around too long, but the sky was
completely empty so I thought I'd circle round and
wait. He just went down absolutely vertically and
carried on until there was an enormous explosion and
he hit the sea and that was that.

I remember thinking to myself, You stupid so-and-so,
you could have saved yourself if you had attacked me.
But he didn't. So then I just pulled up again and flew
back to Middle Wallop, reported what had happened
and that was that. About two days later two of my
fitters presented me with this Iron Cross, which they'd
made in the workshop in celebration of my kill.

The Stukas fleeing the battle had dumped their bombs,
which exploded in the sea, shaking Arthur Hague and his
crew in their lifeboat. When the attack was over, they made
their way back over to their ship. The *Borealis* had been hit
again and was listing heavily to port. As Arthur Hague
wrote in his report to his superiors later in the day, 'There
was a sound of escaping air or gas and a smell that suggested
that the hydrogen bottles on the after deck had been hit.'
Hague decided that it was too dangerous to attempt to
rescue the *Borealis* and reluctantly ordered his crew on to
another ship. 'About twenty minutes later *Borealis* slid, stern

first, beneath the waters of the English Channel.' It was a solemn moment for Hague as his first command went down only days after he had launched from Southampton. In his official report he noted:

> The ensign staff had been carried away by the falling balloon wire in the first attack and I had lashed an ensign to the after rigging. This was still flying when the ship went down. I much regret my inability to bring *Borealis* into port but I can assure you, Sir, that every effort was made to do so and that had she not been severely damaged a second time I had every hope of success.

Hague and his crew made for Portsmouth as the few survivors of the merchant ships limped on to Dorset. Of the twenty-one merchant vessels that had set out from Southend, only four arrived at their destination of Falmouth. There had been losses in the air, too: 145 Squadron alone had lost five pilots, and a total of nineteen fighters had been shot down. The Germans celebrated the action as evidence of their control of the Channel, and propaganda from Berlin claimed that forty-nine RAF fighters had been shot down. In fact the Germans had had the worst of the battle, losing thirty-one aircraft. The Air Ministry, though, were claiming that twice this number had been downed, and in Britain, too, the events of the day were celebrated.

The Prime Minister's secretary Jock Colville was having dinner that night with Winston Churchill, Anthony Eden and top naval and army commanders. He reports the attitude of the high command to the events of the day:

> Winston seemed to think we must go on using these coastal vessels as bait, although he admitted that 'the surviving bait are getting a bit fed up'. In drawing the

German attack thus we stood to lose little (Pound [the First Sea Lord] even pointed out that we had a surplus of coasting vessels) while in the ensuing aerial battles we definitely proved to ourselves and to the world that we were superior to the Germans. Winston said the enemy must be less 'all-powerful' in the air than we had supposed.[3]

Thus while Dowding's picture of the situation judged correctly that only a fraction of the Luftwaffe had been deployed in the fighting so far, Churchill believed that the all-out attack had already started. Dowding must also have been aware that the German losses were partly accounted for by the fact that some of their aircraft were vulnerable bombers, and, as the pilots fighting over the Channel put it, 'We were outnumbered four to one, so we had a lot more targets.' At the same time, the RAF's losses were more important to Dowding than those of the enemy. The day's fighting had seen the largest number of British aircraft shot down of any day so far. While Churchill wanted to draw the Luftwaffe into attacking the convoys, Dowding believed that it was the Luftwaffe that was drawing *him* into battle against his will. That he had managed to preserve his stock of pilots and aircraft at all against this pressure from above is a testament to his strength of will and confidence in his own judgement. That night the RAF order of the day was about the trials to come, rather than the battles fought already: 'The Battle of Britain is about to begin. Members of the Royal Air Force, the fate of generations lies in your hands.'[4]

In spite of the Luftwaffe meteorologists' predictions, the poor weather of 9 August failed to clear, and the opening operations of Eagle Day were postponed. The morning of 11 August, though, dawned bright and clear. Frustrated at the wait, the Luftflotte launched early raids on Dover and

Portland. Gordon Batt's 238 Squadron was scrambled from Warmwell. He describes the action.

> We had rather a shock. We were the first squadron to
> be scrambled to deal with what was thought to be a
> comparatively small attack. As we climbed towards
> Portsmouth, the number of enemy aircraft we were
> being told about increased from the original of twenty
> to thirty, to seventy, to eighty, then a hundred plus.
> Other squadrons were being dispatched to help.

In fact, 150 Ju 88s, He 111s, Bf 110s and Bf 109s had taken off from Luftflotte 3 to raid the Portland naval base. First, though, came the fighters. 'All we could see was the vanguard of fighters, a mixed bag of Bf 109s and 110s at various heights. The controller said, "Split into two flights and attack." We were instantly in a mass of fighter aircraft. We were attacked first by Bf 109s from above, which chopped me off from the other five of the flight.' This was something Batt had been trying very hard to avoid. Unlike some pilots, who were happy on the edge of the mêlée, finishing off lame ducks, he preferred to stay in the middle of the battle. He knew that German aces picked their victims on the fringe. Suddenly on his own now, Batt looked around at the empty sky, before spotting some eight or nine Bf 110s below him.

> I started to dive to attack, when it suddenly felt as if a
> steam-roller had hit me. The aircraft bucked and jumped
> out of my control. I went through the cockpit evacuation
> drill and opened the hood but then noticed there was no
> smell of burning. Looking around, I registered that I
> could no longer see. I then realised that my eyes were
> shut, the instinctive action you take in an emergency. I
> prised my eyelids open; they were gummed shut with oil.

I was by now streaming engine coolant, in a vertical dive, being blasted by cold air from the open hood. Held in the slipstream, a mass of oil hung in a cone from the windscreen. The propeller in front of me had stopped.

But he managed to level off and shut the hood, causing the mass of oil to fall in his lap. Turning his stricken Hurricane north, he broke cloud at 2,000 feet, coming out, to his immense relief, over land.

I was over Selsey Bill, to the east of the Isle of Wight. There was not a field bigger than a postage stamp, so I elected to force-land with the wheels up in a field near to a farmhouse, so that if I did get into difficulties the farmer would come to my aid. As I approach the field, which was covered in barley, I pull my straps extra tight as I know I'm in for a rough landing. As I hit the field, the big air scoop under the Hurricane digs in and rocks me forward. Then it releases as other forces take over, then it digs in again. I thought I was going to knock my brains out on the reflector sight every time my head was shaken forward. Eventually, having made a nasty groove in the farmer's crop, I came to a standstill. I rapidly released my safety straps and parachute harness, heaved myself out of the cockpit and ran along the wing, falling over backwards into the dusty barley and dry earth.

Within moments a troop of Home Guard came rushing across the field, rifles held above their heads so they could run. Covered in oil and barley dust, Batt thought he might look a little like a German pilot and hurriedly raised his hands above his head. Once his identity was established he was taken to RAF Tangmere, where he awaited collection to go back to Middle Wallop.

Eric Bann had seen his friend shot down, and borrowing Batt's car, he hastened to go and see if he was OK. When they both returned to Middle Wallop, they were given twenty-four hours' leave. Eric Bann wrote to his parents, recounting Batt's shooting-down, and requested from his mother three yellow silk scarves for the 'yellow section' friends, Batt, Marsh and himself. They would wear them in combat as lucky charms. She duly went to A.W. Hewittson's in Macclesfield and posted them down to him.

Both Marsh and Bann had claimed to have shot down He 111s and overall the Luftwaffe lost thirty-five aircraft during the day's fighting over Portland and Dover. When the weather failed to improve that evening, zero hour for Eagle Day was again postponed, this time until 5.30 a.m. on 13 August. But the RAF had suffered too, losing twenty-seven fighters, and worst of all, nearly all the pilots of these downed aircraft were reported missing. This was not a rate that could be sustained by Fighter Command.

The next day attacks were launched to soften up the defences before the all-out assault. At first light a group of Bf 109s sped across the coast at Dover and moved rapidly eastwards over Kent. A squadron of Spitfires took up the chase. As the 109s moved north-east, a group of sixteen Bf 110s and 109s, all carrying bombs, began striking at the radar stations on the south coast. This was Experimental Group 210, led by Stuka ace Hauptmann (Flight Lieutenant) Walter Rubensdörffer. Four of the group attacked the Dover station, damaging some huts and shaking the radar pylons. The inland station at Dunkirk in Kent was hit, as was Rye. At Pevensey, bombs cut off the entire electricity supply.

Into the 'radar gap' formed by this destruction streamed the second wave of attacks, this time on the forward airfields. John Gibson of 501 Squadron was landing his fighter at Hawkinge just as a raid by Ju 88s started:

Peter Brothers (right) examining a combat report with a flight lieutenant (*IWM*).

Spitfires from 19 Squadron. Although less numerous than the Hurricane in Fighter Command during the Battle of Britain, it was the Supermarine Spitfire that caught the public's imagination (*TRH/IWM*).

Bill Green, who admits he was the 'most inexperienced pilot in the Battle of Britain'.

The officers' mess at Fowlmere. Most of the personnel on the base had to make do with tents (*IWM*).

George Unwin with Flash, the 19 Squadron mascot (*IWM*).

Felicity Peake, who was in charge of the WAAF contingent at Biggin Hill at the time of the worst raids on the airfield.

Eric Seabourne, who was declared operational with 238 Squadron after just seven hours on a Hurricane. He had never fired the guns before his first encounter with the Luftwaffe.

SERGT. L.G. BATT.   238 SQUADRON

Gordon Batt, who also flew with 238 Squadron. He describes the losses to the Squadron as 'devastating'.

Heinz Möllenbrook, who flew Dornier bombers over England until his luck ran out on 16 August.

Wilhelm Stahl, who piloted a Ju 88, the fastest of the German bombers. Happiest when in a large formation, he was very nervous when called to make a lone raid on London.

London docks burn after the first mass raid on the city, 7 September 1940 (*IWM*).

Fire-fighters battle the flames in Eastcheap (*IWM*).

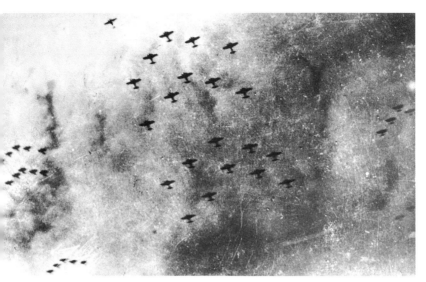

German bombers in formation over England (*The Art Archive/IWM*).

The wreckage of a downed Heinkel 111 (*TRH*).

A Heinkel 111 over the Thames near the Isle of Dogs, as seen from another German aircraft (*TRH/IWM*).

I had just landed and I saw the blur of the bomb right
in front of my aircraft. The next thing the whole aircraft
went on its nose. I thought, This is it. But it didn't go
off straightaway. Instead it went into the grass runway
and made what looked like a big anthill, which caused
the aircraft to end up on its nose. Instinctively I thought,
That's a delay. I was out of there like a cork out of a
bottle. I've never got out of an aircraft so fast. Normally
a delay was about ten seconds so I ran and threw myself
flat on my stomach on the grass waiting for this thing to
go off. But it didn't. The squadron commander on 32
Squadron was standing looking at me. He was laughing
his head off watching this clown.

But Hawkinge had twenty-eight new craters and was out of
action for the rest of the day. Two hangars and station
workshops had also been hit, and four fighters were destroyed
on the ground. Lympne was also hit, but was not an
important airfield. The severest attack was against the airfield
at Manston, which had already become accustomed to being
bombed and strafed. At one o'clock the same group of 110s
and 109s that had attacked the radar stations returned to
Manston, managing to catch several aircraft of 65 Spitfire
Squadron on the ground. They were followed up by eighteen
Dorniers, which had flown from their base near Cambrai.
The youngest pilot in the Dornier formation was Heinz
Möllenbrook. It was his first flight over England. The Dorniers' 150 bombs hit workshops, hangars and other buildings.
As Möllenbrook turned for home, he could see a huge cloud
of chalk dust blotting out the sun. Huddled in shelters in the
chalk beneath the airfield, many of the mechanics and civilian
support staff refused to come out for several days, in spite of
pleas and threats from the pilots.

To the west a large formation of enemy aircraft had been

picked up at noon by the radar station at Poling, in Sussex, which had not been hit. The 100 Ju 88s, together with 120 110s and further 109s high above, moved along the coast in the direction of the Isle of Wight. There, all but fifteen Ju 88s swung north and attacked the harbour and shipping at Portsmouth. The others veered right and came at the Ventnor radar station from behind, dropping fifteen 500kg bombs into the compound. Every building was destroyed and, uniquely of the attacks so far, the radar tower itself was severely damaged. Another hole had now opened up in the radar chain. Quickly a mobile unit was moved to the area to plug the gap and dummy signals were broadcast from Ventnor to try to convince the Germans that it was still operational.

At the end of the afternoon General Martini, the Luftwaffe signals chief who had pressed for the attacks, anxiously monitored radio signals from the radar stations that had been hit. To his dismay he found that all seemed to be back in action. The masts had been difficult to damage and, he surmised, the important machinery and control rooms must have been deep underground. It appeared that radar stations could only be knocked out for a few hours. Eagle Day would have to proceed with the early-warning system in place. Some of the Luftwaffe, full of confidence for the big attack the next day, argued that this was preferable, because if these devices did warn the fighters, that would lure them up to be destroyed in the air. But during the night, the weather, instead of improving, deteriorated.

As the day of the planned great attack dawned, confidence in Berlin in Operation Sealion was beginning to ebb away. Jodl submitted a fresh 'appreciation of the situation' to Hitler that morning. 'Under no circumstances must the landing operation fail. The political consequences of a fiasco might be much more far-reaching than the military.' Unless all preconditions were met, he added, 'the landing must be considered a desperate venture, something which might have to be undertaken in a desperate situation but on which we have no necessity to embark at the moment'. He added, 'England can be brought to her knees by other methods', which, he suggested, would include using the Italian navy to strengthen the blockade against Britain.[5]

Dawn saw fog over the Luftwaffe's French airfields and the Channel lay under thick cloud. Over Britain there was mist, scattered drizzle and some cloud, but otherwise the weather was fair. In all, these were far from ideal conditions for the German tactic of combining low-level bombing with high-level fighter sweeps. The bombers could be attacked without the Bf 109s far above even realising. Göring postponed Adlertag (Eagle Day) zero hour to 2 p.m.

Some pilots had already taken off by the time this order reached their units. One was Oberst (Group Captain) Johannes Fink, commander of a formation of Dornier 17 bombers. He kept his arranged rendezvous with his fighter escort at 5.30 a.m. but there were no 109s in sight, just a few 110s. After a short time, the lead 110 started jiggling about in front of Fink's Dornier, and then dived steeply away. The 110s had at last received the order to abort, but the message had not got through to Fink's Dornier. Unbeknownst to him, his long-range radio was out of action. He did not understand the message the 110 was trying to give him, and was furious when the fighter-bombers turned tail and headed back to France. The Dorniers, though, ploughed on, crossing the English coast at 1,640 feet, still in thick cloud. The RAF radar misread the strength of the formation of fifty-five aircraft as 'only a few', so just one Spitfire squadron was scrambled to intercept them. Finding the bombers over the

Isle of Sheppey, 74 Squadron, led by South African ace 'Sailor' Malan, attempted to break up the formation. By this stage other Do 17s, more through luck than good judgement, had found the airfield at Eastchurch. Many buildings suffered direct hits and five Blenheims were destroyed on the ground. German reconnaissance photographs had shown Spitfires at Eastchurch, but they were only there temporarily – it was a Coastal Command airfield, and therefore less important to Dowding than the vital Fighter Command sector stations. As the Dorniers turned for home, the Spitfires of 74 were joined by 111 and 151 Hurricane squadrons. While the German bombers struggled for the cloud cover, cursing their lack of a fighter escort, four were shot down and four more severely damaged. Heinz Möllenbrook's Dornier group, which had also been earmarked for Eastchurch, had been successfully turned back before it crossed the English coast. He remembers the returned Dornier pilots bemoaning the 'heavy losses' over Eastchurch.

By mid-afternoon, the weather had improved, and the original plans of attack were activated. But the pattern of the morning repeated itself. Airfields at Farnborough and Odiham in Hampshire were targeted even though they were not vital fighter stations. A raid on RAF Rochford got lost and ended up jettisoning their bombs over Canterbury. Low, thick cloud over England made dive-bombing difficult. Decoys sent to lure fighters into the air succeeded, only for the follow-up blows to come hours later, by which time the defenders had had enough time to land, refuel and rearm.

But occasionally the tactics did work. Over Maidstone, a crack squadron of Bf 109s lured the Spitfires from 65 Squadron higher and higher, whilst down below, eighty-six Stukas, commanded by Berndt von Brauchitsch, the son of the German army's commander-in-chief and architect of the army's Sealion plans, wrought havoc on Detling airfield. It was just after 5 p.m. and the mess halls were filling up. A direct hit killed sixty-seven airfield personnel. The operations room was destroyed and twenty-two aircraft on the ground were written off. Had Detling been a Fighter Command rather than Coastal Command airfield, it would have been a harder blow.

To the west, the plotting room at Group 10 headquarters saw several raids building up on their map table. 152, 238 and 609 Squadrons were sent up from Middle Wallop, along with 213 from Exeter, while 601, the 'millionaires' squadron', raced across from 11 Group's Tangmere airfield to cover the Isle of Wight. This time the early decoy actually helped the defenders. By the time the Stukas arrived to attack airfields in the Portland area, 609 Squadron had, for once, gained enough height to attack out of the sun. The Stukas were devastated in 609's best day so far. John Dundas wrote in the squadron diary: 'Thirteen Spitfires left Warmwell for a memorable tea-time party over Lyme Bay, and an unlucky day for the species Ju 87 . . . forty dive-bombers in four vic formations, with about as many Me 110s and 109s stepped-up above them were surprised by 609's down-sun attack.'[6] On their own radio sets the pilots of 609 could hear the German pilots' desperate cries of '*Achtung, Spitfeuer!*' but no mercy was shown. One of 609's pilots remarked that although he had missed the Glorious Twelfth, the 'glorious thirteenth' was the best day's shooting so far. Five Stukas were shot down and many more damaged, with no loss to 609. After all the hard fighting and casualties of the previous month, the West Riding Squadron was now one of the highest-scoring in the country and felt invincible. As Frank Ziegler's 609 Squadron history concedes, however, 'But if, once more, all 609's pilots had come home, this was thanks in part to the enemy's fighter escort having been also engaged by 238. This squadron was not so lucky.[7]

Eric Seabourne, complete with his 'Iron Cross' won five days before, shows the rather different attitude in the inexperienced and badly mauled 238 Hurricane Squadron.

> We were sent off to intercept this raid on Portland, a hundred-plus raid. We were twelve aircraft. There were probably other squadrons coming up but it was a hundred-plus raid! I mean that is a lot of aircraft, and they were all different types. They'd got the bombers down below and then above those were Bf 110s and then above those, 109s. They were all concerned with protecting the bombers so we had to deal with the whole lot of them. As per usual it was about seven or eight to one.

In the fierce fighting that followed, Seabourne engaged the Bf 109s and managed to hit two of them. Then a sickening crunch in front of him indicated that he had been hit. 'I didn't see who it was but I got a cannon shell in the radiator. I watched the oil temperature just going up and up and up until all of a sudden there's a bang and the engine just stopped dead, it was absolutely solid.' Still he was under attack, and this time some bullets hit the gravity tank just in front of him, which 'started burning quite happily'.

> It got hotter and hotter, so I thought it was time to abandon ship. I undid my safety harness and oxygen and radio. I'd read about all the bits and pieces to do and thought, Well, out we go. I pulled the hood but it would only open a tiny fraction. It just wouldn't move, it had been damaged during the attack. It was still getting hotter and hotter and in the end I more or less gave up because there was nothing I could do about it.

This was the nightmare that every pilot dreaded – the aircraft out of control and fire raging in the cockpit. Many stated that they would rather die instantly than be subjected to this torture. Some even carried pistols for this purpose. Already Eric Seabourne's clothes were scorched and his wrists and face burnt. His non-issue rubber goggles had melted on to his face.

All the time the three Bf 109s on my tail kept firing at me and then suddenly my port wing broke off. The aircraft turned over on its back and of course I wasn't strapped in or anything and came down smack in the hood and away went the hood and me with it. And so I was out and of course we were up then at about 18,000 feet and the cold air soon revived me, I can tell you. I knew what height we were and there had been quite a few occasions where pilots coming down had been fired at and killed while they were parachuting down. So I thought, at this height it's going to be a long time before I get wherever I'm going, because I was above cloud. I didn't pull my ripcord until I'd reached the cloud ceiling, which was at about 2,000 feet. So as I approached that I pulled it but the only snag was that when the thing opened up two of the straps were crossed about my neck, so with my burnt hands I had to hold them to one side to ease the pressure on my neck. The next minute there was an almighty splash and I was in the water. The one thing you were always told was to get rid of your parachute. Well I ignored that completely. I don't know why but I still kept my parachute, which billowed out all around me. I blew my Mae West up because we didn't have automatic Mae Wests in those days and neither did we have the single-seater dinghies. So I blew this up and floated around the water for about an hour. After the burning cockpit it even seemed quite pleasant. The next thing I remember is seeing a bow wave approaching. It was a warship and it manoeuvred alongside me and I saw it was a destroyer. They put a scrambling net over, two seamen came down the scrambling net, caught hold of me and hauled me up. The destroyer, the *Bulldog*, was still in action, the guns were still firing at these aircraft above and the skipper didn't want to be stationary for long so he got going. But I still had the parachute tied around my right leg so as he got under way of course there was a nasty crack and the leg snapped. But I didn't feel a thing, nothing whatever, and they hauled me up on the deck and the MO cut a lot of my clothing off and pumped me full of morphine. One of the seamen produced a mug of hot rabbit soup and then, I'm told, I was wrapped in a blanket, put on a stretcher, taken up to the skipper's day cabin and put in there. The MO kept an eye on me and later in the day I was transferred to naval tender when we got near Portsmouth and they whisked me off and in to Hasler [a naval hospital in Portsmouth]. In Hasler I was dumped in a bed next but one to a German pilot who had been shot down. He was an English speaker and he was creating because he had been shot down by a Hurricane, which he thought was much below his dignity. If it had been a Spitfire it would have been OK, but not a Hurricane.

For the British public and the government, it had been a great day. The Luftwaffe had flown nearly 1,500 sorties, and the RAF had done some 700, only 100 more than they were forced to fly while escorting convoys a few weeks before. The RAF had lost thirteen aircraft and only seven pilots to the Luftwaffe's forty-five downed aircraft. Dowding called it 'a miracle'.

———

The Luftwaffe as usual overestimated the damage they were doing both to the airfields and to the British fighters in the air. Nevertheless, it was impossible for the pilots of the Ju 87s and Bf 110s not to realise that their aircraft were becoming Göring's sacrificial victims. Bf 110 pilot Reudiger Proske remembers the atmosphere at his airfield: 'We flew every day and every day someone from amongst us didn't come home. That was no joke. In France we had sometimes had relatively heavy losses but mostly periods of very light losses. But it was hard when we began to lose a colleague or two every day. It had its effect on us.' It was estimated that if a pilot survived three trips in one of these aircraft, he was exceedingly lucky. A Stuka wing commander reported back to his superiors after the mauling by 609 Squadron, 'They ripped our backs open right up to the collar.'[8] There seemed to be no draining of spirit from their British adversaries. Luftwaffe pilots reported seeing RAF pilots remain in burning aircraft to complete a kill, and were by now familiar with fighters daring to approach the bombers until they were at point-blank range. It seemed to some, including the ace Adolf Galland, that the British might not be so easy to overcome after all.

But whatever the confidence in London, for 238 Squadron it had been the toughest day yet. Another pilot who failed to return after the raid was Sergeant Marsh. He had been flying with his friend Eric Bann, who described in a letter home what happened: 'Tony Marsh, my section leader, and I were the last two in action and I think I must have done too much flying for I fainted and I, poor Tony's guard, left him to the mercy of all. Oh dear, I did feel bad, when I learned he never came back.' Gordon Batt was made leader of 'yellow' section, but for him this was scant consolation. 'You get friendly with people and you go drinking with them,' Batt remembers, 'and then suddenly they're not there. You don't see any dead bodies or mutilation or anything like that, they're just not there. It's pretty painful.' With Marsh gone and Seabourne out of action, only Bann and Batt remained of the pilots who had become such a close gang in the sergeants' mess at Middle Wallop. Batt remembers the evening of 13 August: 'We'd lost pilots and, of course, aircraft in a devastating way. I do wonder why I was spared.'

CHAPTER NINE

Fighter Command on the Brink

T HE NEXT DAY, GORDON BATT WENT WITH HIS CO TO visit Eric Seabourne, who was in the naval hospital in Portsmouth. Seabourne was so heavily bandaged it was difficult to see how bad his injuries were. All Batt remembers of the trip is sitting by the bed, asking Eric how he slept without eyelids. Seabourne was one of five 238 Squadron pilots downed in a single day's fighting on 13 August, as they took by some way the brunt of the RAF losses. The exhausted squadron was at last given a few days off and travelled to St Eval in Cornwall. From the sergeants' mess there, Eric Bann wrote to his parents:

> Well here I am an old crock so soon. I am afraid that our duty at the front line has told its tale upon our systems. Our engagements have been really hectic and, unfortunate for us, we've always been there first, waiting for enforcement, with the final result we are all down with nerve trouble and have been sent to this rest camp.
>
> We received a telegram from the Air Ministry congratulating us upon our very good work and wishing us good rest but the cost has been heavy. Just Gordon Batt and I remain among the sergeants and many of our officers have gone.

Although on 'rest', the squadron was still flying, patrolling huge distances in the West Country. But this sector was comparatively quiet and the break at least meant the end of Bann's recurring dreams of huge formations of enemy bombers. 'We shall, I understand, be here for three weeks,' he wrote, 'until we have been re-fitted and new pilots plus our troubles put right.' Bann was desperate to see his wife May, but did not think he would be able to get any leave: 'We have proved good metal for the RAF and they require us back again.' In St Eval word had got around that they had a 'crack squadron' staying and there was free beer for the pilots in every Cornish tavern. 'This good Cornish air has healed our war sores,' Bann wrote some days later, and he had also received the good news that May was going to come and visit and the flight commander had given him a couple of days off. He had also heard of the fund-raising efforts of his home town of Macclesfield to 'buy' a Spitfire. 'How I wish that I could be the lucky local boy to fly the plane,' he wrote to his parents.

Joining the squadron down in Cornwall were its first intake of Polish and Czech pilots. Gordon Batt remembers their skill and dedication.

Domagala flew as my number two, which is one of the reasons I'm still alive. He was an instructor at the Polish School of Flying before the war and was a far better pilot than I was. They could hardly speak any English but show 'em a German and they were deadly, the Poles especially. They were ruthless, they would kill every way and any way they could. I don't think the British had quite the same sort of hatred. If they destroyed an aircraft and the pilot jumped out or went into the sea, it was 'Cheerio, all the best.' But the Poles and the Czechs would finish him off.

The day after the muddled launch of the Eagle Day offensive, there were heavy clouds over England that limited the Luftwaffe to smaller attacks. Many of their bombers had been busy during the night, raiding as far away as Norwich, Aberdeen, Swansea, Liverpool and Belfast, where the Short's bomber factory was hit. More importantly, the Spitfire factory at Castle Bromwich near Birmingham was badly damaged. Even if bombing by night was a notoriously hit-and-miss affair for both sides, Dowding had so far been unable to counter the raids. Neither the Hurricane nor the Spitfire was really suitable for night-time fighting, and the Blenheim aircraft, although now for the first time fitted with a tiny radar to pinpoint enemy raiders, rarely had the speed or firepower to do much about them, although a bomber had been downed at night on 23 July.

But there were some Luftwaffe pilots prepared to brave the weather on the morning of 14 August. A decoy attack on Dover drew the fighter defence away from beleaguered Manston, which was forced to endure further strafing and bombing. Other scattered raids, including one by young Heinz Möllenbrook's Dornier group, hit Hawkinge and Lympne again, and Southampton was bombed. Where possible, the RAF avoided combat. Even so, eight RAF fighters were downed against German losses of nineteen.

Early in the morning of 15 August, the weather looked bad, and the forecast was for it to worsen. Göring took the opportunity to summon his Luftwaffe commanders to Karinhall to account for the failures of 13 August. Top of the agenda was the beloved Stuka, which had reigned supreme over Poland and France but was now being shot down at an alarming rate. Göring ordered that each Stuka squadron should henceforth be accompanied by three fighter squadrons. The first would go ahead to take on the defending fighters; the second would dive with the Stukas; the third would give high cover. This new tactic was to prove unpopular with the Bf 109 pilots and it betrays Göring's lack of technical expertise. It was not possible for the Bf 109s to fly as slowly as the bomb-laden Stukas without wasting the all-important fuel and flying time over the target. Without air-brakes the Bf 109 could never dive with a Stuka anyway. In addition, being tied to the Stukas was the last thing the hunter squadrons of Bf 109s wanted to do. They knew that, unshackled from the bombers, they had the one German machine that could do real damage to Fighter Command in the air.

Other defensive measures hint at a growing fear amongst the Luftwaffe of Fighter Command. The Bf 110 Destroyer was also subject to a post-mortem on its latest set-backs in combat with the faster and more manoeuvrable Hurricanes and Spitfires. It was still, in theory, believed that the Bf 110 was superior to the Hurricane, if not the Spitfire, but it was agreed that this fighter should have its own Bf 109 escort. Also, to stem the loss of experienced pilots, it was decreed that there should be only one officer in any crew flying over Britain.

There was also to be a new focus to the attacks. Operations were to be directed exclusively against the enemy air force, including the aircraft industry. Other targets were to be ignored. Attacks on naval vessels in well-defended harbours had caused losses way out of proportion to the damage inflicted. Göring at last decreed that shipping should be attacked only when circumstances were exceptionally favourable (as per Hitler's original orders).

Lastly, Göring stated that he doubted the value of raiding radar sites, 'as not one of these so far attacked has been put out of action'. No further attacks should be planned, it was decided, although these orders did not reach the Luftflotte in time to affect that particular day's events.

Back in France, the Luftwaffe crews had been enjoying a brief moment of relaxation with their senior officers away. But during the morning the weather changed dramatically. By 11 a.m. there was only a light wind, clear blue sky and bright sunshine. The chief of staff of 2 Group, Oberst Paul Deichmann, whose 800 bombers and 1,000 fighters had been scheduled to lead the day's massive attacks, decided that in the absence of anyone more senior, he should order the offensive to go ahead. Nobody could get through to Karinhall for instructions – Göring had said that his conference should not be disturbed for any reason. Deichmann picked up the phone, and all across northern France the waiting aircraft roared into life. First off were von Brauchitsch's Stukas, bound for Hawkinge, followed by twenty-four more heading for Lympne. Twenty-five Dorniers set off to attack Eastchurch again. More followed vectoring on Rochester, and Martlesham Heath on the Suffolk coast. From airfields in Norway and Denmark bombers from Luftflotte 5 took off to attack targets in the north-east. The Luftwaffe had estimated that Dowding had only 300 fighters serviceable, reporting to the Wehrmacht Chief-of-Staff Halder that 'Ratio of fighter losses 1:5 in our favour . . . We have no difficulty in making good our losses. British will probably not be able to replace theirs.'[1] What was more, thought the Luftwaffe, surely the northern squadrons would have been stripped to reinforce 11 Group?

As the raiders approached, the British radar stations were reporting that there were too many signals to distinguish between individual formations. At 11.35 a.m., von Brauchitsch's Stukas swept down on Hawkinge. Moments later Lympne was attacked. Both were seriously damaged, the latter being put out of action for three days. Manston again suffered, and attacks on radar stations at Dover, Rye and Foreness succeeded in cutting the electricity supply to all three, putting them out of action for several hours.

Just over an hour later, sixty-three He 111s, escorted by twenty-one 110s with drop tanks to extend their range, were intercepted twenty-five miles north-east of Newcastle, having flown from Stavanger in Norway. Their course had been carefully plotted, although the formation was incorrectly estimated at only about thirty raiders and initially only one squadron was sent to intercept. Nevertheless the Bf 110s, stripped of their rear gunners to extend their flying time, proved to be useless at defending themselves, let alone the bombers. After four more squadrons joined the interception, the attack was driven off with the loss of only one British fighter. In the most uneven contest of the battle, Luftflotte 5 had lost eight Heinkels and seven Bf 110s and had not hit any of their targets.

A second raid by Luftflotte 5, this time of unaccompanied Ju 88s flying full pelt from Aalborg in Denmark, was more successful. Bombs fell on houses and an ammunition dump at Bridlington in Yorkshire, and a bomber station in Yorkshire was damaged with ten aircraft destroyed on the ground. But yet again the Luftwaffe had failed to identify the crucial Fighter Command airfields. Six Ju 88s were brought down, and it was clear to the Luftwaffe that Dowding had resisted the temptation to weaken his northern defences in favour of 11 Group. The radar and control system had also proved itself to work with devastating effect over the North Sea. Luftflotte 5 declined to take part in any further daylight raids.

In the south, there were now so many raiders plotted that the group and sector controllers found it impossible to identify the targets the Germans were heading for. All afternoon, German bombers and fighters seemed to pour across the coast. To a *Daily Express* reporter, watching from the cliffs at Dover, the hostile aircraft appeared 'to make an aluminium ceiling to the sky'.[2] The British threw up eleven squadrons, 130 fighter aircraft, but were unable to prevent

Martlesham Heath airfield from being bombed and strafed. Short's aircraft factory in Rochester was severely damaged and there were further raids on Odiham and Worthy Down aerodromes.

Over Folkestone, 501 Squadron's John Gibson was in trouble. He had shot down a Stuka and damaged another before being hit by cannon fire from an escorting Bf 109. His Hurricane caught fire and to his horror seemed to be heading directly for the built-up centre of Folkestone. But by this stage Gibson was a veteran baler-outer, and had the presence of mind to steer his stricken aircraft away from the town before clambering out at just 1,000 feet. Even then, he did not lose his sense of priorities. 'I had a brand-new pair of shoes handmade at Duke Street in London. We used to fly in a jacket, collar and tie, because we were gentlemen,' he laughs. 'I thought I was going to get these shoes wet in the Channel so I took them off while I was still in the parachute.' The shoes were carefully dropped over dry land, before Gibson's parachute took him over the water for yet another dunking. On his return to Hawkinge, he was awarded a DFC, and, even better, his shoes had been sent in by a farmer on the off chance they belonged to a flying officer.

As far as Dowding was concerned, relatively minor targets could continue to be attacked as long as his sector stations escaped. But for the first time, the Luftwaffe plans for 15 August included raids on Biggin Hill and Kenley, the two vital Group 11 sector stations defending London. As it happened, both raids got lost. The Biggin Hill raid ended up devastating West Malling airfield, near Maidstone, and from Biggin Hill itself, 32 Squadron, who had been on call since 3 a.m., sleeping under the wings of their aircraft, scrambled to meet them. The Kenley raid, chased across England by Spitfires, emerged from cloud over Croydon airfield. Taking it for Kenley, the Bf 109s and 110s of Experimental Group 210 destroyed one hangar and damaged two more. But many of their bombs overshot the airfield. Three small factories were hit, all full of workers starting the night shift. No air-raid warning had sounded. Croydon airfield was to be out of action for two days, and to Göring and Hitler's fury, bombs had fallen within London.

Churchill, meanwhile, had heard the news of the great battle going on overhead and had rushed to Bentley Priory to follow the events from the plotting table. He returned to London exalted. 'It is one of the greatest days in history,' he told Colville. Certainly it had been the hardest day's fighting so far; the Luftwaffe had flown nearly 2,000 sorties and the RAF 974. For the Germans, the day became known as 'Black Thursday'. In many cases bombing groups had failed to meet with or had lost their fighter escorts. Over fifty machines had been lost for good and a further twenty made it back to base damaged beyond repair. In return the RAF had lost thirty planes but only seventeen pilots. The Luftwaffe had dangerously underestimated the strength of the RAF, reckoning without the efforts of Beaverbrook's factories. Dowding had almost twice the fighters the Germans thought he had and was able on this day to bring them to bear highly effectively.

Nevertheless, there was no respite as attacks were renewed the next day. Even if the Luftwaffe continued to underestimate the strength of the RAF, they could still bring overwhelming numbers to bear, since while the RAF was spread out, the Luftwaffe could concentrate their forces at will. With the firepower of the bombers themselves improving, Fighter Command were outgunned in almost every encounter.

At noon on 16 August radar on the coast picked up three formations crossing the Channel. One, consisting of 100-plus aircraft, seemed to be heading for the Thames estuary; an even larger force was detected between Brighton and Folkestone; and the third, from the Cherbourg area, was heading for Portsmouth or Southampton. Three fighter squadrons were sent up from Hornchurch, North Weald and Kenley to intercept the Thames-bound raid, but bad weather had already forced the bombers to turn back, as Heinz Möllenbrook remembers: 'Our Dorniers met heavy cloud and the mission was called off. Hitler strictly forbade bombing unseen targets and most particularly dropping bombs on London. Targets were strictly military. On our return flight I was in the last wave of three aircraft.' By now, though, the British fighters had spotted the returning German bombers. 'We were attacked a number of times near Canterbury,' Möllenbrook recalls. 'On the first attack the plane to the left of us was hit and veered off past us. We got it in an engine so were flying on just one. Soon we were on our own. Keeping the plane in trim was taking up all my concentration.' The British fighters were not about to let this stricken straggler get away. They attacked again and again. 'During the second and third attacks my radio operator and mechanic were both wounded. On the fourth attack my right arm was shattered but I was still able to fly the plane. Then a Hurricane attacked us from the front.' This was flown by F. W. Higginson from 56 Squadron. The Dornier's forward firing gun managed to damage his aircraft, which was forced to make an emergency landing near Canterbury. But the brave attack had finished off Möllenbrook's Dornier.

The frontal attack wounded my left shoulder and probably also damaged our steering. The steering column fell from my hand. I baled out with my observer who thought the other two, already badly wounded, were both out of the plane. They were subsequently found dead. I don't know how they got out. We two, however, were in grave danger. The plane was spiralling down and we were caught in its centrifugal force. The observer, in extreme panic, let out the oxygen from his life-jacket kit and it caught fire. Then, suddenly, there was peace.

Anyway, I was lucky. My legs had been shot up but I was caught up with my parachute in a tree hanging fifty centimetres above the ground. I looked around and could see that we had landed on a small farm. I dropped my pistol from my left hand and it remained hidden for forty years in a ploughed field. Next I saw the glint of a gun and two farm workers. I shouted to them to help me and that I was wounded. I had learnt good English at school. They tried to release the parachute without hurting me but had to twist it this way and that. Then they took me into their kitchen and the grandmother bound my arm, and by doing so saved it. She gave me a whisky, or perhaps two, against the pain. My observer, who was hurt all over, had suffered no broken bones but hurt his knee on landing, probably because his parachute was damaged. The two of us were taken to a field hospital near Canterbury. There was an Anglo-German doctor on duty who had studied in Heidelberg. His senior surgeon had wanted to amputate my arm but he held off saying if it turned nasty he could always cut it off on Saturday or Sunday. So my arm was saved.

Meanwhile, three squadrons were sent against the Folkestone/Brighton formation, among them Peter Brothers' 32 Squadron from Biggin Hill. The three squadrons met up and decided to go in en masse against the giant hostile formation in an attempt to break it up. In the fierce dogfight that followed, Peter Brothers downed a Bf 110, among ten hostiles shot down, but the RAF lost five Spitfires and two irreplaceable senior flying officers.

Soon afterwards, at 1 p.m., a raid of 100 Ju 87s was spotted approaching Tangmere. WAAF radio operator Ann Lowe was just coming off duty when the alarm was sounded. 'The sinister sound of the air-raid warning started and loudspeakers over the airfield said, "Take cover, take cover, Stukas sighted over Selsey coming towards Tangmere, take cover, take cover." The warning got louder and louder and then you could hear the approaching aircraft.' The raid had been intercepted by two Tangmere Hurricane squadrons, 601 and 43, but thirty hostile dive-bombers had got through. Ann's sister Tig had been on the night shift and was in bed. 'I rushed to her quarters,' continues Ann, 'hauled her out of bed and began to run with her. She could run faster than me and she got ahead. The next thing, they were coming down – phrommmm. Then the first bomb fell nearby and I was flung about thirty feet in the air, coming down with my stomach on a brick. But I staggered on into the trenches.'

Farm workers in a field nearby took cover under the hay wagon as spent cartridges from the Stukas' machine-guns and the airfield's anti-aircraft guns flew about. On the base, bombs hit the cookhouses, the lines of quarters, and the workshop. Every hangar suffered damage. After fifteen minutes it was all over.

When Ann and Tig emerged from the shelter they were greeted with the sight of a body hanging in a tree where it had been blown by an explosion. With the exception of the operations room, everywhere was in ruins, and the runways were littered with craters. Fourteen servicemen and six civilians had been killed in the raid, which had also destroyed seventeen planes on the ground, including all four of the radar-equipped Blenheims that had made the first ever night-time kill, on 23 July.

Other airfields had fared just as badly or even worse. West

Malling was rendered unserviceable for four days and Manston, by now surely the least popular spot in 11 Group, suffered again. Many non-fighter airfields were attacked and many aircraft were destroyed on the ground, though only three of these were fighters.

The raid from Cherbourg had by now approached its targets. On the Isle of Wight, where technicians had been working around the clock to restore the Ventnor radar, five Stukas undid all their good work in just five minutes. The radar was to be out of action until 23 September. Happily for the Luftwaffe, Göring's orders of the previous day not to attack the radar installations had been ignored. But so too, it appeared, had the strict instructions of target priorities. Naval establishments were still attacked at Gosport and Lee-on-Solent, and the anti-aircraft defences at Portsmouth were dive-bombed by Ju 88s.

Attacks in force continued all across southern England, stretching Fighter Command's resources as never before. For the plotters at Uxbridge, the headquarters of Park's hard-hit 11 Group, there was no more time for reading or making glamorous underwear. The boredom of July had given way to a noisy, bustling urgency. Fifteen plotters hovered over the map table holding sticks to push the marker blocks into position. Instead of plotting just one raid, they could now be following three at the same time. Behind them runners darted about collecting new blocks of various colours as the minutes ticked by on the main clock. At the end of the shift, some of the WAAFs now found it difficult to drag their tired bodies up the hundred steps to the surface.

People who worked at Uxbridge remember the noise that would accompany such a day. A loudspeaker would broadcast orders to squadrons across the room as the teleprinters clattered and whirred. The din was made worse by the sound of squeaking chalk as the day's kills and losses were marked up on a blackboard. As the scores mounted on 16 August, Churchill could not resist rushing with his military liaison officer, General Ismay, to Uxbridge to follow the air battle from one of its crucial nerve-centres. Plotter Vera Shaw remembers that there was no smoking allowed in the ops room, but that an exception was made for the Prime Minister's omnipresent cigar. Ismay recounts the tension at Uxbridge: 'There had been heavy fighting throughout the afternoon; and at one moment every single squadron in the Group was engaged; there was nothing in reserve, and the map table showed new waves of attackers crossing the coast. I felt sick with fear.'[3]

George Unwin's 19 Squadron had come south from Fowlmere to Debden in Essex, and had been in operation the previous day but had failed to make an interception. At 5.50 p.m. on 16 August, they were flying back to Duxford from Coltishall in Norfolk when they were given mid-air instructions to head for a position just off the east coast at Clacton-on-Sea. Soon a part of the squadron made contact with seventy He 111s and about fifty Bf 110s south of Harwich. The rest of the squadron joined in and an intense battle followed. Sergeant Pilot George Unwin was rapidly winning the respect and admiration of his smarter colleagues and his ground crew. Fred Roberts considered him the best pilot in the squadron. Making his first kill since the action over France, he shot down at least one Bf 110. Several more hit the Essex countryside and an He 111 was downed into the sea.

Elsewhere, too, the RAF were showing fighting spirit. In the middle of the afternoon, James Nicolson of 249 Squadron had gone into the attack for the first time. Chasing a group of Ju 88s over the Solent, he was hit from behind by the powerful forward armament of a Bf 110. Heavily wounded, he was hit again and his Hurricane was engulfed in flames. As he struggled with his controls, the Bf 110 overshot him. Ignoring the smoke, his melting instrument panel and the terrible burns to his hands, Nicolson gave chase, eventually shooting down his attacker. Diving head first out of his fiery cockpit, he fell some 500 feet before pulling his ripcord. By now his left eye was completely blinded by blood and as he descended he came under fire from overzealous Home Guarders below and was ignominiously wounded in the buttocks. But he survived and three months later was awarded the only Victoria Cross to go to a fighter pilot during the battle.

At Uxbridge Churchill and Ismay had followed the day's events closely. The score on the blackboard ended with twenty-one RAF losses to over 100 of the enemy. In fact, as usual, just less than half that number of Luftwaffe planes had gone down, but that was still a great achievement. The RAF pilots were making up with courage what they lacked in experience. 'As evening closed in, the fighting died down,' says Ismay, 'and we left for Chequers. Churchill's first words were: "Don't speak to me; I have never been so moved." After about five minutes he leaned forward and said, "Never in the field of human conflict has so much been owed by so many to so few." The words burned into my brain.'[4]

Although the weather the next day was fine, an ominous quiet descended on southern England. The Luftwaffe, weary and disconsolate, flew only reconnaissance missions. At Biggin Hill, 32 Squadron caught its breath. The previous day had seen hard fighting for the squadron. But today there was nothing. In the unofficial squadron diary, Squadron Leader Michael Crossley wrote, 'Not a single sausage, scare, flap or diversion of any description today. Amazing. Heavenly day too.'[5] Across the south, the rest was appreciated. At damaged airfields the mass of unexploded bombs were roped off or destroyed. Battered defences were re-formed. Tangmere, devastated the day before, was operational again within twenty-four hours. Lacking mechanical digging equipment, men and women slaved in the heat to fill in the massive craters that littered the runways. Shot-down German airmen from the station's cells were immediately pressed into repair work. By this stage Ann Lowe was pretty fed up with them.

> As we were marching to the ops room, the Germans
> were digging around at the sides to fill up some shell
> holes, and as we passed, they spat at us. So I broke ranks
> and walked over and went, 'Here, here' to one of the
> chaps and he came up and looked at me and I spat right
> in his face. I thought, 'You'll get as good as you have
> given.' I was charged for bad behaviour.

But Ann had been injured in the explosion the previous day and was later taken to St Thomas's Hospital in London. Her fall on to the brick had caused her womb to collapse. Happily there was no long-term damage, but she stayed on sick leave for several weeks.

After the raid, living conditions at Tangmere understand-ably deteriorated, in spite of the efforts of the repair crews. The electricity and water supplies had both been cut, and most of the buildings had been destroyed. The latrines now consisted of a plank over a ditch, and the WAAFs had to sleep on benches at nearby Goodwood racetrack. Transport proved a problem until an enterprising transport officer flagged down a double-decker bus on the road and, having asked the passengers to alight and given the bemused driver a receipt, proceeded to drive off with his prize. Following the attack, the ops room was moved to St James' School in

Chichester and the accommodation and workshop buildings were dispersed around the airfield.

Even more serious than the damage to the airfields was the loss of experienced pilots. Over the last five days alone, the RAF had suffered sixty-eight pilots killed or missing, and a further seventy had been wounded badly enough to be unable to return to combat for many weeks, if at all. Since 1 August only seventy replacements had entered Fighter Command. At every sector station, commanders used the day's respite to learn from their mistakes and think up new tactics. Up at Duxford, cannon guns like those used by the Bf 109s were fitted to 19 Squadron's Spitfires for the first time. James Coward, still living with his wife in nearby Little Shelford, remembers that the guns worked well on the ground, but tended to jam in the air. For the time being they were withdrawn while modifications were made.

The eighteenth of August was the day on which Göring aimed to smash Fighter Command once and for all. On the British side it has become known as 'the Hardest Day'. Göring had at his disposal 276 Ju 87s; 768 Ju 88s, He 111s and Do 17s; 194 110s; 745 109s; and another fifty-two planes for reconnaissance. Against this onslaught the RAF could put up 419 Hurricanes and 211 Spitfires. It would be vital that the right number of defending aircraft were in the right place at the right time.

At noon, huge Luftwaffe formations crossed the south coast bound for Biggin Hill and Kenley. In total some 108 bombers and 150 fighters had been earmarked for these vital targets. Unlike the control rooms at Bentley Priory and Uxbridge, the vital sector stations' ops rooms were housed above ground in fairly flimsy buildings. A direct hit on one could paralyse the entire sector.

501 Squadron were already airborne and were now ordered to patrol over Canterbury. Four more squadrons, with seventeen Spitfires and thirty-six Hurricanes, were scrambled by 11 Group to patrol the line between Canterbury and Margate in order to protect the docks, the Thames estuary and Gravesend and Hornchurch airfields, climbing as quickly as they could. Four squadrons, with twenty-three Spitfires and twenty-seven Hurricanes, were gaining height over Kenley and Biggin Hill to meet the expected onslaught.

The first victims were four Hurricanes of 501 Squadron, shot down in one pass by the leading Bf 109 of a fighter sweep. The main German bomber formation was fortunate, missing the patrolling squadrons and heading on for the airfields. For the attack on Kenley, Kesselring's plan was for two waves of high-level bombers to pound the airfield and then for Dorniers to finish off the job with a low-level bombing attack. The Dorniers, led by Oberleutnant (Flying Officer) Rudolf Lamberty, crossed the Channel at only 100 feet. They were hoping to avoid high-level fighters, and unbeknownst to them they also succeeded in evading radar detection. They were spotted, though, by the vigilant Observer Corps on Beachy Head. Staying very low, they sped across Kent, hugging the valleys and following the railway lines northwards. On the approach to Kenley, Burgess Hill village was strafed. An auxiliary fireman, flinging himself to the ground as bullets smashed into his vehicle, could clearly see the German crews in their aircraft as they swept past. From the third floor of St Lawrence's Hospital, a patient found himself looking directly into the cockpit of the leading Dornier.[6] As news of the raid spread northwards, sector controllers at Kenley ordered all serviceable aircraft into the air. Those not able to fight should head northwards out of trouble.

The nine low-level Dornier crews had been told that a

mass of smoke from the earlier high-level attack would betray the location of the airfield, but they arrived above a peaceful and undamaged Kenley. Releasing their bombs, they came under fire from the airfield's anti-aircraft Bofors guns at short range, and, from behind, from the Hurricanes of 111 Squadron, scrambled from Croydon on the 'all aircraft in the air' order. The Dorniers returned fire both in front and behind, and the Hurricanes were forced to take avoiding action from their own anti-aircraft guns. At this moment cables were shot into the sky from the airfield perimeter. Parachutes opened at the top of long wires and if they snagged on an aircraft, another opened at the bottom. The drag was enough to stop an aircraft dead in the sky. Several Dorniers became ensnared.

Oberleutnant Lamberty's wing tip was shot off and his bomber caught fire. Coming down in a field near the airfield, Lamberty struggled out of the burning cockpit to be confronted by a troop of Home Guard, determinedly pointing their rifles at him. Lamberty raised his hands, and when the Home Guarders saw burnt shards of flesh falling from them, they lowered their guns.

Above the airfield a lone Dornier still circled, apparently unconcerned by the anti-aircraft fire all around it. In fact the pilot was dead and his slumped body had jammed the controls. Desperately the flight mechanic prised the corpse away. Just as the aircraft's speed had dropped to the critical, he managed to free the controls and guide the stricken aircraft away from the airfield. Even though the mechanic had not flown before, he succeeded in reaching his base in France. Only one other Dornier of the raid made it back. Low-level attacks of this kind were subsequently abandoned by the Luftwaffe.

But now, at last, the delayed high-level attack arrived. While 151 Squadron of Spitfires kept the top cover busy, 'A' flight of 32 Squadron, led by Squadron Leader Crossley, closed in on the bomber formation. Crossley let out the 'Tally ho!' signal and headed into position to attack the bombers directly from the front. Leading 'B' flight just behind, Peter Brothers spotted the fighter cover of Bf 110s wheeling around to attack the Hurricanes, their cannon and machine-guns already opening up, and veered his flight up and to the right to engage them. Intent on chasing one of them, he pulled the nose of his Hurricane past the vertical and it stalled. Moments later he was spinning away from the battle out of control.

'A' flight had by now managed to shoot down a bomber and significantly break up the formation. Some were forced to carry their bombs home, others dropped them indiscriminately in the area, hitting Croydon aerodrome nearby and damaging residential property all around the airfield. Peter Brothers recovered from his spin and joined the continued attacks on the bomber formation and its escort, shooting down a Dornier 17 and a Bf 109. The third wave of bombers scheduled for Kenley, Ju 88s, arrived to find a thick pall of smoke obscuring the airfield, making dive-bombing impossible. Veering eastwards, they headed for their secondary target of West Malling, where they were attacked by 501 Squadron, eager for revenge for the earlier disaster. On the way home, Park's Spitfires and Hurricanes continued to harass the German bombers and fighters, now low on fuel and in no mood for combat.

Down below, at Kenley, there was hardly a building left standing. Six Hurricanes had been destroyed on the ground, ten hangars were flattened and six more damaged, and the vital ops room was well and truly out of action. Straightaway, plans were put in motion to set up a new operations room in the disused Spice and Wallis butcher's in nearby Caterham high street. By contrast, Biggin Hill had escaped lightly. Most of the bombs from the high-level attackers had landed wide of the eastern periphery of the airfield.

To the west, all had been quiet as 10 Group waited to see how Luftflotte 3's attack would compare with Kesselring's in the east. At Poling radar station near Tangmere, Avis Parsons was beginning her shift. She had joined the Auxiliary Territorial Service in March 1939, when she was twenty-two. Volunteering to work on RDF, she had been sworn to secrecy, trained for three weeks, and then posted to Poling in November 1939. When she came on duty on 18 August with a fellow radar operator, her sergeant told them there was a need to change over quickly. He wanted one of them to go into the switchboard hut to man the line from Truleigh Hill, an RDF station which did not have its own direct link-up to the system. Avis volunteered; she'd never been in this new building before. The single WAAF on duty was working on a switchboard with two headsets, feeding the information from both Poling and Truleigh through to the filter room at Fighter Command. Avis relieved her and from then was on her own; the officer and NCO on watch at the time were located in the receiver hut, a wooden shed in the same compound.

Avis knew from the plots that she was hearing and from the squared-off map in front of her that a raid was imminent. In fact what had been building up on the airfields of Lufflotte 3 was the biggest Stuka strike yet. Over a hundred of the dive-bombers, each with a 550-pound bomb under its fuselage and four 110-pounders under its wings, accompanied, as per Göring's new orders, by over twice the same number of Bf 109s, were heading on a four-pronged attack on coastal targets. Included were three Coastal Command and naval airfields at Gosport, Thorney Island and Ford, and the Poling radar station, in direct contravention of Göring's orders. Just before 2 p.m. Poling had picked up the first warnings. Now Avis Parsons was reporting through plots rapidly increasing in number and frequency.

Thirty-one Stuka aircraft, peeling off from the main formation, were detailed to attack the Poling site. Major Helmut Bode led the first attack of three dive-bombers coming in from a north-easterly direction, diving.

Inside the hut, the phone went by the plotter table and Avis picked it up. Her sergeant, on his way to the shelter, shouted down the phone, 'Duck!' Avis replied in a flash, 'I can't, there's too much information coming through.' Then the Truleigh Hill station came through on one of the sets of headphones. 'Poling? That block's right on top of you!'

'I know, I can hear them, the bombs are nearly dropping on my head!' replied Avis. She remembers:

Then there was a scream as the Stukas dived and then the noise of the explosions was terrific. Anyway I carried on and a man appeared. For all I knew at the time he could have been a spy. I just handed him one of my phones and asked him to repeat everything I said to him. He got the one to Fighter Command, poor chap, it must have been Double Dutch to him. After about quarter of an hour, the line from Truleigh Hill went dead.

The raid had lasted about twenty minutes, in which time eighty-seven bombs had been dropped. In R Block, where Avis was working, every window and door was blown in and one of the main walls cracked. Several 550-pound bombs had fallen alongside the building. When Avis emerged it was to a scene of devastation – cars were ablaze, the hut roof was resting on the receiver itself, there were huge craters everywhere and chunks of metal from the aerial littered the ground. A new building for the CO, which had lacked just a roof, was now a pile of rubble. Avis discovered that her mysterious helpmate was a Post Office engineer who had been working on the site. She never found out why he had not taken to the shelters like everyone else.

Air Vice-Marshal Sir Quentin Brand, commander of 10 Group, had put up just about every fighter he had to counter this raid. Even so, the sixty-eight British fighters were outnumbered by more than two to one by the hostile fighters alone, and the fighters of 11 Group, returning to their bases after the bruising encounters over the airfields, were unable to reinforce them.

The Prime Minister's secretary Jock Colville, visiting a friend in the south-west, was amongst many watching the action going on overhead.

> We were sitting on the terrace looking towards
> Thorney Island . . . Suddenly we heard the sound of
> AA fire and saw puffs of white smoke as the shells
> burst over Portsmouth. Then to our left, from the
> direction of Chichester and Tangmere, came the roar of
> engines then the noise of machine-gun fire . . . shading
> our eyes to escape the glare of this August day, we saw
> not far in front of us about twenty machines engaged
> in a fight. Soon a German bomber came hurtling
> towards us with smoke pouring from its tail and we
> lost sight of it behind the trees . . . Out of the mêlée
> came a dive-bomber, hovered like a bird of prey and
> then sped steeply down on Thorney Island. There were
> vast explosions as another and another followed, and
> my attention was diverted from the fight as clouds of
> smoke rose from the burning hangars of Thorney
> aerodrome. In all, the battle only lasted about two
> minutes and then moved seawards, with at least two
> German aircraft left smouldering on the ground.[7]

Brand's gamble was paying off. The Bf 109s, as their pilots had predicted, found defending the diving Stukas difficult.

The Stukas had suffered losses, particularly those over Thorney Island. Of the twenty-eight Stukas that had attacked there, ten were shot down and many more only just made it back to base. The British, who had underestimated the size of the raid, claimed to have shot down nearly half the attackers. In fact losses on the other strikes were not so severe, but confidence was irrevocably shaken in the Nazis' favourite dive-bomber. The eighteenth of August would be the last time that the Stukas would be used in any number during the battle.

On 5 September 1940 Avis was awarded the Military Medal for her actions that day. She says, 'I wasn't thinking about being brave, I had a job to do and I loved my country – I knew I only had a fifty-fifty chance of surviving.' At Poling the damage was repaired quickly. Within two days of the raid the station was operating again. A mobile unit was brought in and hidden in the woods and the WAAF officers had to work off slightly smaller cathode screens.

But the day's fighting was still not over. By 5 p.m. another formation, estimated correctly at about 250 aircraft, was mapped by radar massing over the Calais area. Luftflotte 2 had refuelled and rearmed since their attacks against the airfields and were back in the sky. Fifty-eight Dorniers were preparing to attack Hornchurch and fifty-two Heinkel 111s were aiming for North Weald. Their escort consisted of some 140 Bf 109s and 110s.

Then 32 Squadron was scrambled again, along with three other squadrons. Together with 501 Squadron they intercepted the Dorniers bound for Hornchurch. As Peter Brothers' 32 Squadron closed in on the bombers, their fighter escort of Bf 109s swooped down. Turning sharply to the right as one flashed past him, Brothers was able to let off two bursts directly into the fighter, which caught fire and crashed into a field near Chilham; 501 lost a flight lieutenant to the fighter escort, but their two new Poles each shot down a Bf 109. The bombers continued, however, and both British squadrons took further losses.

Weather was to defend Hornchurch and North Weald more effectively. As they neared their targets, the German bombers found thick cloud covering the area. Mindful of Hitler's strong warnings against indiscriminate bombing over London, they turned tail and started carrying their bombs home. Emboldened by this, the British fighters continued to attack, as Park put up more squadrons to cut off the retreat.

In Britain there was jubilation. The bombers had been turned back, it appeared, by anti-aircraft fire, and the Air Ministry was certain that 141 enemy aircraft had been downed with a loss of only ten RAF pilots. Individual squadrons had been hit hard – 501 had seen seven Hurricanes shot down and two pilots killed – but surely the Luftwaffe must be hurting. In fact the Luftwaffe had lost some sixty planes, still a great number, and, just as importantly, they had lost to active service five times more pilots and crew than the British. Those surviving complained, 'Only a few of us have not yet had to ditch in the Channel with a badly damaged aeroplane or dead engine.' 'Utter exhaustion had set in,' remembers another Luftwaffe flyer. 'For the first time pilots discussed the prospects of posting to a quieter sector.'[8] There was growing disquiet at the disparity between what Göring claimed was the state of the RAF and the strong defences still encountered by Luftwaffe crews over Britain. Göring himself was forced to admit that the total air superiority demanded prior to an invasion was still proving elusive. Operation Sealion was delayed until 17 September.

In fact both sides were to have a short rest as bad weather until 24 August prevented any large-scale attacks. At Karinhall, Göring decorated his fighter aces Galland and Mölders but told them that their squadrons were not doing their escort duties well enough. To concentrate his forces, Göring moved almost all Luftflotte 3's Bf 109s to the Calais area under Kesselring and ordered renewed concentration on the RAF's airfields and factories, which was just what the British feared. From Uxbridge, Park ordered his pilots to avoid combat over the sea and to concentrate on the bombers within the formations. He also appealed to Leigh-Mallory for help from 12 Group in defending 11 Group airfields. Three days later the Air Ministry at last introduced improved sea-rescue facilities.

But boats in the Channel had a new threat to deal with. On 22 August, giant railway guns installed on Cap Gris Nez opened fire on ships for the first time. That evening the gunners turned to a larger, stationary target, the British mainland, and for the first time in history, enemy shells started landing on British soil. In the first attack several houses were destroyed and four civilians injured, and thereafter the shelling became a fact of life in the extreme south-east of the island, which became known as 'shellfire corner'. The British, on Churchill's insistence, countered with their own guns, but they could not match the firepower on the other side of the Channel, and as their attacks almost always brought a heavier retaliation, their activity was highly unpopular with the dwindling number of residents of Dover.

On the south-easternmost tip of the country, these attacks coincided with a wide-held belief amongst the remaining residents that they would be in the front line of the forthcoming German invasion. Everywhere noticeboards were posted with pictures of German airborne troop carriers, so that the locals would know when they were under attack. Fighters from nearby Manston were encouraged to fly low over Ramsgate, Margate and Dover to impress upon the civilians that they were still in existence. But very early on 24 August came the heaviest attack so far on RAF Manston.

At just after noon, twenty Ju 88s, heavily escorted by Bf 109s, began attacking the airfield. A bomb hit the communication lines and 248 circuits were cut in one strike. On the ground the defenders were throwing up everything they had – anti-aircraft weapons, parachute rockets, even Very pistols were fired at the diving aircraft. The water main was hit and buildings and aircraft on the ground were flattened or set on fire. Unexploded bombs littered the area. As a huge cloud of chalk dust rose obscuring the airfield, the Ju 88s who had not attacked dropped 500 bombs on nearby Ramsgate, damaging 1,000 houses in three minutes, before heading triumphantly for home.

At North Weald, as another raid approached, personnel began fleeing the airfield until warned by the station CO that anyone deserting their post would be shot. Hornchurch was hit as well, and on the way back Manston was bombed by those driven off from Hornchurch by anti-aircraft fire, confirming in the minds of Fighter Command that Manston was the top 'opportunity target' for enemy bombers returning still laden from missions further north-west. Later that day, Manston was abandoned and the shell-shocked personnel were evacuated. Churchill visited the airfield four days later and found it still covered with the flags that denoted unexploded bombs. Until 5 September, it would operate as an emergency landing field only. As far as the Luftwaffe were concerned, Manston, such a crucial location for air control over the Channel, no longer existed.

To the west, at Portsmouth, a raid largely missed the docks, but the town itself was heavily bombed instead, causing many civilian casualties. Rushing to its defence, a Canadian squadron, active for the first time and with only the briefest of aircraft recognition courses under its belt, managed to shoot down a British Blenheim fighter and damage two more when it took them for Ju 88s.

Both 11 and 12 Groups kept their pilots on readiness or in the air for most of the day, if nothing else to prevent the aircraft being destroyed on the ground. But the British fighters found it hard to penetrate the massed fighter escorts. Peter Hairs with 501 Squadron was scrambled eight times. On the last occasion, as a crushing tiredness descended on him, the customary dogfight took on a strange new light.

There were six of us flying back from Hawkinge to Gravesend when we were told there were some bandits in the vicinity and we were given a course to steer. It was a beautiful evening; it was just getting dark and there was a little bit of stratus cloud directly below us. We were told we should be very close to these enemy aircraft but we couldn't see them anywhere. Then we descended through this rather flimsy cloud right into the middle of a formation of 109s. They must have been quite surprised; everybody started firing at a great rate, and as I fired, I saw not just the smoke trails but also the bright lights of the tracer. I remember thinking, Look, isn't that pretty? It was like a fireworks display. The next thing, I had a 'whoomph' at the back and the 109 behind me had knocked part of my tail plane off.

Constant readiness took its toll, and the sheer number of flying hours also wore down the pilots. Flying to heights greater than Mount Everest in unpressurised aircraft made the combat flying all the more exhausting. At these heights tiredness, a weak disposition or an oxygen tank failure could be fatal. Wing Commander D. Allen had one such fatality in his flight: 'I once watched one of our pilots peel off and go into a vertical dive . . . he never recovered and felt nothing as his Spitfire made a hole in the ground big as a bomb crater. God knows how his oxygen dried up, but it did.'

With fighter training slashed from one month to only two weeks, newcomers to the squadrons would now be unlikely to have fired the guns or done more than twenty hours on operational aircraft. Peter Brothers remembers, 'All the ones who were killed were the new boys, of course, with lack of experience.' After the death came the 'dreaded letter to parents'. 'We'd say what a good fellow this chap was and how sad it was that he'd been shot down, that sort of thing,' says Brothers. 'It was difficult because you can't really express feelings in a letter. All you can do is try and sympathise with them and say that at least it was quick. You'd usually do the letter the next day or in a quiet period. The squadron adjutant would help you draft it and make suggestions.' Funerals were rare during the battle. Ones that did go ahead were sometimes 'a bit traumatic. Often you knew the coffin merely contained some bricks or something because everything else had vanished.'

Tig and Ann Lowe adored the pilots at Tangmere. But taking boyfriends from among the flyers led to inevitable heartbreak. 'We used to wave them out and wave them back in,' Ann Lowe remembers. Often they would hear the battle itself. Working on the radio was 'a horrifying experience at times'.

They'd leave their transmitters on and you'd hear their sweet voices calling out in glee when they saw a German aeroplane, and you'd hear the crackle of the machine-gun and then sometimes you'd hear them go down, you'd hear the last cries as bullets hit the aeroplane and the transmitter went off.

We'd be with them in the Nag's Head in Chichester one day and on the next day they would be gone. Wiped out, their names removed from the board in the ops room. You always knew when they were dead when they

took their names off the board. But never from our
hearts and memories. There were so many. They
mourned each other so simply and with no fuss and went
off rushing into the air again. Now at last, we began to
know and understand a little and now we knew war.
Always there was the sound of weeping. Every day some
girl was weeping.

Several squadron leaders pleaded unsuccessfully with Park for
a week or two away from the front line to train the new pilots
and give the veterans a badly needed rest. In the absence of
rest or leave, many pilots would try to off-load the stress with
drink. 32 Squadron CO, Squadron Leader John Worrall,
remembers, 'If you weren't in the air, you were plastered.'[9]
For others it meant fraying tempers. Peter Brothers remembers at Biggin Hill a young pilot who lost his cool when his
boiled egg wasn't properly cooked. He threw it at the WAAF
waitress, hitting her in the chest. As she ran out of the dining
room in tears, Peter Brothers remembers thinking, 'Ah yes.
Time for a rest.'

Brothers, who had shot down another Bf 109 on
24 August, winning a DFC, was not immune himself.

The CO had been shot down and I was leading the
squadron. We arrived at Hawkinge, our forward base, and
there was a little airman waving a little blue flag for
where I was to park, or would have done if the CO was
there. I ignored him and taxied over to the operations
tent where I could have the aircraft close by and be on
the spot for any orders that came through. This poor little
airman came rushing over and said, 'Sorry, sir, you have
got to move your aircraft, B flight is supposed to be over
here.' I let fly at him and told him what he could do
with his little blue flag. After I'd cooled down I got the

sergeant to go and fetch him and he came in looking
very sheepish and I apologised to him for being so rude.

Others, says Brothers, got eye-twitches. He himself, he says,
became 'totally fatalistic'.

> I thought, I am going to die. If it doesn't happen today
> it'll happen tomorrow. So you then did stupid things. I
> was shot at by an anti-aircraft gun over France and I
> handed over to my number two and went down and shot
> up the gun. Well, that was quite stupid; you might kill
> the gun crew, a couple of Germans, but a head-on shot
> for them was going be just as easy as it was for me and
> they'd got every chance of shooting down a valuable
> aeroplane. My little pellets wouldn't have harmed their
> gun; they would have bounced right off it. I was getting
> a bit tired by then.

With his fighter pilots either green or exhausted, Churchill
knew that to keep them flying their spirits would have to be
lifted. On 20 August he addressed the House of Commons,
describing the current conflict as one of 'strategy, of organisation, of technical apparatus, of science, mechanics and
morale'. 'The gratitude,' he continued, 'of every home in our
Island, in our Empire, and indeed throughout the world,
except in the abodes of the guilty, goes out to the British
airmen who, undaunted by odds, unwearied in their constant
challenge and mortal danger, are turning the tide of war by
their prowess and by their devotion.' Next came the phrase
that had 'burned' into the brain of Ismay a few days earlier.
'Never in the field of human conflict was so much owed by
so many to so few.'

But to the Fighter Command pilots, wrapped up in a cycle
of scrambling, flying and snatching sleep, the wider picture

seemed far away. Peter Brothers remembers commenting on reading the speech in the next day's papers, 'He ought to see my mess bill, never was so much owed by so few to so many!' But out of the fear, exhaustion and daily losses, a different feeling was being born: that of anger. It was to be a hatred of the enemy, rather than any oratory from Churchill, that kept the pilots going.

Several of the pilots had by now been shot at while descending on parachutes. John Gibson, on one of his bale-outs, had to be protected by another Hurricane as a Bf 109 came bearing down on him, guns blazing. For Peter Morfill and the rest of 501, it marked a change in attitude. 'When we realised that one of our chaps was shot at coming down with his parachute, it was no longer friendly, I'm afraid.' Morfill's wife's house had also just been bombed. 'She woke up with the ceiling coming down on her head. I was phoned so I dashed down there in someone's car I'd borrowed and there she was, so I thought, Right, personal war from now on.' Sailor Malan said that rather than downing enemy aircraft, he preferred to allow a bomber pilot to return home with his crew dead as a warning to the others.

This feeling was widely shared as August came to an end, even amongst those happy at the beginning of the conflict to entertain downed German airmen in their mess bars. Peter Brothers remembers:

[With] chaps being shot at on parachutes, you then began to say the Germans aren't playing this as it should be played, the chivalry's gone out of it. So then you got a bit tougher, I think. I certainly did anyway. You got angry; then you got frightened which made you more angry, and so on. I had an occasion when, during the battle, we'd been engaged and all got split up as usual. I was peering around and I saw five 109s heading for home up above me and I thought, Oh gosh, simple, I'll just stalk these and knock them off. I caught up behind and the one on the right of what was the vee formation was obviously looking over his shoulder my way because he started turning round. I thought he'd spotted me coming up behind. Oh well, I thought, I'll make do with him and forget the others. I got right up within range but as I opened fire all hell broke loose behind me from the other four. Of course it had been a wonderful decoy action. They'd watched this chap pull away, they'd watched me follow and go after him, then the whole lot of the other four had come in and filled me full of holes. I was frightened and I was angry that I'd been so stupid that I'd been outwitted. I only got out of the situation with difficulty and a lot of holes.

If a pilot of Peter Brothers' experience was being outwitted by the Luftwaffe, what would be the fate of an RAF pilot who had never flown combat operations until now? While 238 Squadron had been inexperienced, as Gordon Batt concedes, at least they got to learn when there were only small raids coming over. Pilots thrown into the combat now were facing hundreds of enemy attackers. For some, it was difficult enough keeping the aircraft in the air, let alone fighting in it.

Bill Green, who describes himself as 'probably the most inexperienced pilot in the RAF', had done his first flight in a Hurricane on 3 August. It had been a hair-raising début, during which Green had blacked out and found himself in a spin. Nevertheless, after just seven hours and forty-five minutes flying in a Hurricane, he was made operational with 501 Squadron at Gravesend on 20 August. As he says now, 'I really didn't know what it was all about. I was Green by name and green by nature, as anyone would have been in the situation. I'm sure I wasn't alone in having this little amount of experience. But I don't think they had any option but to make me operational. We had lost people in 501 on the eighteenth, and my early recall was a simple necessity.' On his first flight with the squadron he lost the others while trying to weave at the back of the formation, but succeeded in finding the airfield at Hawkinge. Four days later he was with the squadron when they were vectored to Manston, during the attack by Ju 88s. 'We were peeling in behind them,' says Green, 'when I was hit.' It seems that it was not the bombers or their escorting Bf 109s but anti-aircraft fire that had done the damage. 'I felt the aircraft shudder. The engine coughed, and the whole windscreen went black with oil.' Nevertheless, Green managed to get the aircraft back to nearby Hawkinge. Forced to pump the undercarriage down by hand, he glided the damaged aircraft into a landing approach. Although half of his undercarriage had been shot away and the nose of the aircraft dug into the ground, ending up in a vertical position, Green clambered unharmed from the cockpit.

During the night of 24 August, Göring was keen to keep up the pressure on Fighter Command. One hundred and seventy bombers were sent to attack air force installations and industrial targets throughout the south-east of England, as well as further afield to Cardiff and Swansea. Of these about a dozen were sent against the oil refineries at Thames Haven and the aircraft factories at Rochester and Kingston. But through navigational errors, bombs were scattered over the City of London and at least nine other London districts. Ron Harvey, then an East End schoolboy, lived in the first house to be bombed out in London.

I was twelve years old at the time of the bomb. My brother was away in the army, there was my mum and dad and my sister and her boyfriend. When the warning sounded I was woken up by Mum or Dad and I went downstairs through the kitchen into the back yard to the shelter where there were already some neighbours. Being sleepy, I didn't realise at the time that my sister and her boyfriend had stayed in the house. I remember it was a bright moonlit night. Being twelve years old, I wasn't taking notice of the grown-ups. I was just at the door of the shelter and I heard this German plane come over and I knew it was German because of the drone of the engine. A few seconds passed and then there was a whistle of a bomb coming down. I was just by the door. Someone shouted, 'There's something coming down. Duck!' and I ducked and I must have had my face to the right because I saw the two black balls fall on the house. The bombs exploded and it wasn't like a 'boom' or a blast, more like the crack of a thunderbolt, which echoed through the street for a few seconds and that was that. The shelter was full of dust and someone said, 'Gas!' but I knew it wasn't, it was brick dust. The next thing I remember is being out of the shelter and looking up at the vicar and him looking down at me. Then I looked to my right and there was all this activity going on – I suppose it was rescue work. And there were lots of people digging out my sister and her boyfriend. They were roughed up a bit, a few bruises; all the chimneys had come down.

There was no damage for miles and miles around before that. I was going to school just round the corner, it was as if there wasn't a war on. That was the beginning of war to me, when things started happening.

☆ ☆ ☆

In Bethnal Green, where Ron lived, large fires were started. St Giles' Church at Cripplegate was damaged and bombs also hit Oxford Street. Nine people were killed and fifty-eight more injured. It was the first time that bombs had fallen on central London since 1918.

The next day, as his Luftwaffe bombers returned to England to attack Warmwell, Dover and the Thames estuary, Göring furiously demanded to know the names of the pilots who had broken the Führer's orders not to drop bombs on central London. When found, the crews were transferred to the infantry. But for Göring, who had promised that no bombs would ever fall on the German capital, the damage had been done. The next day, in spite of the reluctance of the Air Ministry, Winston Churchill ordered a retaliatory raid on Berlin.

CHAPTER TEN

The Few

O N 25 AUGUST THERE WAS A STIR IN THE BRIEFING room of 49 Bomber Squadron. A few days earlier the station commander had called all the officers together to warn them that invasion was probable. 'It was a poignant moment,' says bomber officer Wilf Burnett. 'We all went away with our own thoughts and determined to do our bit.' On 25 August, they were to have their chance. For the first time as they entered the briefing room they saw a flag stuck in the map against Berlin, remembers Burnett. 'We had expected Berlin to be one of our targets at one time or another once the hours of darkness allowed us to cross the coast in safety. The orders came through on 25 August. We were given industrial targets in Berlin. All the crews wanted to have a go, purely and simply for no other reason than to refute Göring's boast that Berlin would never be bombed.'

As Burnett points out, whatever the heroics of Fighter Command, the Spitfires and Hurricanes were defensive weapons. The only way of carrying the war to Germany was through Bomber Command. 'From a morale point of view,' he says, 'it was very important that we were able to retaliate.' Churchill, not for the first time, had judged the mood of the people correctly.

As night fell, the squadron took off from its base in Lincolnshire and headed out across the North Sea. As they settled into their jobs, the tension of the briefing room evaporated. They had been attacking other industrial targets in Germany and were used to long night-time flights. Although their Hampdens bombers were manoeuvrable and easy to fly, they were also very cold and cramped for the four-man crew, packed into 'the Flying Suitcase', as the planes were known. The worst spot was to be isolated in the tail as rear gunner. As Wilf Burnett's crew crossed the North Sea, he hailed his tail gunner through the intercom: 'How are you down at the back there?'

'Bloody cold,' came the inevitable reply. The crew chatted and joked to keep each other warm and focused on the long flight, which they knew would keep them in the air for at least nine hours. In these conditions certain necessities had to be taken care of.

One inherent disadvantage of the Hampden was you were unable to relieve yourself once you were in the cockpit, although there was a device called a 'peeto'. This had to be fitted on when you were dressing for flight with a rubber tube running down inside your trouser leg. The end of a tube then fitted loosely in a lavatory in the navigator's position venting to the outside of the aircraft. It proved disastrous both for the pilot when it froze and for the navigator when it didn't.

Along with the weather, navigation at night threw up many other problems. At this stage, the crews had to rely mainly on landmarks. Soon the first of these on the way to Berlin, the distinctive Dutch coastline, came into view. As the bomber crossed into mainland Europe, the joking stopped. 'Once you got into enemy territory you were focusing on your job – flying the aircraft, navigating, or, as a gunner, being alert to enemy aircraft. Fighter attacks were usually unannounced and devastating, they came in and that was it. It wasn't the time for casual talk.'

Although there were eighty other bombers on the raid, the crew of Burnett's Hampden could not see any of them in the darkness, and each plane did its own navigating. Unable to fly at more than about 10,000 feet, they were keen to avoid built-up, heavily defended areas such as Hamburg. But at the same time they had to fly as direct a route as possible, as the nine-hour flight left the Hampden fairly tight on fuel. The key navigational aid was water. On a moonlit night canals and rivers shone; with no moon the water was darker than the surrounding land. Following these landmarks, Burnett's Hampden slowly got closer to Berlin, whose nearby lakes they had been briefed to look out for. But as they approached the German capital, they came into thick cloud. Dropping down in order to be able to see the target, the bomber came under fire from anti-aircraft guns. 'You could see these sort of puffballs with a nasty red look inside them. I heard this bang and told my rear gunner to shut the door in the middle of the aircraft. "That isn't the door banging, skipper," came the reply from the back of the Hampden. "That's anti-aircraft fire, and it's getting nearer." '

Over Berlin, there were nothing like the air defences that Burnett would encounter later in the war, but there were still searchlights to avoid as well. These were controlled by a sound detection device, and to fool this, the bomber crew carried with them a crate of milk bottles. In theory, the whistling noise the bottles made as they fell would deceive the equipment. However far-fetched the idea, it was well worth trying anything to put off the searchlights, which were liable to dazzle you; worse still, you could get 'coned'. This was when more than one locked on to you. 'The next thing you could expect after that was pretty accurate anti-aircraft fire,' says Burnett.

Keen to be away, the bomber let go its load and headed back from Berlin. As Hitler's Europe was left behind, the crew relaxed and conversation flowed, 'sort of dilly-dally', Burnett remembers. Flasks of coffee, chocolate and fruit were got out and gratefully consumed. Talking continued, if nothing else, 'to keep each other awake'.

Like most night raids at this stage of the war, the bombers had found it almost impossible to bomb their industrial targets accurately. For the first time in the war, explosives had fallen on residential areas of the German capital. Although no one was killed on this occasion, Göring, who had promised it would never happen, was ridiculed from all sides. Churchill was delighted, minuting the next day to the Chief of Air Staff, 'I want you to hit them hard, and Berlin is the place to hit them.'[1]

If Bomber Command was celebrating, Fighter Command was in the middle of suffering its worst period in the battle so far. After weeks of trying to do everything at once, the Luftwaffe was now at last focusing its might on its primary target, RAF Fighter Command. At 11 a.m. on 26 August, 150 German aircraft attacked once more the vital sector stations at Biggin Hill and Kenley. For Biggin Hill it was a foretaste of what, from 30 August, would be a nightmare three days in which the airfield was bombed no fewer than six times.

Felicity Peake was in charge of the 250 women on the station. Aged twenty-six, she was already a war widow. On 3 October the previous year, after she had spent a day frantically helping with the recruitment of WAAFs, she had received the news that her husband, Jock, had been killed in an accident during night-flying exercises. Posted to Biggin

Hill in May 1940, she loved the beautiful surroundings. 'But on 30 August,' she remembers, 'the storm broke.'

A couple of hours before, a lucky hit had caused the radar stations at Dover, Pevensey, Rye, Foreness, Fairlight, Beachy Head and Whitstable to be out of action for a few hours after the electricity mains were damaged. At 6 p.m., ten Ju 88 dive-bombers, loaded with 1,000-pounders, feinted towards the Thames estuary and then headed directly for Biggin Hill. They were spotted by the Observer Corps and news of the raid was passed to Biggin Hill. When the local civilian air-raid warning sounded, Felicity Peake was talking to a WAAF flight sergeant.

> The main station siren hadn't gone yet, so we finished our chat and waited to see what, if anything, would happen next. However time passed and nothing further happened so I started on my way to my own office in the station HQ building about 300 yards away. I had nearly got there when the station sirens wailed their alarm. Our instructions were, once the station warning had been given, to go at the double into the nearest trench. I went . . . The trench rapidly filled and there we sat, packed like sardines, with tin hats on, waiting. One could hear the aircraft taking off – first one, then another, then another until all our squadrons were airborne. Then things happened quickly.

As the Ju 88s began their diving descent on the airfield, the RT frantically radioed for help, trying to contact 501 Squadron, who were patrolling from Hawkinge. Peter Hairs heard over his RT, 'Bandits approaching . . . they're approaching Biggin Hill, they're bombing Biggin Hill, they're bombing me!' Then the line went dead.

From her trench, Felicity Peake heard the bombing begin.

Bombs fell at the far side of the aerodrome, each one seeming to come nearer until one fell just outside our trench. I remember thinking, I suppose one feels like this in an earthquake. The vibration and blast were such that one felt that one's limbs must surely come apart. Bombs fell pretty continuously, the noise was indescribable, yet through the intervals I could hear the put, put, put of machine-guns as plane after plane dived on its target.

Then there was a lull and the only sound heard was British fighters returning to refuel and rearm. Felicity Peake didn't wait for the all-clear.

I climbed over the earth and rubble that had been blown into our trench and out into that lovely summer day. All was strangely quiet. I wound my way back the way I'd come towards the WAAF guard room. As I approached I saw a woman lying on the ground on the other side of the road into the station. When I started to walk across a voice said to me, 'Don't bother, she's dead.' I distinctly remember to this day saying to myself and thinking to myself, This is the first dead person I have ever seen. I've got to get used to this. So I made a point of standing and looking at her and then I did find that my feelings were at least controllable. When I arrived at the guard room, or what was left of it, I found that the airwomen's trench had had a direct hit.

A bomb had fallen at one end of the trench, shooting all twelve occupants violently against one end and burying them all in earth.

Many airmen were already digging to reach the airwomen who had been trapped in their trench. The

dry summer had made the ground unusually hard and
their task was no light one. As the work went on, we
must all have had the same thought: What shall we find
when we reach them? Ambulance and stretcher parties
were standing by, a way was cleared, and gradually, one
by one, the airwomen were brought out.

Miraculously, although several were badly injured, only one
in the trench had been killed. It was a popular New
Zealander, Corporal Lena Button. 'She was the only one,'
says Peake, 'and she would be from New Zealand, bless her
heart, and she would also be our one medical orderly. I, like a
fool, went around calling out, "Corporal Button where are
you? You are needed!" '

Thirty-nine people had been killed and another twenty-six
injured. Several aircraft had been burnt out on the ground
and the water, gas and electricity lines had been cut. Most of
the barracks and workshops had also been destroyed. The
next day, in spite of unexploded bombs and a leaking gas
main, Post Office engineers worked to reconnect the cable
that linked the airfield to the outside world. Felicity Peake
busied herself with checking on the injured airwomen,
finding new billets, writing the 'ghastly' letter to Corporal
Button's next of kin, and generally doing her best 'to get
things straightened out'. It was to be an uphill task. The next
day, when Peake was off the airfield seeking new billets, the
Observer Corps reported that an unknown quantity of raiders
was approaching from the south-west. All the station's squadrons were scrambled, but they could not prevent a bomber
scoring a direct hit on the operations room. Incredibly, there
were few deaths, but the ops room was a write-off. All the
hard work of the Post Office engineers had also been undone
and two more Spitfires had been destroyed on the ground. As
at Kenley, a temporary ops room was set up in the nearest

village, but for two days the airfield could have only one fighter squadron based there. Interviewing some WAAFs the next day for positions at the station, Felicity Peake remembers them looking around and asking, please, could they be posted somewhere else?

Attacks continued on 1 and 2 September; even the funeral service for all the killed personnel was disturbed by a raid. The cemetery bordered the airfield, and as Felicity Peake and the station CO stood rigidly to attention saluting, the relatives of the deceased scattered and the padre was so frightened he took shelter in one of the freshly dug graves. 'He was escorted away out of control,' remembers Peake. The Roman Catholic padre was found, and the ceremony continued as dogfights raged overhead.

To deter further attacks on Biggin Hill, the station CO ordered the demolition of the remaining hangars, an action that did not endear him to the Air Ministry – they even presented him with a bill after the war – but which seemed to work. After 2 September, Biggin Hill was spared until an inaccurate raid on 6 September.

Although Biggin Hill was the worst hit, other important airfields suffered too between 26 August and 6 September. Day after day, and even at night, 11 Group's important bases were bombed or strafed. On 26 August, Debden, north of London, was badly damaged when a squadron from Leigh-Mallory's 12 Group airfield at Duxford failed to protect the 11 Group sector station. Whether Park was too slow in requesting help, or whether Leigh-Mallory was too slow in providing it, is difficult to establish. Wherever the blame should be laid, relations between the two men worsened as recriminations flew about.

After a quiet day on 27 August, bombers returned on the 28th to hit Eastchurch in Kent and Rochford in Essex. As well as the raid on Biggin Hill on 30 August, the Luftwaffe also damaged Kenley, Luton, Tangmere and Detling, flying more than 1,300 sorties. The following day saw an even greater effort – over 1,400 sorties hit North Weald, Croydon, Hornchurch, Debden and Detling. Soon, it seemed, Park's stations around London would, like Manston, have to be abandoned.

On 29 August Kesselring's fighter commander, General Kurt von Döring, claimed that 'unlimited fighter superiority' had been achieved.[2] The next day Hitler announced that he would decide whether or not to launch the invasion on 10 September. If everything continued to plan, the order on the 10th would mean that the invasion fleet would set sail ten days later.

With the scale of the build-ups over the Channel growing, radar became less effective at judging where the intended targets were. Once the large formations split up, it was impossible to tell which were bombers and which were fighters trying to draw away the defenders or scramble them early so that they would be back on the ground or at the limit of their endurance when the main raid arrived. So RAF fighter squadrons only scrambled when it was clear that a raid contained bombers and that it was not a decoy. But every minute of delay in scrambling meant 2,000 feet less of altitude for climbing fighters, and the defenders often found themselves in vulnerable positions when they intercepted.

With the crucial advantage of radar thus to a certain extent neutralised, the RAF suffered accordingly. By the end of August it had become a war of attrition. On 28 August, the British lost twenty-eight aircraft to the Luftwaffe's thirty; on 30 August it was twenty-five to the Germans' thirty-six; the next day it was thirty-nine to forty-one. Squadrons were rotated as much as possible. During this terrible period 32 Squadron were just too tired to deal with being at Biggin Hill and were withdrawn to Northumberland for a rest. For Peter

Brothers, this meant a very welcome seven-day leave. 'We were down to seven pilots. Funnily enough, of the original pre-war squadron, many had been shot down, wounded, some burned, but nobody had been killed. It was only the new boys who had died.'

The squadrons that replaced these weary veterans, flying from Scotland or the north, were often entirely inexperienced. Many had been itching to join the battle and charged in to suffer terrible losses. On their first day down south 222 Squadron lost seven planes. Almost all arrived still flying the suicidal vic formation – what the Luftwaffe now called 'the bunch of bananas, ripe for the plucking. By now even squadron leaders and flight commanders might never have flown in combat before going into action. Richard Hillary, author of *The Last Enemy*, was told on arriving at Hornchurch with 603 Squadron, 'You don't have to look for them – you have to look for a way out.'[3]

Still in the front line were 501 Squadron, who had been in almost continual action since 10 May. But they, too, had their share of inexperienced replacement pilots. On 29 August Bill Green, shot down five days previously, returned to Gravesend after twenty-four hours' leave. As soon as his flight had been stood down, he left the airfield to visit his wife Bertha in Bristol. They had been married on 3 June 1940. As usual, they didn't talk about the war. She had knitted him some new socks. Returning to rejoin 501 Squadron, he was on readiness, but one look at the low cloud indicated that there would be little action that day. He sat down and started a letter to his wife, saying how nice it had been to see her and telling her not to worry too much about him. 'Everything will be fine,' he wrote. 'We won't be flying today as the cloud is almost on the deck.' But just as he finished the letter, at six o'clock in the evening, his section was scrambled. As they shot up through the cloud they were vectored to 'Red

Queens', the code-word for Deal. They approached the port at 20,000 feet, circling and watching out for the reported 200 Bf 109s, code-named 'snappers'. He didn't see a thing until he was hit.

There was a crash of glass, and a hole appeared in the middle of the supposedly bulletproof windscreen about the size of a tennis ball, or a little larger. I heard bits falling into the cockpit and I was immediately covered in glycol liquid coolant. The aircraft was finished, the stick was just like any old bit of stick. I realised I had to get out and I already had the hood back and I got as far as just taking the weight on my feet and I was gone. I think my head must have been exposed to the wind and I was just sucked out. I found myself in space and I started to roll around trying to find the parachute release and thought to myself, I'm never going to find this ripcord.

Eventually he found it, and gave it a good pull. To his horror nothing happened, and he found himself still falling from the sky. 'I was going through the air at one hundred and forty miles an hour, terminal velocity, and the wind noise was quite terrific, like sticking your head out of a car window at the same speed.' His flying boots came off and seemed to shoot up past his ears. His main parachute pack was trapped between his legs. 'I kept falling and falling, forlornly doing a kind of breast stroke trying to push it into its proper position. I really thought my number was up, and I remember so clearly thinking, I wonder if Bertha, my wife, would wonder if I wondered too much as I was falling what my end was going to be like.'

Suddenly, at just 300 feet above the ground, with Green less than a second from death, a gust of wind opened the parachute folds.

There was a jolt when the parachute kicked me
backwards and a secondary jolt when the rigging lines,
which are fastened up and down your back, burst away
from their buttons. I grabbed the main parachute cord
thinking, having seen one bit go off, the whole lot might
be going, but it didn't. After the noise of the free-fall, I
was struck by the sudden quiet. It made more impact
upon me than any noise I'd ever heard. I thought, Gosh,
I'm all right. So I sat in this field, bootless, surrounded
by thistles and cow pats and just looked around and
thought, Oh dear, just think, I've got to go for a walk
through this lot with my new socks on. It wasn't bravado
because I was anything but brave, one just thinks about
these stupid things. At that point these two people came
running down the field with a shotgun, realised I was
British and took me into a farmhouse and made me a
cup of tea.

I'd picked up some cannon splinters in my leg and it
was swollen and in the centre there was a hole, just as
though you'd stuck a pencil right through it. When I got
back to Hawkinge I went to sick quarters and the doctor
laid me out and started probing around with what looked
like a steel knitting needle. I fainted. That really put me
out of action then for the rest of the Battle of Britain.

Also shot down in the same action was John Gibson. But he
had by now been downed no fewer than four times, and was
an expert on getting out of the aircraft.

People all had different ideas of baling out. Some people
said you turn the thing upside down and fall out, some
people climbed over the side. Some people thought that
if there was fuel in the cockpit of the aircraft, and you
turned it upside down, it would douse you in fuel. I

think you were so pleased to get rid of the thing you
didn't think about how you did it.

We had an unwritten rule that we didn't chase people
over the water too far, the idea was to get back to the
UK for the next operation. So most of our flying was
done over the water but fairly close to the coast.

On this occasion Gibson was confident of being picked up.

Practically everybody that came down on a parachute was
observed by our people or the navy or someone, and
obviously when I baled out I took quite a long time to
come down, because I baled out at 15,000 feet or
something.

I did a free drop for a while and knew I was coming
down over the sea. I was, in those days, a very good
swimmer, but in a Mae West it is impossible to swim,
you can only lie on your back and do a kind of a
backstroke. Very soon I saw creaming directly towards me
an MTG, a gunboat similar to the MTB motor torpedo
boats, a Vosper, eighty-three feet long with three big
Merlin engines in it. This boat never altered course at all
and just at the last moment did a bloody great turn. I'd
blown my Mae West up so high that when I got in the
water I hadn't even got my hair wet up till then. But this
thing nearly drowned me with a huge wave. Then he
came right round on top of me and I was looking down
the barrels of two Lewis guns in the bow of this boat.
The gunner barked, 'Friend or foe?' I told him in a way
that left him in no doubt at all that I was not a foe. The
navy never had any ladders or nets and to climb on to
the counter of that MTG was a long way. 'How am I
going to get into this thing?' I asked. They threw a rope
over the side with a noose in it and said 'Put your foot in

this thing.' So I was hauled out of the water like a tuna fish. At last I was on deck and I fell flat on my stomach, and some chap pulled my shirt open and rubbed my chest. Then I was sent below and was given a bottle of whisky and a tin mug, no water. I thought, I'll just get myself a bit jolly on this stuff. The boat took me to Dover and when I got off I was met by a lieutenant commander surgeon, navy, who said, 'Are you all right, lad?' I replied, 'Yes, sir.' He took me into a hotel and gave me some more drinks, so I was quite drunk when they finally took me back to Gravesend. In the meantime they had collected Bill Green, and once again I'm not sure how we married up but we went back in the same car. We got back to Gravesend gone midnight and I remember there was a Wren driving this car and one nursing the pair of us in the back seat.

Our CO then was a great chap, Harry Hogan, and he was waiting up for us. He asked us how we were and I said I was fine. 'Good,' he said, 'you're on readiness tomorrow morning, four-thirty again, so go and get a couple of hours' sleep.'

Gibson would be needed. The next day, 30 August, saw the RAF at its fullest stretch, flying 1,054 sorties, the most of any day of the battle. In the morning sixteen squadrons were sent up against a stream of Luftwaffe raids, and eight were in action trying to prevent the afternoon attacks on Biggin Hill, Tangmere, Kenley and Shoreham. Diversionary raids into the Thames estuary stretched Fighter Command effectively. But although the interceptions did not succeed in breaking up the raids, it was a shock for the Luftwaffe crews, who had repeatedly been told that Fighter Command was on its last legs, to see so many British fighters still arrayed against them. The pressure continued. By night, also, the Luftwaffe bombed the airfields, Liverpool, the London docks and industrial targets in south Wales.

The following day, Leigh-Mallory's sector station at Duxford was targeted as well as Park's airfields south of London. From Fowlmere, 19 Squadron were scrambled at just after eight in the morning to intercept. Twelve of the squadron took off, but one turned back with engine trouble. Almost directly over Little Shelford, where his heavily pregnant wife was bathing her sister's baby, James Coward spotted a formation of about twenty Dorniers with an escort of nearly fifty Bf 110 long-range fighters. Even though it was almost his first sortie of the battle, Coward was leader of 'green' section. Crying out, 'Tally ho!' he climbed into the attack with his section. At this moment, the Bf 110s, with the advantage of height, came in to counterattack. As Coward was on the point of firing at the bombers, something hit him in the leg. Feeling nothing more than a brief knock, he looked down. 'I could see my foot hanging loose on the pedal, but you thought you were invincible and I still went in to open fire.' But immediately the cannon in his Spitfire jammed. Cursing and still heading directly for the German Dornier bomber, he ducked as the top of his aircraft grazed the bomber's underbelly. The hood of his plane ripped off and the Spitfire spiralled down, out of control, its petrol spilling on to Coward. 'I baled out at 22,000 feet,' he says, 'and got caught on the back of the cockpit as I went.' Thrashing around on the top of the Spitfire, suddenly he was free.

I was going to free-fall for a bit in case they shot up my parachute, but my foot was thrashing around up by my thigh and the pain was too much. I pulled the ripcord and I swung there in a great figure of eight. The blood was pumping out of my leg – it was amazing how bright it was so high up. I thought I'd bleed to death so I used the radio wire from my helmet to put a tourniquet round my thigh. After that, I felt no pain, apart from the petrol that had drenched me and was stinging my armpits and crotch. I drifted across Duxford towards Fowlmere and then the wind took me back again.

Coward was lucky that a doctor was nearby when he landed painfully in a field. Taken to Addenbrooke's Hospital by ambulance, he had his left leg amputated below the knee. Three weeks later, he got out of hospital just in time for the birth of his first child, a daughter. After another spate of the cannons jamming in action, 19 Squadron got rid of the cannon-fitted Spitfires on 4 September.

The Squadron had lost two other planes in the engagement. One pilot baled out unhurt, but young Pilot Officer Ray Aeberhardt struggled to get his damaged Spitfire down at Fowlmere. For the watching armourer Fred Roberts, it was the worst moment of the war: 'He went up on his nose on landing and the plane caught fire, we were there and we watched him burning, we couldn't do anything, we couldn't get near him. We hadn't got the fire-fighting facilities at Fowlmere and that sort of thing, you know.' Aeberhardt did not survive. At only nineteen years of age, he had been the youngest man on the squadron.

The same day, Winston Churchill had been back at Uxbridge. He had seen all of Park's 11 Group fighters committed in battle. Writing his diary that night, Jock Colville noted, 'The PM was deeply moved by what he saw this afternoon at Uxbridge: he said that what he saw brought the war home to him.'[4] Park and Dowding were now refusing to commit to interceptions until after the raiders had crossed the coast. Desperate to engage the Bf 109s only when they were at the limit of their endurance, enemy fighter sweeps over the south coast flew unmolested.

To Churchill, it must have looked as if the front line was moving inexorably northwards. Fighter Command was showing the strain.

On 1 September, although five airfields were attacked again, the Luftwaffe flew only just over half of the sorties of the previous day. Attacking by night and day, many German crews were as exhausted as their RAF counterparts. Furthermore, the Luftwaffe had by now lost 800 aircraft in the previous two months, and for them the supply of new fighters in August had actually declined.[5] Nevertheless, Park had his back up against the wall now; through poor communication with Leigh-Mallory, he was forced to hold his squadrons over his airfields, rather than send them forward to intercept the bombers before they reached their targets. At Rochford an attack by eighteen raiders succeeded in hitting an ammunition dump and destroying five planes on the ground. Eastchurch, like Manston before it, was abandoned after a heavy attack. Raids continued on Debden, Kenley, Digby, Hornchurch and Detling. On 3 September North Weald was severely hit; at the end of the day the two Hurricane squadrons at the airfield could only muster two serviceable aircraft between them.

On 4 September, as Göring's directive of three days earlier to attack aircraft factories was initiated, the RAF succeeded in shooting down only one bomber for the loss of six Hurricanes and nine Spitfires, with nine pilots killed. A further four Hurricanes and two Spitfires force-landed. Six Bf 109s and thirteen Bf 110s were downed, but not only was this not a satisfactory rate of exchange, it was an indication that Kesselring, by insisting that his formations be 75 per cent fighters, was at last conducting the air war on his terms. Some of the fighter pilots of the RAF seemed to have had enough. Peter Brothers returned to the action on 5 September, joining 257 Squadron.

> Two flight commanders had been killed and I arrived as one of two new flight commanders. The squadron morale was absolutely zilch because the CO was unpopular and having lost both flight commanders on the same day, obviously the young chaps thought, well, if the flight commanders can get shot down, what chance have we got?
>
> The CO was a strange chap. We were told to patrol over Maidstone flying at 20,000 feet. Once in position, we saw this great horde of German aircraft. 'There they are!' we said. But the CO came back, 'We were told to patrol Maidstone and that we will do until we're told otherwise.' We all pissed off, got stuck in and left him on his own. I had second thoughts that maybe he had been right, maybe the ground controller was holding us for a second phase or something. But on the third occasion of this happening, we decided that he just didn't like combat. He was avoiding it, I think, so it was time he departed. I think he was old for the game. He was probably thirty or thirty-five and he was past it from our point of view.

Even if the pilots were enthusiastic, many thrown into the battle for the first time at this stage did not stand a chance. On 2 September, Ross Price, the brother of actor Denis Price, arrived at 501 Squadron, as Peter Morfill remembers:

> One lunchtime, at Gravesend, a chap came in a beautiful Riley car and as it stopped, we looked in and saw squash rackets, tennis rackets and even golf clubs, I think. The

CO asked the newcomer, 'Where have you come from?' He replied, 'So-and-so Spitfires.'

'Hurricanes here,' said the CO. 'Same thing, anyway. Grab yourself some food but forget sleeping quarters at the moment, we'll do that later on. We're on readiness in a quarter of an hour so you've just got time to grab something. We lost three blokes today, so you're on.'

'Yes, sir!' replied Price. I will always remember his face. Anyway, we took off at about two o'clock and he was dead at quarter past. So after the day was over, the CO phoned his mother, and she didn't want to know anything, not the car, nothing, so now we had a squadron car. We used to go from Gravesend down the hill to the pub down the bottom there and could get seven people in this car.

As the experienced pilots hardened their hearts against such losses, Dowding, too, was having to have a hard look at his casualty figures. The period from 24 August to 6 September had been the worst so far for the RAF. In the week ending 6 September, Fighter Command lost 161 aircraft in air battles alone for only 189 German planes of all types brought down. During the entire fortnight 103 British pilots were killed and 128 wounded, a weekly wastage rate of over 10 per cent of Fighter Command's combat strength.[6]. The training schools, however much they dangerously slashed their instruction period, could not make good these sorts of losses. Of those still flying, many were averaging only four hours' sleep a night. For the first time also, Fighter Command's available aircraft numbers were being hit hard. Beaverbrook's short-term push could not last for ever. In August fewer aircraft were produced than he had managed in July. As workers on long hours got tired, so productivity fell off, and it would not improve in September. In the two weeks following

24 August, 466 fighters had been damaged or destroyed, and only 269 new or repaired aircraft arrived to take their place. Furthermore, six of the seven 11 Group sector stations were bombed almost to collapse. To the Germans the road to London seemed open.

—CHAPTER ELEVEN—

The Many

O N WINSTON CHURCHILL'S INSISTENCE, BOMBER Command had been repeating the nine-hour round trip to Berlin. As on the first raid, many of the bombers failed to locate the city, let alone military targets within it. On the evening of 28 August, German civilians were killed in the city for the first time, near Goerlitzer railway station.

Until August 1940 both sides had tried to avoid all-out bombing of civilians. In August 1939 Göring had used a Swedish go-between to obtain assurances from the British that they would not be the first ones to bomb heavily populated areas. When Rotterdam had been bombed, the British had taken it to be the end of this mutual agreement and had launched attacks on the Ruhr, against, in theory, industrial targets. With the inaccuracy of bombing it was inevitable, however, that some if not all the bombs would fall nowhere near their targets. Nevertheless, there was still reluctance on both sides to bomb each other's capital cities.

Initially, Hitler ignored the bombing attack of 25 August. Still hoping that Britain would see sense and come to the negotiating table, he held back from retaliation for this 'atrocity'. But after the civilian deaths of the night of the 28th, his attitude began to change. On 30 August, Hitler gave Göring the go-ahead to launch retaliatory attacks on London. The same night he personally witnessed a further raid on his capital.

Part of the motivation for this about-turn was simple retaliation. The citizens of Berlin demanded revenge. On 4 September, Hitler addressed an audience of nurses and female social workers. His speech soon had them in a frenzy of applause. 'Mr Churchill is demonstrating his new brain-child . . . the night air raid . . . When they declare they will increase their attacks on our cities, then we will *raze* their cities to the ground. We will stop the handiwork of these night pirates, so help us God!' At the same time, the threat of invasion was restated: 'In England they're filled with curiosity and keep asking "Why doesn't he come?" Be calm. Be calm. He's coming! He's coming!'[1]

As well as a chance to terrorise the inhabitants of London into demanding peace, bombing the city offered a seemingly unmatched strategic opportunity. Not only did London contain a fifth of the country's population, it was also the centre of industry, commerce and finance, the hub of national road and rail transport, the biggest port and the seat of government, legislature and judiciary. A blow to London would be to strike the head and heart of the entire country and empire.

For the Luftwaffe leadership, meeting at the Hague on 3 September, there were other considerations, too. The meeting was undecided about the remaining strength of the RAF. Luftgruppe 2's Kesselring felt that they were down to their very last planes. Sperrle, in charge of Luftgruppe 3, wasn't so sure. Kesselring was adamant, however, that only by attacking London would the RAF be brought to complete destruction. Dowding could always move his fighter bases out of reach of the short-range Bf 109 fighters, so destroying southern airfields was never going to bring the battle to a conclusion. A great attack on the capital would surely draw Dowding's carefully marshalled reserves south to destruction. Furthermore, Kesselring argued, just two more heavy attacks would end the war. 'If you can pull off these attacks,' he told the assembled officers, the invasion would be unnecessary and 'you will have saved the lives of 100,000 German soldiers.' The go-ahead was given for a massive strike at the capital on 7 September.

Before this time, the Luftwaffe had not espoused strategic bombing. In 1933 a hard look at its industrial capacity had convinced the Luftwaffe planners that to produce a fleet of heavy long-range bombers was beyond its means. Instead, as we have seen, production was devoted to building the Luftwaffe into an army support operation. Many of its chiefs were ex-army officers, and in the early actions of the war, it retained this role. Göring, however, ignored this, confident that the attack would be decisive. He had it on reliable authority that Hitler had gone cold on the invasion plans. Therefore, he felt, more than ever it was up to his Luftwaffe to defeat Britain single-handed. Previously it had been desirable; now it seemed the only option.

Especially for the great attack on 7 September, Göring had his personal train brought to Cap Blanc Nez, within sight of the English coastline. Code-named 'Asia', the train needed two of Germany's heaviest locomotives to move it. One coach held his bedroom and that of his wife, as well as a study. Another was a private cinema. A third was a command post with a map room, another a dining car. All were luxuriously appointed and specially weighted for a smoother ride. Guest cars were attached for other officers and at the front and back were anti-aircraft guns on their own carriages.

Göring himself watched as the huge two-mile-high formation of over a thousand planes crossed the French coast. The city had been divided into two 'target areas'. Target Area A comprised the East End of London with its extensive docks; Area B the western half of London. Heavy bombing raids against Area A, it was hoped, would close the docks and cut off the city's power supplies. In the face of advice from his senior commanders, Hitler still preferred that the targets in the city should be commercial or industrial. In fact, with cheap housing for the dock-workers in some cases lying adjacent to depots and warehouses, the German bombers were never going to be accurate enough to avoid hitting civilians. The Luftwaffe's orders of the day finally concede this: 'The intention is to complete the operation by a single attack. In the event of units failing to arrive directly over target, other suitable objectives in Loge [Göring's code-name for London] may be bombed from altitude of approach.' This crucial clause revoked Hitler's previous precise orders against the bombing of civilians. Effectively it was the go-ahead for terror bombing. It seemed as if all the doom-laden theories of the 1930s were finally going to be put to the test.

For the Luftwaffe, it was also a question of asserting what it felt was its virtual air superiority. Just to demonstrate that a mass attack on the capital was possible would cheer the public in Germany and perhaps even finally break the will of the people of Britain. As the orders conclude: 'To achieve the necessary maximum effect it is essential that units fly as highly concentrated forces during approach, attack and especially on return. The main objective of the operation is to prove that the Luftwaffe can achieve this.'[2]

As usual, the Luftwaffe formations were spotted by radar massing over the French coast and plotted in the ops room at Uxbridge. But this gave little indication of the intended target. Park was away from Uxbridge at a conference with Dowding, and in his absence it was decided that this must be another attack on the desperate sector stations south and north-east of London, or on the Thames Haven oil depot, which was still burning from previous attacks. The controllers were also under strict orders to guard the aircraft factories on the west side of London. British fighters were sent to protect the factories and oil installations but, not trusting Leigh-Mallory's 12 Group to do the unglamorous work of defending the 11 Group airfields, Park's controllers kept many fighters back circling over their bases. Too late it was realised that London itself was the target. As the lead Dornier bombers moved up the Thames, twenty miles short of their target their fighter escort found themselves short of fuel and forced to turn back. But in spite of the German bomber crews' nervousness, they reached London with few attacks from the RAF. Less than half the British aircraft airborne when the raid arrived were near enough to make an interception before the bombers closed on their sprawling target, the largest city in the world.

It had been an especially beautiful morning and early afternoon in east London. As usual, the markets and dog tracks were busy, and at Upton Park an improvised West Ham team were taking on local rivals Tottenham Hotspur. When the air-raid siren went, the Hammers were ahead 4–1, and the crowd began, grumbling, to disperse.

Eighteen-year-old factory worker Betty Roper of Bow was helping her younger sister Nellie with the preparations for her wedding the next day. It had been a busy morning and there were important tasks still to be fulfilled. 'We were about to head over to the Roman Road to get a ring when we heard the sirens. Nobody went into the shelters at first, but then we saw them. There were hundreds of them . . . the sky was black and you could see the bombs falling. They were like silver. Soon the docks were all alight.' Nevertheless, Betty and her sister headed across Victoria Park, in the hope that there might still be some shops open on Roman Road. In the park they came across an old man whose face was bleeding. Having taken him to a nearby wardens' centre, they continued on their way. 'So we hurried through the park to the Roman and luckily enough the shop had just opened up for another half-hour so she got her ring. We came back to my nan's house.'

On the flat roof of the Walthamstow Sainsbury's, eighteen-year-old shop porter Robert Barltrop was on fire-watching duty. It was a typical busy Saturday, and the shoppers ignored the air-raid warning. 'This time, though, the all-clear didn't come,' remembers Barltrop.

> I had a view across to the east and I saw the planes coming from the Dagenham and Barking direction; they were following the Thames like a little swarm of flies. They puffed some anti-aircraft fire all around them and as I sat there watching, the planes got more and more numerous. Then clouds of smoke began to rise from the East End. Then the clouds gradually became one huge cloud.

Soon stories reached the shoppers of the damage to the East End, and the shop was hurriedly closed.

Fifteen-year-old Charles Turner had already had a taste of the combat. During August, in the Kent and Sussex fields, the hop-picking was beginning, and as usual, cockneys from London had made the journey down. Charles had been travelling down to Cousley Wood near Wadhurst in East Sussex since the age of eight or nine. At the end of August he had been working in a field when a Bf 109 crash-landed nearby. Immediately he and his friend Johnny Grange had wanted to go and have a look, but were forbidden from doing so by an aunt. Half an hour later the plane had exploded violently. Now back in London, Charles was at the Granada cinema in East Ham as the raid began. 'They put a slide up on the screen,' he recalls, 'saying, "Those who want to leave the cinema should do so now." No one did 'cos there had been no daytime raids so far.' Once the film had finished, Charles made his way out into the open. 'I caught the bus home. It went over the bridge that crosses the River Lea. I could smell the smoke and as we crossed the bridge I could see the East India Dock burning and there was a ship on fire.'

The first wave of bombers consisted of more than 150 He 111s and Dorniers, flying over three miles high. Many of these were carrying incendiaries, which were dropped over the docks. At once the fire services were at full stretch. In the Surrey Docks, one and a half million tons of timber was set alight. Stores of pepper caught fire, sending stinging particles into the air. Rum supplies were soon burning; barrels exploded as liquid fire sloshed around the firemen's feet. Burning paint and rubber, also, threatened to choke the firefighters.

American military attaché Raymond Lee, who was staying at his club at 42 Half Moon Street in the West End of London, went out into the square to see for himself:

> I could see little flecks like bits of tinfoil darting about
> overhead, so high that they were almost out of sight.
> Only an occasional burst of machine-gun fire showed
> that fierce combat was going on in the heavens . . . Over
> beyond the Houses of Parliament, a huge mushroom of
> billowing smoke had risen so high as to blot out the
> sky . . . In the heart of it fierce red glows showed that
> immense fires were raging.[3]

Like Charles Turner, sixteen-year-old Bert Martin had also encountered the enemy over the hop fields of the Weald.

Cycling from the fields to the primitive huts where his family was staying, he had heard a 'whoosh' over his head and had fallen off his bike. A German fighter had opened fire, stripping the nearby apple trees of their leaves and hitting Martin in the leg. On his return to London he had joined the fire and rescue division of his local Civil Defence unit in Homerton, east London. Now, as fires broke out all over the East End, it was a question of learning on the job, working the stirrup pumps and handling the hoses with their fourteen-pound brass nozzles. 'I was terrified and resigned,' he says. 'I would be holding a hose amid burning buildings – I couldn't touch the buttons on my tunic because they were so hot. My face blistered. I don't think you ever get immune to it – the wreckage, the dead bodies. It was a kaleidoscope of hell.'

In far-away Uxbridge, plotter Hazel Gregory was in the small canteen at the top of the ops room.

We stood there and we looked towards London and the whole sky was on fire. It was terrible; it really looked as if the whole of London and the whole sky was on fire. The sky was brilliant with light. Oh, the feeling of helplessness! It wasn't like the earlier part when we were plotting the day raids. There was nothing we could do about it.

George Wheeler, another auxiliary fireman, was called to a shelter in Wick Road, Hackney, at around 7 p.m. The brick-built structure had received a direct hit. 'The bomb had blown out a wall and the concrete roof had come down on the people inside. There were men, women, children; some alive, most dead. Everything was covered in this thick grey dust . . . I think there were about thirty dead. It was a terrible sight.'

Worst hit were the docks of West Ham and Bermondsey, Stepney, Whitechapel, Poplar, Bow and Shoreditch. In Silvertown, a very poor area bordered by the Thames, the river Lea and the docks, over 13,000 people were trapped for many hours as fires raged all around them.

The all-clear was sounded at 6.30 p.m., but the fires on the docks were still raging. Nine miles of waterfront were now ablaze and 75,000 tons of food supplies were in the process of being destroyed. Quebec Yard in Surrey Docks suffered the fiercest fire ever recorded in Britain, and fire crews were called in from as far away as Coventry.

Vera Shaw, who had finished her shift at Park's 11 Group headquarters at midday, had been to a twenty-first birthday party a few miles away from Uxbridge. Needing to be back at work at midnight, she had left the party early. On her way back she got stuck for an hour, and was concerned about being late. 'All the fire engines and ambulances were coming from Slough, Windsor, from everywhere, dashing to London, and we couldn't move.' Her friend Philippa Robertson had been on leave in Woking and was returning to Uxbridge via Ealing. 'As we approached London, we could hear it all going on and see the searchlights lighting up the sky, as well as all the flames.' To George Wheeler and the London auxiliary firemen, 7 September was to be known thereafter as 'Red Saturday'. 'As darkness came,' he remembers, 'the whole of the sky line on the river as far as you can see from down river to up river into the centre of London was one big, red glow. You could see all the outlines of tall buildings against the redness, and in the middle of it smoke rising. For five or six miles it was all one big red glow.'

By midnight, there were nine huge conflagrations in the city, each three times the size of the biggest peace-time blaze, as well as a host of smaller fires, guiding to their target the night raiders that had followed from 8 p.m. in a continuous stream. From Luftflotte 3, Sperrle had sent over 247 bombers to pour high explosives and further incendiaries into the blaze until 4.30 in the morning. Betty Roper spent the night in the Anderson shelter in her grandparents' garden. The wedding party of eleven had assembled, bottles were opened, and amid the noise, discomfort and excitement there was little sleep to be had. At some time in the night a loud thump indicated that a bomb had hit at the top of the road.

For most people in England the intensity of the attack meant only one thing: the invasion was underway. The Joint Chiefs of Staff, who met that evening at 5.20, had further evidence. Photographic intelligence showed a considerable build-up of barges at Ostend. On 31 August there had been eighteen; now there were 270. German radio decrypts had also revealed that dive-bombers were being moved to France from Norway to cover the Straits of Dover, and that all German army leave had been cancelled from 8 September onwards. The British assumed that the barges would not be brought within range of the RAF bombers unless invasion was imminent. The meeting also heard that the conditions in the Channel as far as tides and moon were concerned would be 'particularly favourable' for landings between 8 and 10 September. The Chiefs of Staff's meeting, not attended by Churchill, who was at Chequers, concluded that the invasion was 'imminent' and ordered all defence forces in the UK to 'stand by at immediate notice'. The General Headquarters, Home Forces, on its own initiative, issued at 8.07 p.m. the code-word 'Cromwell', to bring all home defence forces to 'immediate action'.

Many units, particularly amongst the Home Guard, interpreted this as meaning that invasion was actually taking place. Church bells were rung, several bridges were blown up, and all over the country Home Guard units, having wished their families an emotional farewell, spent a bleary night on lookout, sharing with Londoners what must have been one of the most sleepless and miserable nights the country has ever had.

The next morning it soon became apparent that the warning had been a mistake or had been misinterpreted. Some accused the government of panicking in the face of the terrible raid. Over London, 11 Group's commander Keith Park was flying his personal Hurricane across the city to survey the damage. 'It was burning all down the river. It was a horrid sight. But I looked down and said, "Thank God for that," because I realised that the methodical Germans had at last switched their attack from my vital aerodromes on to cities.'[4]

Later that morning the Roper wedding party left the shelter. After a hurried wash they groggily changed into their best clothes. As they left the house they were confronted by their first sight of bomb damage. At the end of the road, a pile of debris was all that remained of a stables and a nearby house in which two old ladies had lived. Volunteers were helping pull the dead bodies from the ruins but it would be a further week before the stinking corpses of the horses would finally be removed. Further on, they were amazed at the number of fire engines clogging the streets, and gazed in awe at the heat glow in the sky over the docks. Although the flames were not visible, they could see their flickering light. But the simple church service at St Mark's just by Victoria Park was miraculously undisturbed by air-raid warnings, and by 10.30 in the morning Nellie was married.

Four hundred and thirty civilians had been killed on the first night, and another 1,600 had been seriously injured; as many casualties in one night as Fighter Command suffered in the whole of the Battle of Britain. It was now the battle not just of 'the Few', but also of the many. As Angus Calder writes in his *The People's War*, 'While the Battle of Britain was still very much in progress, what is sometimes called the Battle of London had begun. It was the battle of an unarmed civilian population against incendiaries and high explosive; the battle of firemen, wardens, policemen, nurses and rescue workers against an enemy they could not hurt.'[5]

But the ghoulish pre-war estimates of the effect of terror bombing had not been met. There had been no unspeakable new weapon, and no poison gas beyond that caused by the huge fires. A mercifully large number of the bombs dropped had proved to be duds, and the casualty figures had been a tiny fraction of what had been predicted. In the same way, in the East End, the much-predicted breakdown of civil order and discipline failed to materialise. Hitler had hoped through bombing the capital to bring about an upsurge of opinion against the 'warmonger' Churchill. He knew that Churchill, with his defiant rhetoric, had burnt his bridges as far as suing for peace was concerned, and that only a new leadership would come to the negotiating table. Certainly the British ruling class had not had high hopes of the East End putting up with night after night of bombing. For nervous civil servants, there existed in the East End of London if not the potential for revolution, at least the capacity for a turning against the war and the leadership of the country who had taken Britain into it. Certainly if you went looking for it you could find confusion and resentment amongst the bombed. 'In dockside areas the population is showing visible signs of its nerve cracking,' a government intelligence report noted gloomily the next day. The East End had been the cradle of both the British Union of Fascists (BUF) and the Communist Party, which remained opposed to the war until the invasion of the Soviet Union in 1941. Sir Oswald Mosley had spoken at a successful BUF rally at Bethnal Green eleven weeks after the beginning of the war, and when a by-election was held in

West Ham on 22 February 1940, two of the three candidates had opposed the war. But even before the bombing started, support for anti-war candidates had fallen away. In July the Information Minister Harold Nicolson wrote in his diary, 'When bombing begins on a large scale, people will ask "What are we fighting for? Would we not be better off with peace plus Hitler?" '[6] These fears, based in part on a low opinion of 'the people', turned out to have been unfounded.

Many of those most fearful of bombing, and therefore most likely to panic or lose control, had already left the city. Over the days following the first raid, many thousands more would trek out to Epping Forest and camp there while the attacks continued. Some 5,000 took refuge in deep caves at Chislehurst. Those who remained soon learned what to expect. Not that the East Enders liked the fact that they seemed to have been singled out for destruction. There was resentment, too, that the rich were able to get out of London easily. The first bombs had revealed the flimsiness of their cheap terraced housing and few had gardens in which to build Anderson shelters. On 8 September many headed for Liverpool Street, then the nearest station on the tube network. There they were refused entry amid angry scenes. There were no facilities on the rail network for sheltering people, it was said. The possibility of using the underground for shelters had been discussed but the authorities had feared a 'deep shelter' mentality – once the people were in, it was thought they would never come out and vital war work would go neglected. But at Liverpool Street force of numbers prevailed and people streamed down on to the platforms. Over the next few days the numbers increased and by the end of September there were 177,000 Londoners sheltering in the underground system, many in the long tunnel, then under construction, that now links Liverpool Street to Bethnal Green and Mile End. During the night, the live rail would be switched off and people found space where they could to grab some all-important sleep. Privacy went by the wayside. Few of the stations had deep-level sanitation and soon the stench was terrible. In these conditions lice and mosquitoes flourished.

Other shelters were far worse. Near Liverpool Street, a goods station covered by flimsy railway arches was deemed an official shelter for 3,000. Soon there were 14,000 people using it, with nothing but the most rudimentary sanitation. In Victoria Park, just north of Mile End, 1,450 people packed into a shelter and had to remain standing all night as filthy water lapped around their ankles. Many of those sheltering had nowhere else to go. After the first day and night of bombing thousands of people were made homeless. Officials who had expected that many of these people would have been killed were in some cases ill-prepared. Rest centres were poorly supplied with sanitation, too few in number and vulnerable to bombing. Delays in shipping out homeless people from the danger area led to the deaths of 400 when a bomb hit a crowded rest centre in Canning Town.

But London had at least made some preparations, and a mass of volunteers stepped into the breach. Even if not attached to any of the ARP bodies, neighbours helped extinguish fires and dig out victims. Where the normal chains of command broke down, other community leaders, such as priests, took over. The government also moved quickly to improve shelters and evacuation of the homeless. When, over the next few days, the bombing moved westwards, resentment of the rich West End was modified by fellow feeling. On 13 September Buckingham Palace was bombed. Although no one was hurt, for many it seemed evidence that the whole city, however rich or privileged, was in it together.

Across the capital a combination of frayed nerves, sleeplessness and outrage was funnelled not towards Churchill's bellicose leadership, but at the Germans. Now it was not just Hitler and the Nazis, but the 'whole German race' that should be 'wiped out. All of them,' one East Ender remembers thinking. Nobby Clark was a young policeman based in Charing Cross Road. When a German airman parachuted down nearby, he was called on to rescue him from a heated throng.

> We had a cabby call in the door and shout out, 'One
> of your chaps is in trouble down the road with a
> parachutist.' So of course we were out like a shot. He
> had landed almost on our doorstep fortunately for him
> or I swear they would have killed him. They were
> really vicious, particularly the girls. People had appeared
> from nowhere, wanting to tear this joker apart, and he
> was terrified. They really meant business, I'm not
> kidding, and the worst were the women. We went into
> that web of people like a wedge of steel till we got to
> the guy, because we thought it was one of our blokes.
> He was pretty bedraggled. I don't know what happened
> to the parachute – it had probably been cut up by that
> time because the girls were very keen to get parachute
> silk. We dragged him into 82 Charing Cross Road
> where we all sat down. We gave him a fag.

The German airmen, though, had left the Londoners' city with terrible damage on the morning of 8 September. Telephone lines had been cut, gas, water and sewage pipes breached, electricity cables smashed to ribbons. Unexploded bombs meant whole blocks had to be evacuated, and the city's roads were in many places unpassable. The railway network, too, had been severely disrupted, with hits on important stations and tracks. At midday Raymond Lee walked over to Victoria station to inspect the damage: 'The station is closed but one can see that a bomb came through the roof all right and knocked things about badly. The sign said, with true British restraint, "Closed on account of obstructions." '[7]

The RAF too, out of position and outnumbered, had suffered, losing twenty-five aircraft and nineteen pilots. The Luftwaffe had lost thirty-seven aircraft, but it was a small total compared to the size of the attacks. Only one in thirty German planes had been harmed at all. For Göring, the operation had been a triumph. The next day, in an impromptu radio address, he announced, 'I personally have taken over the leadership of the attacks against England . . . for the first time we have struck at England's heart . . . this is an historic hour.'

Just after 8 p.m. on the night following the first attack, the bombers returned, killing a further 400 Londoners. On Monday 9 September the death toll was 370. From now on, for seventy-six consecutive nights (with only one night off), London was raided. After the destruction of 7 September, General Pile, in charge of the country's anti-aircraft defence, ordered that every available gun be sent to London. On 10 September, the German raids were met with more than double the amount of fire from the ground as gunners pushed their weapons to the limit. Although there were few hits, the attackers were forced to fly higher, and Londoners' feelings of helplessness receded. Even Raymond Lee, who as a military attaché might have been expected to know something of the limited effectiveness of the anti-aircraft guns, wrote in his diary, 'It is a pleasure to reflect that so much metal is going up instead of coming down.'[8]

But the anti-aircraft barrage did not deter attacks. The

following night, the 11th, there were over 200 bombers over London. The next day Harold Nicolson noted in his diary, 'The people in the East End are still frightened and angry.' That night he had to walk back to his ministry from the Reform Club. 'I have no tin hat and do not enjoy it. When things get very hot, I crouch in a doorway. In one of them I find a prostitute. "I have been drinking," she says. "I am frightened. Please take care of me." '⁹

For the pilots of 501 Squadron, the night raids were terribly frustrating. Although they attempted interceptions in the dark, they were ineffective at stopping the onslaught, as John Bisdee remembers:

> I flew a number of night-fighter sorties from Biggin Hill.
> Of course it was awful to see, particularly the dockland
> area and the East End of London absolutely in flames.
> There were an awful lot of these parachute flares dropped
> by the Germans that formed quite a pyrotechnic display
> quite apart from any ack-ack or anything like that. There
> were all these hanging chandeliers in the air and it was all
> very impressive. The trouble was that it was practically
> impossible to locate a German bomber at night if you
> didn't have radar.

Almost unopposed, the German bombers came back night after night. Raymond Lee noticed people 'looking tired and preoccupied . . . the strain does tell'. On the night of 13 September, he survived a near miss. 'About midnight I was awakened by two tremendous explosions which jarred the whole building and then by a whistling bomb that seemed to come down just outside my window. It was an hour before I could get to sleep once more. In the morning, I found two large craters just across Piccadilly about 150 feet from my bedroom.'¹⁰

☆ ☆ ☆

During the day, however, the battle was continuing and Fighter Command had some success in turning back or breaking up daylight raids. On 9 September, Ju 88 pilot Wilhelm Stahl flew over England for the first time. A civilian weather-forecasting pilot before the war, he was an experienced flyer and had been in action in France. During August he had been stationed in Denmark, and only heard rumours of the air war over England. On 25 August he wrote in his diary: 'It is being said that the British are already on their last legs, but when one hears what the operational pilots – and in particular the bomber crews – have to report, we're obviously still a long way from victory.' On 2 September he was transferred to an airfield near Mons in Belgium, where his crew were put up in an old deserted castle. Exploring the nearby area, the German airmen came across some locals. 'In the evening we pay a visit to the nearby village where a lot of beer and wine is consumed in a cheerful bar of sorts. The locals are quite willing to join in conversation and tell us we should beat the British as quickly as we can, so that the war will be over soon. Political subjects are avoided by both sides.'[11]

Now, on 9 September, Stahl was at last in the action after several frustrating last-minute cancellations due to technical problems with his Ju 88. 'We set off from bases in Holland, France and Belgium and collected over Lille,' he remembers. 'Eventually there is an assembly of at least 200 bombers that gathers into some sort of order and sets course for London. Soon afterwards we are joined by an escort of Bf 109s and Bf 110s. There were 500–600 aircraft with me in tight formation.' This gave Stahl a much-needed feeling of security. 'Wherever one looked,' he recalls, 'one saw our aircraft, all around, a marvellous sight. Among us we estimate that the total load destined to fall on London soon afterwards amounts to at least 200,000kg. And this had been going on for some days already. Poor London!'

While crossing the Channel, Wilhelm Stahl saw the fighters around him start to zigzag about, underneath and above the bombers, watching for interceptors diving out of the sun. As they crossed the coast, visibility improved and they could see trains moving below them. Soon the navigator gave Stahl a signal and pointed ahead, where 'black smoke pillars' from fires still burning gave away the location of the capital. Soon he could see the first bombs dropping from his formation. Later that night he wrote in his diary:

> Then it is my turn to press the red release button. The aircraft makes its usual jump of relief and we look down. The Thames' bends, the docks and the whole colossal city lie spread out before us like a giant map. Then come the explosions of our bombs which we observe while banking in a wide turn eastwards, then south . . . the effect of our attack is an enormous cloud of smoke and dust that shoots up into the sky. One cannot imagine that a town or a people could endure this continuous crushing burden for long.

But as it turned away, the formation began to break up. The next thing Stahl knew, there were British fighters amongst them.

> At first I take them for our own escorts and wonder about their tactics, twisting around among bombers in such a foolhardy way. Then I realise that they are British . . . there is tracer all around us, and a wild twisting turning air combat has broken out between our 109s and the Spitfires and Hurricanes. Now everything is happening right underneath us! I get away to hide in the thickest bunch of our bombers I can spot nearby.

Stahl saw several He 111s downed or damaged, and one of his own engines had been hit and was leaking oil. Suddenly, though, the 'Tommies' disappeared and all was quiet again. By now, the Ju 88 had only one engine running, but Stahl managed to return to an airfield at Amiens.

The Germans were surprised by the number of defending fighters sent up to intercept them over Canterbury and south London. Many ended up dropping most of their bombs over the residential areas of Purley, Norbiton and Surbiton. Following this unexpected resistance, the next day Hitler decided to again postpone his decision on the invasion. Admiral Raeder had informed him that the Kriegsmarine would be ready with the transports on 15 September, and Hitler had replied that although the Luftwaffe had scored 'tremendous successes', the conditions for invasion – namely the defeat of the RAF and daylight air superiority – had still not been met. The moment had not yet come to issue the ten-day warning. But now that the decision had been postponed until 14 September, it meant that the invasion itself would not happen until 24 September. As the date slipped, the risk of bad weather in the Channel worsened for the Germans. It became even more vital for the Luftwaffe to press home its attack and engage the British fighter force.

On 11 September, Kesselring launched his third daylight raid on London. A hundred bombers managed to hit their targets in the City and the docks, and at the same time a smaller force badly damaged a brand-new aircraft factory near Southampton. For the first time RAF losses had exceeded those of the enemy: twenty-nine to only twenty-four Luftwaffe aircraft destroyed. As night fell, the now customary raid devastated London further.

While the nation's attention was focused on the capital, Churchill and his commanders were increasingly worried about the signs from across the Channel of an impending invasion. On the evening of 11 September, Churchill broad-cast to the nation, saying, 'We cannot tell when they will try to come; we cannot be sure that in fact they will try at all; but no one should blind himself to the fact that a heavy, full-scale invasion of this Island is being prepared with all the usual German thoroughness and method, and that it may be launched at any time now.' Explaining that the weather conditions meant that the invasion would have to be tried soon, he went on: 'We must regard the next week or so as a very important week for us in our history. It ranks with the days when the Spanish Armada was approaching the Channel, and Drake was finishing his game of bowls; or when Nelson stood between us and Napoleon's Grand Army at Boulogne. Every man and every woman,' he continued, 'will therefore prepare himself to do his duty, whatever it may be, with special pride and care.'

There followed Churchill's reading of the Blitz, and a direct political appeal to the people of London not to allow the attacks to separate them from the country's leadership.

These cruel, wanton, indiscriminate bombings of London are, of course, part of Hitler's invasion plans. He hopes, by killing large numbers of civilians, women and children, that he will terrorise and cow the people of this mighty imperial city, and make them a burden and anxiety to the Government . . . Little does he know the spirit of the British nation, or the tough fibre of Londoners, whose forebears played a leading part in the establishment of Parliamentary institutions.[12]

By now exaggerated rumours of the East Enders blaming Churchill's government for the attack on their homes had reached Berlin via the American embassy there. Two days later Hitler told von Brauchitsch that he was confident that air attack alone would bring about the defeat of Britain and that the invasion in force would surely now not be necessary.

After two days of bad weather, Kesselring attacked again on 14 September by day and only fourteen German aircraft were shot down for the loss of the same number of RAF fighters. That night 140 bombers were over London. The Luftwaffe were convinced that Fighter Command was on its last legs.

Back in the fighting, 238 Squadron had been taking heavy casualties. On 14 September Eric Bann wrote to his parents: 'Old 238 have been right in the thick of it. London every day.' One of 238's Polish pilots had been killed and Gordon Batt's trusted number two, Domagala, was in hospital. 'Things have been rather warm,' wrote Eric Bann.

The uneven performance of the RAF defenders had persuaded Hitler that all that was keeping the RAF above water were the odd days of bad weather that disrupted the Luftwaffe attack. All that was needed, he thought, was a short run of successive good flying days and it would all be over. Consequently he decided to gamble on delaying the final invasion decision until 17 September in the hope that the intervening period would see the Luftwaffe triumph.

The great attack of 15 September was planned to finally break Fighter Command and the morale of Londoners through engaging the remaining British fighter aircraft and at the same time raining down an unprecedented amount of high explosive on the capital. It would prove to be the last decisive day of the battle.

What the Luftwaffe had crucially failed to realise was that since 7 September, when the weight of their attacks had shifted away from Fighter Command installations and on to London, Park's 11 Group airfields had received a vital respite. Craters were filled, the vital web of communication lines restored and buildings reinforced. New squadrons from the north were brought in and a large number of Polish airmen made operational. Even if things had been bad in the air, Fighter Command was stronger on 14 September than it had been a week earlier, and had more planes than four weeks before.

—CHAPTER TWELVE—

Air Superiority

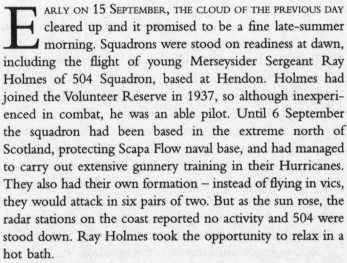

E ARLY ON 15 SEPTEMBER, THE CLOUD OF THE PREVIOUS DAY
cleared up and it promised to be a fine late-summer
morning. Squadrons were stood on readiness at dawn,
including the flight of young Merseysider Sergeant Ray
Holmes of 504 Squadron, based at Hendon. Holmes had
joined the Volunteer Reserve in 1937, so although inexperienced in combat, he was an able pilot. Until 6 September
the squadron had been based in the extreme north of
Scotland, protecting Scapa Flow naval base, and had managed
to carry out extensive gunnery training in their Hurricanes.
They also had their own formation – instead of flying in vics,
they would attack in six pairs of two. But as the sun rose, the
radar stations on the coast reported no activity and 504 were
stood down. Ray Holmes took the opportunity to relax in a
hot bath.

In London, reported the Berlin newspapers, draft-
dodging playboy plutocrats were living it up with good-
time girls and prostitutes while abandoned women and
children were left to find shelter in a city largely gutted by
fire. By contrast, the *Sunday Times* was reporting the latest
football game interrupted by an air raid – Arsenal versus
Fulham – and the racing correspondent was wistfully
hoping for a day's uninterrupted running. At the cinema at
Marble Arch, *The Westerner*, starring Gary Cooper, had been
playing to full houses. There was great celebration in the

morning when a huge unexploded bomb that had threatened St Paul's was finally, after three days' effort, extracted from under the wall of the cathedral. It was straightaway rushed into a lorry and driven at top speed to Hackney Marshes, where it was exploded, making a crater one hundred feet wide.

At 10.30 a.m. Churchill arrived unannounced at the Uxbridge control centre with his wife, Clementine. He was shown around again by Keith Park, who told him, 'I don't know if anything will happen today. For the moment everything is quiet.' Vera Shaw, on plotting duty there since seven, was reading and writing letters.

Then, not long after Churchill had arrived, she took a message that a raid of 250-plus aircraft had been picked up by the coastal RDF stations. Her sergeant didn't believe it and asked her to query the number. But soon other messages started arriving as the size of the first formations was established. Park quickly put up twelve squadrons of fighters to attack the enemy over Canterbury. A further six were ordered to circle high over London. Ray Holmes was still in the bath when the call came just before eleven o'clock. Hurriedly dressing, he raced down to the transport, which instantly sped off, rattling and bumping, towards their dispersal point. Within minutes, the squadron was airborne and climbing.

Churchill, in his *The Second World War*, describes the action he witnessed at Uxbridge.

Presently the red bulbs showed that the majority of our squadrons were engaged. A subdued hum arose from the floor, where the busy plotters pushed their discs to and fro in accordance with the swiftly changing situation. . . .The Air Marshal himself [Air Vice-Marshal Park] walked up and down behind, watching with a

vigilant eye every move in the game, supervising his
junior executive hand, and only occasionally intervening
with some decisive order, usually to reinforce a
threatened area. In a little while all our squadrons were
fighting and some had already begun to return for fuel.
All were in the air. The lower line of bulbs was out.
There was not one squadron left in reserve.[1]

There were by now over 200 British fighters airborne and 12
Group, commanded by Air Vice-Marshal Leigh-Mallory,
were quickly asked to reinforce Park's squadrons. Leigh-
Mallory and his star pilot, Douglas Bader, had been urging a
policy of attacking the German formations in strength even if
it meant that they would have already dropped their bombs,
and were scathing of Park's careful use of small numbers of
aircraft. But Park had been unconvinced – the time spent
assembling big 'wings' of several squadrons of aircraft would
mean that help would come too late, and he couldn't afford
to have his sector airfields bombed at will by the Germans.
Now, though, Bader's wing assembled in record time and
sixty aircraft were soon over London.

The bomber formation of Dorniers, accompanied by
Bf 109s, had crossed the English coast near Dungeness and
was intercepted by two Spitfire squadrons over Maidstone.
Other units quickly joined and a giant dogfight started. Soon,
the Bf 109s were running short of fuel and by the time the
bombers fought their way through to London, the escort had
had to turn back.

Waiting for the bombers over south London were Ray
Holmes and 504 Squadron. Spotting a formation of Dornier
bombers that had got through, Squadron Leader John
Sample led the attack. As the formation broke up and,
jettisoning its bombs, began a fighting retreat, 'arse-end
Charlie' Ray Holmes suddenly found himself alone in the

sky. Then, to his west, he spotted a formation of three Dorniers also separated from their fellows. These were still heading stubbornly for the centre of London. To Holmes, it seemed he was the last-ditch defender. Picking the port-side plane, Holmes dived to attack.

I made my attack on this bomber and he spurted out a lot of oil, just a great stream over my aeroplane, blotting out my windscreen. I couldn't see a damn thing. Then, as the windscreen cleared, I suddenly found myself going straight into his tail. So I stuck my stick forward and went under him, practically grazing my head on his belly. I pulled away and when I looked around he was going down. So that was one. Then I came back at the second one in this little vic of three and I attacked him from the right-hand side. I got to the stern of the aeroplane and was shooting at him when suddenly something white came out of the aircraft. I thought that a part of his wing had come away but in actual fact it turned out to be a man with a parachute coming out. I was travelling at 250 miles per hour, it all happened so quickly, but before I knew what had happened this bloody parachute was draped over my starboard wing. There was this poor devil on his parachute hanging straight out behind me, and my aeroplane was being dragged. All I could do was to swing the aeroplane left and then right to try to get rid of this man. Fortunately his parachute slid off my wing and down he went, and I thought, Thank heavens for that!

The third Dornier was still heading onwards and there was no sign of any help for Ray Holmes' Hurricane. Climbing quickly ahead of it, he then swung around to attack from the front.

As I fired, my ammunition gave out. I thought, Hell, he's got away now. And there he was coming along and his tail looked very fragile and very inviting. So I thought I'd just take off the tip of his tail. So I went straight at it along him and hit his port fin with my port wing. I thought, That will just take his fin off and he'll never get home without the tail fin. I didn't allow for the fact that the tail fin was actually part of the main fuselage. Although I didn't know it at the time, I found out later that I had knocked off the whole back half of the aircraft including the twin tails.

Far below, young Jim Earley was playing football at the corner of Ebury Bridge Road, near Victoria station. The air-raid siren had gone off, but as usual he and his friends ignored it. Suddenly they heard gunfire. 'All of a sudden there was this rat-ta-tat-ta-tat. We ran up to the Ebury Bridge and I can remember the Hurricane seemed to go underneath the Dornier, which split and all of sudden – wallop! – it came down in no time. Obviously the Hurricane pilot had no care for his own safety, he couldn't have done. He just hit it and the back of it came off.'

Holmes' own plane began to dive to the left, and was no longer responding to the controls. As the Hurricane went into a vertical dive the clouds rushed up to meet him. He was already halfway down when he undid his safety harness. As he climbed out, the air-stream caught him and smacked him down on to the roof of the Hurricane. Then, as he was thrown backwards, his shoulder hit his own tail fin. When he finally managed to pull his ripcord, the jolt shook off his flying boots and he found himself swinging violently about. Above him he could see the damaged Dornier begin a lazy-looking dive to the ground below.

I got hold of the guy ropes and stopped the spinning and looked down. I was right over the railway lines running into Victoria Station. I thought, 'Hell, I'm going to get electrocuted now after all this!' Then I was swinging towards a row of houses. I hit the roof of one and could not get any grip on the slates in my stockinged feet. I slithered down the roof until I got to the gutter and thought, Now I'm going to break my back and kill myself falling off a three-storey house! But as I fell there was a sudden jerk and I stopped with just my toes on the ground. My canopy had snagged over an up pipe running past the gutter and that had stopped me. But both my feet were inside a dustbin, the lid was on the ground; the bin had obviously just been emptied. My two toes touched the bottom of the bin but my heels were off the ground.

Unbeknownst to Ray Holmes, the episode had been watched through a break in the cloud by a large group of people in nearby Hyde Park. Even nearer, Jim Earley had seen Holmes' Hurricane crash twenty yards from where they had been playing football. 'As soon as it hit the road, it went straight down and burst the water main. Water was all over the place, my feet were soaked.' Holmes himself had come down in a narrow back garden. Calmly, he undid the parachute harness and dusted himself down. In the next garden were two girls who had seen him come down. 'I went over the fence,' Holmes remembers, 'and we all kissed each other.' Jim Earley recalls the ecstatic crowd that greeted the downed pilot as he made his way out into the street. 'The blokes were shaking his hand, but it was mostly women gathered around him. I wish it had been me, they all cuddled him and kissed him. Then he was carried over their heads towards Chelsea Barracks. Everybody was touching him as he was taken over the bridge.

You know, I don't think he wanted to go to Chelsea Barracks, I think he wanted to stay where he was being made a fuss of!'

It is likely that the third Dornier had already been damaged, but it was still the first German bomber brought down over the centre of London. Pieces were scattered over a large area and a part of the plane landed on Victoria station. The pilot, wounded, had baled out and landed in Kennington. There, he got a different reception from that which greeted Ray Holmes. He was set on by an angry crowd and died of his injuries the next day.

Not all the German bombers had been turned away, however. As noon struck on Big Ben, 148 bombers broke through over London, showering their bombs over the city. But as they turned to head home, they met Bader's wing of three squadrons of Hurricanes covered from above by two further Spitfire squadrons. At the same time, more 11 Group squadrons came into the attack. The outnumbered German aircraft were soon streaming back down the Thames in disarray. On the way back they were harried mercilessly as Park put up four squadrons to bring down any stragglers. Peter Brothers, in action with 32 Squadron from Biggin Hill, got one and a half Dorniers before nearly being shot down himself:

> I never thought I'd have the guts to bale out of an
> aircraft. Then when I got badly shot up I was halfway out
> before I realised there was still a bit of control left in the
> aircraft and got back in. I managed to get it back down
> on the ground and saved it, and so it was repaired. But it
> was amazing how quickly and totally unthinkingly I was
> straps off and hood open and halfway over the side before
> thinking, Hang on a minute.

Safely on the ground, Peter Brothers even had time for a

quick bite to eat before Park's entire force was back in the action. At 2.30 p.m., the bombers returned – 300 machines in two waves, heavily escorted by fighters. Amongst them was Bf 109 pilot Gunther Büsgen. 'The nearer we got to London,' he remembers, 'the more we were afraid of being shot down and losing our lives.' Kesselring had hoped that the second wave would catch the British fighters on the ground refuelling and rearming after the first attack. But it arrived too late, and Kesselring had not counted on the speed and efficiency of the ground crews all over southern England. This time the defenders met the attack before it reached London, and by the time Chatham docks came into sight below, fifty bombers had already been forced away. In tight formation the remaining Dorniers flew straight into the beefed-up anti-aircraft battery at Malling, which succeeded in breaking up the attack. The Duxford wing were again called into the action but arrived too late, out of position below the Bf 109 fighter escort. Part of the German plan had been to force Dowding into a great air battle. Now they got their wish as fifteen British squadrons fought a half-hour dogfight with about the same number of German fighters over south-east London.

While this battle was continuing, many of the bombers managed to slip through to the centre of London, although heavy cloud cover meant that the German attack failed to hit any strategic targets. But for the inhabitants of the East End this was scant consolation for another pounding. Newspaper reports of dinners and dancing continuing in the well-protected basement of the Savoy Hotel in central London had infuriated some of the poorly sheltered East Enders. About a hundred of them, led by communists, arrived at the hotel during the raid and demanded entry. An ugly situation was only dispelled when the all-clear sounded soon afterwards. The incident sent a frisson of fear through the establishment. Harold Nicolson wrote in his diary on 17 September:

Everybody is worried about the feeling in the East End, where there is much bitterness. It is said that even the King and Queen were booed the other day when they visited the destroyed areas. Clem [Attlee, Labour leader in the coalition] says that if only the Germans had had the sense not to bomb west of London Bridge there might have been a revolution in this country. As it is, they have smashed about Bond Street and Park Lane and readjusted the balance.

Nevertheless, the government remained worried. A few days later Nicolson noted: 'Already the Communists are getting people in shelters to sign a peace petition to Churchill.'[2]

For the RAF, though, it had been a day of triumph. For once they had had numerical advantage and had found themselves in a position to do real damage to the bomber formations. For the Luftwaffe pilots, who had repeatedly been told that Fighter Command was down to its last fifty Spitfires, to encounter 180 fighters over London and 300 or more over the south-eastern counties in the same day was utterly dismaying. Of the eighteen He 111 bombers that Gunther Büsgen's wing had been assigned to protect, he remembers, eleven were shot down. As much as the day's events depressed the Luftwaffe, they raised the spirits of the RAF. The next day Eric Bann wrote to his parents: 'What about the RAF yesterday? My gosh, for every bomb dropped upon the King and Queen old 238 gave them hell. We got 12 Huns in one scrap. We just went in as one man and held our fire until very close range and then blew them right out of their cockpits.'

As well as having a flight commander shot down, 238

Squadron also lost twenty-two-year-old Sergeant Leslie Pidd, who baled out safely but was dead when he reached the ground. Eric Bann described what happened and the reaction in the squadron: 'Yesterday the Yorkshire boy Sergeant Pidd fell victim to these swines, machine-gunned whilst coming down by parachute. Now after seeing poor Pidd go, I shall never forgive the Hun. We're all just mad for revenge. Never again shall any one of us give any mercy.'

Hazel Gregory remembers an outburst of cheering at the end of the day at Uxbridge as the figures were announced. One hundred and eighty-three German aircraft were claimed; the figure was later amended to fifty-six, but it was still the greatest German losses of the campaign, and there was no doubt who had won the day, even though the RAF had lost twenty-seven planes and thirteen pilots. The *Daily Express* commented gleefully, 'Göring may reflect that this is no way to run an invasion.'[3] Many of the bomber formations had been broken up before they reached their targets, and crucially, Fighter Command had shown itself to be far from defeated. The Luftwaffe attempt to assert daylight superiority had failed.

Furthermore, in spite of the incident at the Savoy, the inhabitants of the East End were still bucking the predictions of their 'superiors'. On 16 September, 'Chips' Channon noted in his diary:

I drove back to London via the East End, which is a
scene of desolation; house after house has been wrecked,
debris falls from the remaining floors, windows are gone,
heaps of rubbish lie in the pavements. A large hospital
and a synagogue still stand, but they are windowless.
Some streets are roped off because of time-bombs. The
damage is immense, yet the people, mostly Jewish,
seemed courageous.[4]

On the same day, even after the disasters of the 15th, Göring continued to claim he could destroy Fighter Command in four to five days. No one disputed, however, that he was still a long way from doing so. On 17 September Hitler again delayed the invasion decision. Bad weather restricted the Luftwaffe's sorties for the next few days and although the night-time assault on London continued, during the day the Germans were restricted to fighter sweeps and light bombing. The Luftwaffe was also prevented from pushing home its attack by its own crippling losses. Only needing to survive to threaten an invasion, Fighter Command had never hoped to destroy the Luftwaffe, but this was what was now happening. On 18 September, for a daylight raid on London, Kesselring could put only seventy bombers into the air. Meanwhile, on the part of the British, there had been redoubled reconnaissance over the Channel ports, where the build-up of barges, together with hints from deciphered radio signals, convinced them that the invasion was still imminent. On 18 September a large raid was ordered against the invasion ports along the northern coast of Europe in which British bombers destroyed 150 barges and blew up a large quantity of ammunition, stored to supply the invading troops.

This operation was much easier than the attacks on Berlin, as Wilf Burnett, with 49 Squadron Hampdens, recalls.

You are operating over water and land so on a moonlit night particularly, you could see the outline of the coast pretty clearly and then you came down to 6–7,000 feet so you had a better chance of hitting your target. We could see the inlet where they were based, as we'd been shown on aerial reconnaissance photographs. I could see the explosions and you knew whether you had been on target. In some places there were fires, where there might have been fuel, particularly in the areas around the docks.

The next day Hitler ordered the partial dispersal of the invasion barges, and as the possibility of Operation Sealion faded away, he concentrated more and more on plans for Barbarossa, the invasion of the Soviet Union. Kesselring, meanwhile, tried another tactic, of sending over very high-level fighter sweeps. As the British radar was unable to tell if the formations contained bombers, Park was forced to send up interceptors. On 19 September, 238 Squadron suffered in one such attack, losing many of their senior officers. 'Only one pilot returned from "B" Flight,' wrote Eric Bann to his parents, 'so we now have only pilots without a CO or Flight Commanders. I think they will have to make me Squadron Leader.' Although the battle was beginning to peter out, 238 were still in the front line. 'My leave has gone for six, even my 24 hours today has gone. Still, never mind,' wrote Bann. 'May God keep me alive and I'll be with you all one of these fine days, so don't worry.'

Meanwhile, attacks on aircraft factories continued. On 25 September a factory in Bristol was badly hit, killing many of the workers, and the following day the Spitfire factory near Southampton was heavily damaged. By now, however, much of the production had been dispersed, and although it was a set-back, it was too late to be decisive. At the same time Kesselring would send over single bombers on nuisance raids over London. This task fell to the fastest of the German bombers, including Wilhelm Stahl's Ju 88. The exultance he had felt pitying 'poor Londoners' was now a thing of the past, as he writes in his diary:

> We're a bit more modest: it's not so much a matter of achieving some kind of success, but mainly to ensure there's at least an air-raid warning in London. However for us poor sausages it is anything but easy. During the previous large-scale raids one could to some extent hide

inside the large formations, but flying alone, one is always exposed like a practice target to a well-coordinated defence organisation.

Setting off on the morning of 25 September, the nearer they got to their target, the more, to their dismay, the cloud broke up. Stahl remembers that their nervousness increased.

All four of us are anxiously searching the sky around us for Spitfires. Sure enough, exactly at the spot where we could assume the sirens would begin announcing an approach raid on London we see them: four fighters below us in a steady climb in our direction. It does not take us long to decide that there is nothing to be done here now. I break off our approach, tipping the aircraft on a wing and whipping round in the fastest turn of my life.

The British fighters took on the race, but just as they were about to fire, Stahl managed to get his Ju 88 into a small cloud.

Inside the cloud it is so bright that I know we will be through it and shoot out the other side in moments . . . The British fighters – they are Hurricanes – have obviously recognised this too, and make no attempt to follow me. There follows a flying game which, if played in sport, would have been no end of fun. In our case it is a game played for our skins! My Ju 88 does not let me down, and every time one or two Hurricanes get into a firing position I succeed in diving back into the cloud, forcing the enemy to manoeuvre for another attacking position on the other side. How often we repeat this game of hide and seek I have no idea: all I know is that I hold on to 'my' cloud for dear life. Finally, using a favourable moment, I manage to jump to another, larger cloud floating in the southerly direction, and from there into ever thicker cloud cover . . . I finally succeed in shaking off the fighters, but it was a close-run thing.

Stahl's navigator kept his cool and steered the Ju 88 towards Hastings, where they successfully dive-bombed the railway station. Then, as darkness fell, Stahl headed for home.

For the British, such raids added to the weariness of a long campaign. Eric Bann was approaching exhaustion:

Things are really warm [he wrote to his parents], never a night without a visit from Jerry and all day long we are knocking him away from London. Still such is the day's work.

I wonder if you could forward to me my alarm clock. I am having great trouble in getting up these days for we are going to bed and getting up at very odd times.

Our squadron may well be called the International Squadron for we have in our midst English, Scotch, Irish, New Zealanders, Australians, Polish, Czechs and Canadians. Not so bad but they are all a grand lot and good to know.

My report and recommendation for commission has now gone through,. My word, my C/O did give me a nice report . . . I have now decided to hold the first commission in our family.

On 27 September came Kesselring's last great daylight attack on London. Driven back before their target and losing a further fifty-four aircraft, it seemed that the morale of the German pilots was at rock bottom. George Unwin, fighting with 19 Squadron, noticed a change: 'They didn't want to fight. The 109s used to come forth and escort their mates but they now ran away as soon as they saw us; they were not made of the same stuff as the original boys, they were good pilots the first ones, but they had lost nearly all of them.' Following these losses, the Luftwaffe withdrew its twin-engined bombers from daylight attacks. Instead Göring ordered that his Bf 110s and 109s be equipped with bombs and sent over for precision raids. Losses continued on both sides – it was not until 21 October that the RAF had its first day without having an aircraft shot down.

On 28 September, Eric Bann was in combat over the Isle of Wight. He did not return from this mission. His parents, to whom he had written so regularly, tried to find out what had happened. A few months later they received a reply from W. Butcher of the Isle of Wight Constabulary:

I will try to give you the facts as near as possible as I know them. On the fatal day your son was engaged with other splendid fellows of the RAF in aerial combat with the enemy over this district and his machine later crashed.

I cannot give you any details as to what caused his machine to crash but can only assume that it was hit by enemy fire. While his fight was still in progress, the machine your son was piloting was seen flying at great speed towards Portsmouth, probably hoping to retain its base as I believe that it was on fire although not to any great extent.

When at a good height over Brading Marshes your son was seen to bale out quite safely but watchers who saw him come down say that his parachute did not open and this was found to be correct when Police and Military recovered his body shortly after. As regards the machine, this continued for a considerable distance out of control, pilotless, before finally crashing on the north side of

Bemridge Downs about a mile away.

The machine was in little pieces strewn over about 200 yards of ground and I can only assume that the petrol tank exploded otherwise this would not have happened in the way it did.

As far as I could see your son was not wounded by the enemy as no gunshot wounds could be found on him at all but it was perfectly obvious that he died from a fractured skull . . .

There was no chance of life when found I am sorry to say. Had there been I would have worked hours as also would my men to have brought him round, but, under the circumstances, I could see that it was perfectly hopeless from the first.

One blessing is that your son did not suffer for death according to the doctor was instantaneous.

I agree with you that at that time these gallant men must have been very much overworked but they have performed a most marvellous feat against overwhelming odds and have earned the gratitude of all the civilised world and such is the spirit of the British RAF that their names will live for ever as the saviours of our country of which we are all so proud.

On 3 October, Bann's death was the headline news in the *Macclesfield Courier.* 'Hero of all the air-minded boys in the town, Sergeant Pilot E. Bann, of 121 Bond Street, fighter-pilot who had expressed a wish to fly the Macclesfield Spitfire, was killed in air combat last week-end.' After describing Bann's continued desire to 'have a go' at the enemy, the article continued:

Can one wonder at the successes gained by the RAF over the disillusioned Luftwaffe when we have men of the calibre of Sergeant-Pilot Bann manning our deadly little fighters? It is with intense regret that we learn of his death, and we sympathise greatly with his family; but they can find comfort in the knowledge that their son died defending his home and the women and children of his land from the threat from the air.

For Gordon Batt, losing the last of his yellow-scarved section was almost too much to bear.

When Bann disappeared, I was even worse, I didn't make friends at all. You do get to a point where you do not wish to be hurt any more. I just did my job, to the best of my ability, had jovial off-duty parties, but no friends, no more than that. I do not even know the names of many of the people I later flew with and were killed. I just blotted that out of my mind. I just concentrated hard on doing my job, and staying alive. Otherwise you'd go barmy, I think.

In October Peter Hairs left 501 Squadron. Like many he was utterly exhausted. 'I'd decided that I'd had enough and I was quite happy to have rest. I was very, very tired. Getting the fighter's twitch, you know.' In November Eileen had a child, but it was stillborn. The doctors told her that the strain of worrying about her husband and suffering air raids had caused problems. 'The midwife said she was a lovely little girl, but they put it down to inward worry. I used to worry about Peter, of course, and once or twice I had to dive under a table when I heard a bomb coming down, and that's really no way to behave when you're pregnant. I often felt it was probably as well; perhaps the child, if she had lived, would have been very nervous.'

CHAPTER THIRTEEN

Hitler's First Defeat

BY THE END OF THE FIRST WEEK OF OCTOBER, Bf 109
pilot Gunther Büsgen had shot down six British
fighters and had flown nearly eighty sorties over
London. At last, on 12 October, his luck ran out:

On the eightieth occasion I copped it. On the way
home I was attacked by a Hurricane and the hits were
unfortunately all in the cooling system and when that
was hit you had perhaps ten minutes' flying time before
you had to bale out. We were told at that stage that if
you were hit over England you had to get back over the
Channel. What a nonsense! It was quite impossible. I was
shot at at 3,000 metres and, not following orders, went
into a glide, but noticed that the plane was losing height
rapidly. I lifted my cockpit roof and started to get out,
but made a mistake and banged my left arm, cutting it.
After a few more flying minutes I landed the plane at an
aerodrome at Chatham. There were two Home Guards
there immediately with weapons, it seemed, out of the
Tower of London. 'Hands up!' they said. I was quite
good at English during my school days and explained, 'I
can't take my hands up because one is broken.' They
accepted this, took me prisoner and took me to hospital,
where I was well treated. There was a junior officer
guarding my single room who brought me some smart

English cigarettes. He himself was smoking Woodbines and when I asked why he had brought me something better he said it was because I was a more senior officer!

Part of Gunther Büsgen was relieved to be out of the war and still alive. After 15 September he had ceased believing in a German victory. 'The flights to London we regarded as completely unnecessary,' he says now. 'They brought no results for us. In October the Battle of Britain was all over – the first part of a lost war.'

On the same day that Büsgen's war ended, there was an announcement by General Keitel that effectively shut the book on Operation Sealion:

> The Führer has decided that from now until the spring, preparations for Sealion shall be continued solely for the purpose of maintaining political and military pressure on England. Should the invasion be reconsidered in the spring or early summer of 1941, orders for renewal of operational readiness will be issued later. In the mean time military conditions for a later invasion are to be improved.[1]

Although exercises continued, and many of the barges that had been converted to carry tanks, now useless in inland waters, remained in the Channel ports, slowly important personnel were transferred away from the operation to pressing duties elsewhere. As early as August some detachments of infantry had been moved east, and now the trickle became a flood. Soon all that remained of Operation Sealion was a skeleton crew. On 21 December the Führer Directive No. 21 was issued for the campaign against Russia: Barbarossa.

For 'conditions for a later invasion' to be improved would

mean trying again to establish air superiority over southern England. Outside the range of the Bf 109, the Luftwaffe were never going to be able to dominate the skies as they had done over France and Poland, where advancing ground troops kept allowing the Luftwaffe to push their bases forward. They had also already demonstrated the difficulties of establishing control over a hostile, uninvaded country even within the range of their key fighter. Any field would have done eventually for the British fighters, which, had they not been let off by the switch to the attacks on London, could have continued the policy of dispersal practised at the airfields almost indefinitely. As long as the RAF did not allow all of their aircraft to be destroyed in the air, they would remain to protect the Royal Navy as it attacked the vulnerable barges and ferries of an invasion force.

But it had been a near thing. During the critical months of August and September the RAF had lost 832 fighters to the Luftwaffe's 668. Only the 600 downed German bombers make the figures look so favourable to the RAF. Nevertheless, by September, the RAF could afford the losses better than the Luftwaffe, who had less effective supply, repair and replacement mechanisms for aircraft than the British. Had the Luftwaffe been better led, and concentrated from the outset on destroying the RAF, it might have been a different story. But the Luftwaffe's aims, as we have seen, were confused from the start, a symptom perhaps not just of the strategic ineptitude of Göring, but also of the indecision right at the top of the German leadership. Without the interest and involvement of the Führer himself in Sealion and the wider campaign against Britain, it has been argued, 'there was little chance of sustained progress'.[2] Even Göring spent most of the campaign at Karinhall, in distant eastern Germany.

Against the background of this uncertainty about Sealion, the Luftwaffe's efforts were divided between three distinct strategic objectives: forcing a surrender through blockade; defeating Britain through a more general air attack; and creating the necessary conditions for a seaborne invasion. Even as late as 15 September, the great attack on London had had two objectives – to destroy fighters and to terror-bomb. Part of this seeming lack of focus had been forced on the Luftwaffe through the actions of the defenders. Kesselring had discovered that he could only lure the British fighters into the air if his attacking formations contained bombers, but if they did, the fighters would be shackled to them in escort duties, making them far less effective at what was supposed to be their primary aim – destroying the British fighters in the air.

This general uncertainty of priorities, based in part on an overestimation of the effectiveness of air power on its own, percolated right through the ranks. Had the Luftwaffe stuck to one aim alone, each on its own could have been decisive – when a blockade was pursued determinedly in 1941, it had a catastrophic effect on Britain's imports of vital food and raw materials – but the Luftwaffe was not strong enough, quite, to achieve all its aims at the same time. Designed to support ground troops, the Luftwaffe's bombing attacks lacked not only precision, but also weight. The two-engined 'fast bombers' had a fraction of the bomb-carrying capacity of the Allied aircraft that would later, also without decisive effect, pour explosives on German cities and factories. A major raid in 1940 was 100 tons of bombs. Later in the war the RAF and USAF were dropping 1,600 tons a night on Germany. Fifty-seven raids on London resulted in 13,561 tons of bombs being dropped. Over Germany in 1944–45, the RAF often exceeded this total in a single week.

In other ways the Luftwaffe suffered technical defects. The Bf 110 and Ju 87s proved to be too slow and vulnerable against determined opposition from fast monoplane fighters.

The Bf 109, although in many respects a match for the Spitfire and the Hurricane, had insufficient fuel-carrying capacity to fight effectively over London. The Luftwaffe intelligence, too, proved unreliable. Radar, and the vulnerability of the radar stations themselves, was underestimated. The chief operations officer of Luftflotte 3 would later concede that RDF and the associated command and control system had doubled the efficiency of the RAF fighters. Although it may be partly a symptom of the imprecision and overestimation of the attacks, the Luftwaffe also seemed to have a poor understanding of which were the vital airfields and factories for Fighter Command. Often bomber airfields and factories would be devastated, while the key sector stations and the vulnerable Spitfire factory at Southampton went unattacked.

There has been much debate about Sealion, and there is no doubting the difficulties of the operation or Hitler's unwillingness to involve himself in it, let alone give the go-ahead. Nevertheless, the Wehrmacht had performed miracles before, and certainly the British, although hoping to cause grievous losses during the crossing, had no confidence that the German army would not establish bridgeheads if the invasion went ahead. Indeed, the defence tactic ordered by Churchill was to hold forces back from the coast to attack the Germans once they were ashore. Happily for Britain, though, it was air power, rather than the relative strengths of the opposing armies, that was to be decisive. General Ismay's verdict holds true:

Personally I always felt that if we won the Battle of
Britain the Germans would not invade, and that if we
lost it they would have no need to invade . . . the
Luftwaffe could have proceeded to wipe out in their own
time and without any significant hindrance, first our air

stations, then our aircraft factories, then perhaps our other munitions factories, then our ports and so on. The point would have been reached, perhaps quite soon, when we would have been bereft of all means of serious opposition. We could have continued the war from Canada – I hope that we would have done so. But the physical occupation of Britain would have presented no serious difficulties.[3]

From the Luftwaffe's point of view, the switch to the night bombing of London and other large cities in the winter of 1941 made a virtue of the necessity of abandoning daylight raids. Night bombing was imprecise, but large cities were easy targets, however strictly the blackout regulations were enforced. For Kesselring, October 1940 saw not a defeat for his Luftflotte, but a change in priorities. As far as he was concerned, the Battle of Britain continued until May 1941 and only ended because of the switch to Barbarossa. In the meantime, the Blitz by night continued on London and other great cities with increasing ferocity. On the day of the first deliberate raid on London the heaviest bomb had weighed 110 pounds. By October bombs of up to 2,200 pounds were being dropped.

Two weeks after the first raid, Betty Roper's house took a direct hit, starting a nightmare twelve hours for Betty and her family. The Ropers were in the public shelter on their street, where bunks and primitive toilets had been installed. Betty's father, like many, was helping out where he could, damping down fires and aiding in the rescue of people from demolished homes. As the raid worsened, he went to the shelter to check on the family. Just as he was entering a bomb fell and he was blown inside, cracking his head on a pillar. Betty's mother was in the toilet when the explosion went off nearby. 'All the plaster and ceiling and that came down on her,' remembers Betty. 'Anyway, she managed to get herself out and she came in looking a sorry sight.' Amid the scenes of confusion a neighbour was holding up a chicken and shouting at Betty's dad, 'Look at this, Bill! The blast must have blown it from somewhere.' Another neighbour appeared white-faced. The blast that had hit Betty's house had caught her in the open. She had been holding a string-handled paper bag containing her important insurance policy documents. Now safely in the shelter, she was still clutching the string but the bag had been blown away. Soon the police arrived and ordered everyone to leave the shelter and make for the comparative safety of Victoria Park, where more public shelters had been dug. Arriving back out on the street, the family saw that the glue factory behind the house had also been hit. 'Lumps of glue were going everywhere,' recalls Betty's brother Jim, then a boy of eleven. 'We were lit up like daylight by the fire.' While Betty's dad plunged off to help with the fire-fighting, Betty's mother insisted on trying to rescue her insurance documents from her bombed-out house. Betty and Jim followed the rest of the shelter dwellers.

But the first shelter they came to by the gates of Victoria Park was deemed full, and they had to visit four more before they found one that would let them in. 'We got in that shelter,' says Betty, 'and we'd just sat down when there was a thud. The warden came down and shouted, "Everyone out! There's a time-bomb on top of the shelter!" ' Eventually, Betty remembers, she and her brother ended up in Bell Street in Hackney.

This is the beginning of the evening, about eight o'clock. All night long people were coming in and calling out for people. Everybody had become separated and they were looking for their families. We're sitting there and I'm saying to him [her brother], 'Dad's bound to come and look for us, they're bound to send him up here.' All night we sat and waited, everyone that came in we thought, That's bound to be our dad. But our dad didn't come and at six o'clock the next morning the all-clear was sounded.

Emerging 'tired and dirty and in a state', the two made their way back across Victoria Park, where there was a 'greeny-brown mist from the smoke of the burning docks'. At last they met up with their father, who, between helping out, had been searching through shelters looking for them. Their mother, who had taken shelter in a sweet factory, had, like the children, been scanning every new person who came in, hoping that it might be Betty and her brother. 'That was that night,' says Betty. A week later she and her brother volunteered to be evacuated to the country, but ended up in Paddington. By this stage west London was being bombed as well, for which the urchins from the East End were blamed. 'Nobody liked us because we had brought the raids with us,' remembers Betty. Soon they decided that they might as well be bombed in their own neighbourhood, and returned to the East End. They never saw any of the high-profile visits by Churchill or the royal family – the only visitor they had after being bombed out was the landlord, worried in case they weren't going to pay the rent.

Remembering that time now, Betty and her brother are amazed at how uncomplaining and obedient they all were. As Bert Martin, then a young auxiliary fireman, says, 'We were brought up not to protest about anything.' The concern to earn money was ever-present. 'Even when we got bombed,' Betty says, 'you still got up in the mornings and went off to work.'

As the bombing continued, sixteen-year-old Bert Martin, helping out with fire-fighting and rescue, came across some strange sights, now engraved on his memory. Glass from explosions could be buried several inches into brick walls. 'There was a car parked in a bedroom in Hackney Wick, it looked as if it had been lifted up and stood there. The windscreen was still intact, the headlamps were still there, it was perfectly all right.' Other, darker images, stay with him still.

The whole thing was pretty horrific. When a bomb dropped it would blow the buildings and people to pieces. The sickening part was that the body parts would be mixed up with the rest of the debris and for a young lad it was a pretty nauseating experience. I can remember one occasion I saw a child's hand sticking out from a very low pile of rubble and I thought, I'll get hold of it and see if it's warm and if it's warm the child's alive. But as I got hold of it the rubble moved and the arm came out with no child attached to it and I dropped it and I felt a bit sick at the time. But that was in the early days and I gradually became accustomed to finding bits of people everywhere. People died which way you liked – they'd be crushed, suffocated, drowned, electrocuted, gassed, die of loss of blood. I think the worst part for me was playing God – who do we get out? When the rescue parties arrived, there would be a debate about who was going to be the easiest to get out. You could dig somebody out and they would be dead or could die on the spot whereas somebody that you hadn't dug out might have survived. I heard so many children crying and heard so many people screaming that I want to run away when I hear it now, it tears me up emotionally. When I walk through a supermarket and see the meat, I get vivid pictures of body parts; if my wife's cooking roast pork or leg of lamb or something, the smell takes me back and I can smell body parts burning. It's lots of silly things that

sort of turn a switch and the pictures turn on. I'm sure
that it must affect lots of people like me. But the fire
crews and the rescue parties, they were my superheroes.
They really stuck it, bombs or no bombs they stuck it
and dug people out.

Amid the heroics, some, racked by endless fear and sleepless
nights, were unable to cope. Whatever the immense pressures
of army, RAF or navy life, almost all servicemen report
being far more afraid in an air raid than in combat.
Cowering under air attack, the fear is made worse, more
debilitating, by the feeling of helplessness. Some, says Bert
Martin, accepted it, others could not. 'I've seen grown men
crouched up against the wall, covering their heads and
crying. I've seen them standing and wetting themselves. I
never thought any worse of them because I was terrified
myself. When people talk about cowards, they're the sort of
people who never had to experience it so they don't know
what being a coward is.'

To cope with the pressure, Bert, like many other Londoners,
would find refuge in the demands of ordinary life, and in the
escapism of the cinema.

I'm just amazed at the fact we took it like we did,
because every day was sheer hell. But the general
population still used to go to work, used to go to school,
used to go to church, they'd go out for the day as though
in a way it wasn't all happening. We'd sit in the cinema
and watch Errol Flynn winning the war, getting excited
about the things happening on the silver screen, and just
outside the door and over the top there was all hell let
loose. We were just shut off to what was going on
outside. We went to music hall and they'd say, 'There's a
raid on. If you want to leave you can.' But of course

what was the point? We might as well stay there and
enjoy ourselves if we were going to get killed. We might
as well all get killed together, that's the best thing.

The Blitz continued until May 1941, when the Luftwaffe
bombers were moved east to attack Russia. In the course of
the attacks, 30,000 people died; up until September 1941,
more British civilians had been killed in the war than
servicemen, and after the first six weeks, 250,000 people had
been made homeless in London.

Fighter Command seemed powerless to prevent the
onslaught, and on 25 November, Air Chief Marshal Dowding, the architect of the system that had successfully repelled
the German daylight air invasion, was replaced. Park, too, was
removed from his command, which went to Leigh-Mallory.
Both men were to some extent the victims of professional
rivalry and personality clashes. It was also felt that as well as
giving insufficient urgency to the night-bomber problem,
Dowding had been ineffective at stopping feuding between
his subordinates, Leigh-Mallory and Park. Lastly, it was
decided after the Battle of Britain that it was vital to get the
country on an offensive footing. Churchill was still concerned about Britain adopting a Maginot mentality. Dowding
was considered a good defender but a poor attacker and was
replaced by Air Vice-Marshal W.S. Douglas. Douglas' subsequent move on to the offensive showed that he had learnt few
of the lessons of the Battle of Britain. However good for
national morale, his daylight fighter sweeps over France lost
more pilots than the Battle of Britain (426 against 414). At
the time he claimed to have killed over 700 German pilots,
but the actual number was 103.

Dowding had always insisted that his role was to prevent
the successful invasion and overrunning of his country. In this
he and Fighter Command succeeded. The invasion was

indefinitely postponed and Britain survived unoccupied. As John Keegan writes in his *The Second World War*, 'the pragmatism of Dowding and his Fighter Command staff, the self-sacrifice of their pilots and the innovation of radar inflicted on Nazi Germany its first defeat. The legacy of that defeat would be long delayed in its effects; but the survival of an independent Britain which it assured was the event that most certainly determined the downfall of Hitler's Germany.'[4]

The air offensive was perhaps most importantly an attack on morale and on the willingness of the British people to continue the war. Had the RAF been driven noticeably out of the skies, there would have been widespread panic, as well as the strategic considerations. Had the bombing of London been heavier, or the remaining Londoners less hardy, then civil breakdown could have occurred or Churchill could have been forced to make peace. But the British, with scant regard to military realities, had decided on war, and the British system, whatever its imperfections, was strong enough to hold the country together. Much of this was down to the leadership of Winston Churchill, who in May 1940 was widely disliked but by the end of the year was a national idol, in spite of the failure of several military operations under his direction. But it was also down to the hopes that many had that victory, when it came, would sweep away the old systems and empower the ordinary person, just as the war had involved them with this national, communal effort. Broadcasters and politicians on the left energetically sold this scenario to their traditionally more anti-war constituency. It was to be unity with a positive purpose – not just to defeat Hitler, but to build a better world after the war.

The wider world had been following the battle, and the exploits of 'the Few' made good copy from Sydney to New York. In America, Roosevelt's fears of a rebuke in the

November elections for his perceived leaning towards intervention receded. Military attaché General Lee, for one, was won over by the effort made by the British. At the beginning of the battle he had written, 'What a wonderful thing it will be if these blokes do win the war! They will be bankrupt but entitled to almost unlimited respect.'[5] Nevertheless, it was not until February 1941, with the election safely under his belt, that Roosevelt was to send his envoy Averell Harriman to London to 'recommend everything we can do, short of war, to keep the British Isles afloat'.[6]

Britain was to remain a mere annoyance, a pinprick in Hitler's side for the duration of 1941. Churchill got his offensive – he had started moving troops to North Africa to fight the Italians even at the height of the invasion scare of mid-1940. But it was not until December 1941, when Hitler declared war on the US in the wake of the Japanese attack on Pearl Harbor, that the failure to defeat Britain really became the 'two-front' scenario that Hitler had always feared. In the meantime, there were dark days to be endured as vital shipping was sunk in the Atlantic and rationing began to bite. But the intense Spitfire Summer would sustain the British people for the duration of the long war ahead. Hitler's attack on morale had backfired and at the end of 1940 he faced a enemy in Britain far more determined to fight than had been the case at the beginning the year. The threat of invasion, together with the heroism and sacrifice of the RAF fighter pilots and the great sufferings of the civilian population, coalesced to form a unique heroic narrative. In his account Churchill described it as 'a white glow, overpowering, sublime, which ran through our Island from end to end'.[7] In her 1941 *The Oaken Heart*, author Margery Allingham would write:

In those weeks in May and June [1940], I think 99 per cent of English folk found their souls, and whatever else it may have been it was a glorious and triumphant experience. If you have lived your life's span without a passionate belief in anything, the bald discovery that you would honestly and in cold blood rather die when it came to it than be bossed about by a Nazi, then that is something to have lived for.[8]

If the summer of 1940 had brought changes to the country as a whole, it also altered forever the lives of those who fought in the RAF. Mostly from educated middle- or upper-class backgrounds, many had joined up with an awkward, embarrassed attitude to country and a wariness of nationalistic militarism. They went to war resigned, without illusion. But with hostile bombers over the country and invasion threatened, they were not immune to the national mood of defiance. The Luftwaffe pilots were fighting, they hoped, to end the war, but the RAF were fighting to save their homes and families. 501 Squadron pilot Bill Green tells of how one day in July his father-in-law had taken down his shotgun and showed it to his wife and three daughters, telling them that if the Germans invaded he would shoot them all and then himself. Green believes he would have carried out his threat. Laurence 'Rubber' Thorogood, the good friend of Sid Wakeling in 87 Squadron, said after the war: 'We were fighting over our home ground and this had a great bearing on our morale. The Luftwaffe certainly had the numbers but this only seemed to spur us on. We certainly got tired but we were fit and young.'[9]

Many by the end of the summer felt anything but fit. Peter Hairs would need a long break in Canada to put himself and his family back together. Bill Green's nightmare fall from the sky caused him to wake up shuddering violently for several years. Many had troubling dreams, sleepwalking and nervousness, as well as long recoveries to make from painful injuries.

Eric Seabourne, who had been horrifically burned on the face and hands, was one of several pilots operated on by pioneering plastic surgeons. He was in the care of Sir Harold Gillis, who painstakingly put him back together. James Coward could not fly again until he had been fitted with an artificial leg. In the meantime, he was posted to Churchill's personal staff in charge of roof-spotting at Chequers and Chartwell. He and Cynthia are approaching their diamond wedding anniversary. Cynthia says that the war taught them not to bother with petty arguments, as each morning their 'Goodbye' could have been their last. But for them too the memory of the fear they experienced at the time is still vivid. 'I remember going to the premiere in Australia of a film about the Battle of Britain twenty years after the war,' Cynthia Coward recalls. 'When a bomb fell I suddenly wanted to get up and get out of the cinema and James put his hand on mine and said, "It's all right. It's only a film." Then there was this shot of a horde of Heinkels and I had my hand on his arm and all the hairs were standing up on end and I said, "It's all right. It's only a film." '

Select Bibliography

Allen, D., *Fighter Station Supreme*, Granada, 1985.

Barker, Ralph, *That Eternal Summer*, HarperCollins, n.d.

Batt, L.G., *Sgt Pilot 741474 RAFVR: A Flying Memoir 1938–1959*, privately published, 1990.

Bickers, Richard Towshend (ed.), *The Battle of Britain*, Salamander, 1999.

Calder, Angus, *The People's War*, Jonathan Cape, 1969. *The Myth of the Blitz*, Jonathan Cape, 1991.

Churchill, Winston, *The Second World War*, 2 vols., Cassell, 1948–9.

Collier, Basil, *The Battle of Britain*, Batsford, 1962. *Defence of the UK*, HMSO, 1957. *The Leader of the Few*, Jarrolds, 1957.

Collier, Richard, *The Sands of Dunkirk*, Collins, 1961. *Eagle Day*, Hodder & Stoughton, 1966.

Colville, John, *The Fringes of Power*, Hodder & Stoughton, 1985.

Deere, Alan, *Nine Lives*, Hodder & Stoughton, 1969.

Deighton, Len, *Fighter*, Jonathan Cape, 1977.

Dilks, D. (ed.), *The Diaries of Sir Alexander Cadogan OM, 1938–1945*, Cassell, 1971.

Dundas, Hugh, *Flying Start*, Penguin, 1990.

Erickson, John (ed.), *Invasion 1940: The Nazi Invasion Plan for Britain by SS General Walter Schellenberg*, St Ermin's Press, 2000.

Faulks, Sebastian, *The Fatal Englishmen*, Hutchinson, 1996.

Ferguson, Niall (ed.), *Virtual History*, Picador, 1997.

Flint, Peter, *RAF Kenley*, Dalton, 1958.

Galland, Adolf, *The First and the Last*, Methuen, 1973.

Gilbert, Martin, *Finest Hour*, Heinemann, 1983.

Harman, Nicholas, *Dunkirk: the Necessary Myth*, Hodder & Stoughton, 1980.

Hillary, Richard, *The Last Enemy*, Macmillan, 1942.

Ismay, James, *The Memoirs of General the Lord Ismay*, Heinemann, 1960.

Keegan, John, *The Second World War*, Century Hutchinson, 1989.

Kieser, Egbert, *Operation Sealion*, Bechtle Verlag, Esslingn, 1987 (Arms and Armour Press, 1997).

Lee, General Raymond E., *The London Observer*, Hutchinson, 1972.

Longmate, Norman, *Island Fortress*, Hutchinson, 1991.

Mason, Francis K., *Battle Over Britain*, McWhirter, 1969.

Nicolson, Harold, *Diaries and Letters II, 1939–45*, Collins, 1967.

Overy, Richard, *Why the Allies Won*, Jonathan Cape, 1995. *The Air War, 1939–1945*, Europa Publications, 1980.

Palmer, Alan, *The East End*, John Murray, 1989.

Ponting, Clive, *1940: Myth and Reality*, Hamish Hamilton, 1990.

Price, Alfred, *The Hardest Day*, Jane's Publishing Co., 1979.

Ray, John, *The Battle of Britain*, Cassel, 1994.

Rhodes Robert (ed.), *'Chips' The Diaries of Sir Henry Channon*, Weidenfeld & Nicolson, 1967.

Shephard, Ben, *War of Nerves*, Jonathan Cape, October 2000.

Stahl, Peter W., *The Diving Eagle*, William Kimber, 1984.

Stockmer, R., *History of RAF Manston*, RAF Manston, 3rd ed., 1986.

Taylor, A.J.P., *English History 1914–45*, Oxford University Press, 1965. *Beaverbrook*, Hamish Hamilton, 1972.

Taylor, Telford, *The Breaking Wave*, Weidenfeld & Nicolson, 1967.

Townsend, Peter, *Duel of Eagles*, Editions Robert Laffont, Paris, 1969 (Weidenfeld & Nicolson, 1970).

Warlimont, Walter, *Inside Hitler's Headquarters*, Weidenfeld & Nicolson, 1964.

Wood, Derek, and Derek Dempster, *The Narrow Margin*, Hutchinson, 1961.

Wynn, Kenneth G., *Men of the Battle of Britain*, Gliddon Books, 1999.

Watkins, David, *Fear Nothing*, Newton, 1990.

Ziegler, Frank, *The Story of 609 Squadron*, Macdonald, 1971.

Ziegler, Philip, *London at War*, Sinclair-Stevenson, 1995.

Notes

PREFACE
1   In extract from Ian Gleed's *Arise to Conquer*, quoted in *Hurricane Squadron* by Perry Adams, Air Research Publications, 1988.

CHAPTER ONE: BLITZKRIEG
1   Rhodes (ed.), *'Chips', The Diaries of Sir Henry Channon*, p.243.
2   Letter of 7 February 1940: Fox papers, quoted in Gilbert, *Finest Hour*, p.148.
3   *Hansard*, 7 May 1940.
4   Churchill, *The Second World War*, Vol. II, pp.523–4.
5   Dilks (ed.), *The Diaries of Sir Alexander Cadogan OM 1938–1945*, p.280.
6   Churchill, op. cit., p.527.
7   *Hansard*, 13 May 1940.
8   Telegram of 15 May 1940: Premier papers, 3/468, folio 204 21, quoted in Gilbert, op. cit., p.345.
9   Churchill, *The Second World War*, Vol. I, pp.441–2.
10   Churchill, *The Second World War*, Vol II, p.42.
11   Colville, *The Fringes of Power*, p.134.
12   Ibid., p.136.
13   Quoted in Keegan, *The Second World War*, p.66.

CHAPTER TWO: DUNKIRK
1   F. Ziegler, *The Story of 609 Squadron*, pp.77–87.
2   Collier, *The Sands of Dunkirk*, p.129ff.
3   ibid., p 135.
4   Quoted in Ponting, *1940: Myth and Reality*, p.92.
5   'Strictly Confidential' minute of 29 May 1940: Premier papers, 4/68/9, folio 954 60, quoted in Gilbert, *Finest Hour*, p.428.
6   War Cabinet No. 142 of 1940, 27 May 1940, 4.30 p.m. Confidential Annex: Cabinet papers, 65/13, quoted in Gilbert, op. cit., p.413.
7   Quoted in Ferguson (ed.), *Virtual History*, p.293.
8   Cabinet papers of No. 142 of 1940, 27 May 1940, 4.30 p.m., Confidential Annex: Cabinet papers, 63/13, quoted in Gilbert, op. cit., p.412.
9   Gilbert, op. cit., pp.411–12.
10   War Cabinet No. 145 of 1940, 29 May 1940, 4 p.m. Confidential Annex: Cabinet papers, 65/13, folios 84–9, quoted in Gilbert, op. cit., p.419.

11   Churchill, *The Second World War*, Vol II, p.88.
12   *Hansard*, 4 June 1940.
13   Gilbert, op. cit., p.468.
14   Nicolson, *Diaries and Letters II, 1939–45*, p.93.
15   Colville, *The Fringes of Power*, p.154.
16   Churchill, op. cit., p.138.
17   Quoted in Harman, *Dunkirk: the Necessary Myth*, p.246.
18   Keegan, *The Second World War*, p.70.
19   Colville, op. cit., p.154.
20   Keegan, op. cit., p.70.
21   *Hansard*, 18 June 1940.
22   Colville, op. cit., p.181.
23   George Orwell, 'The Lion and the Unicorn: Socialism and the English Genius', in *Collected Essays*, Vol II.
24   Quoted in Calder, *The People's War*, p.111.

CHAPTER THREE: BRITAIN ALONE
1   Quoted in P. Ziegler, *London at War*, p.11.
2   Quoted in Ferguson (ed.), *Virtual History*, p.286.
3   Quoted in Ponting, *1940: Myth and Reality*, p.151.
4   Ibid., p.150.
5   *Hansard*, 7 May 1940.
6   Quoted in Calder, *The People's War*, p.124.
7   'Impressions of a visit to XII Corps Area', 23 June 1940, copy in: Foreign Office papers, 800/326, folios 136–8, quoted in Gilbert, *Finest Hour*, p.591.
8   Churchill, *The Second World War*, Vol. II, p.148.
9   Nicolson, *Diaries and Letters II, 1939–45*, p.90.
10   Kieser, *Operation Sealion*, p.73.
11   Colville, *The Fringes of Power*, p.197.
12   Ibid., p.149.
13   Ibid., pp.149, 194.
14   Draft telegram of 9 June 1940: Churchill papers, 20/14, quoted in Gilbert, op. cit. p.486.
15   Kieser, op. cit., p.112.
16   Lee, *The London Observer*, pp.11–12.
17   Colville, op. cit., p.172.
18   Note of 30 June 1940: Premier papers, 3/38, folios 52–3, quoted in Gilbert, op. cit., p.619.
19   Ronald Lewin, *Ultra Goes to War*, London, 1978, p.64.
20   Gilbert, op. cit., p.621.
21   Colville, op. cit., p.187.

CHAPTER FOUR: OPERATION SEALION
1   Warlimont, *Inside Hitler's Headquarters*, p.106.
2   Ponting, *1940: Myth and Reality*, p.113.
3   Kieser, *Operation Sealion*, p.85.
4   Longmate, *Island Fortress*, p.490.
5   Bickers (ed.), *The Battle of Britain*, p.211.
6   Kieser, op. cit., p.274.

7   Longmate, op. cit., p.491.
8   Warlimont, op. cit., p.109.
9   From Erickson (ed.), *Invasion 1940: The Nazi Invasion Plan for Britain by SS General Walter Schellenberg.*
10   Quoted in Kieser, op. cit., p.38.
11   Albert Speer, *Inside the Third Reich*, Collier Books, New York, 1981 (paperback), pp.178–9.
12   Overy, *The Air War*, p.22.

CHAPTER FIVE: THE ROYAL AIR FORCE
1   Lee, *The London Observer*, p.30.
2   Deighton, *Fighter*, p.44.

CHAPTER SIX: THE CHANNEL BATTLE
1   F. Ziegler, *The Story of 609 Squadron*, p.114.
2   Ibid., p.119.
3   Deighton, *Fighter*, p.152.
4   Townsend, *Duel of Eagles*, p.276.

CHAPTER SEVEN: DOWDING HOLDS BACK
1   Bickers, *The Battle of Britain*, p.225, and Overy, *The Air War, 1939–1945*, p.33.
2   Allen, *Fighter Station Supreme.*
3   Quoted in Kieser, *Operation Sealion*, p.277.
4   Colville, *The Fringes of Power*, p.205.
5   William Langer and S. Everett Gleason, *The Challenge to Isolation 1937–1940*, Harper Bros., New York, 1952, p.744.
6   Premier papers, 3/493, quoted in Gilbert, *Finest Hour*, p.733.
7   Colville, op. cit., p.219.

CHAPTER EIGHT: EAGLE DAY BEGINS
1   Deighton, *Fighter*, p.148.
2   145 Squadron newsletter, Autumn/Winter 1995.
3   Colville, *The Fringes of Power*, p.213.
4   Bickers, *The Battle of Britain*, p.220.
5   Warlimont, *Inside Hitler's Headquarters*, p.110.
6   F. Ziegler, *The Story of 609 Squadron*, pp.120–1.
7   Ibid., pp.122–3.
8   R. Collier, *Eagle Day*, p.72.

CHAPTER NINE: FIGHTER COMMAND ON THE BRINK
1   Keegan, *The Second World War*, p.78.
2   Collier, *Eagle Day*, p.86.
3   Ismay, *The Memoirs of General the Lord Ismay*, pp.179–80.
4   Ibid., p.182.
5   Price, *The Hardest Day*, p.19.
6   Flint, *RAF Kenley*, pp.65, 67.
7   Colville, *The Fringes of Power*, p.225.
8   Bickers, *The Battle of Britain*, p.228.
9   Collier, op. cit. p.108.

CHAPTER TEN: THE FEW

1 Colville, *The Fringes of Power*, p.230.
2 Collier, *Eagle Day*, p.104ff.
3 Hillary, *The Last Enemy*, p.95.
4 Colville, op. cit., p.236.
5 Overy, *The Air War, 1939–1945*, p.33.
6 Calder, *The People's War*, p.153.

CHAPTER ELEVEN: THE MANY

1 Overy, *Why the Allies Won*, p.35.
2 Bickers, *The Battle of Britain*, p.233–4.
3 Lee, *The London Observer*, p.47.
4 Calder, *The People's War*, p.155.
5 Ibid., p.156.
6 Nicolson, *Diaries and Letters II, 1939–45*, p.101.
7 Lee, op. cit., p.48.
8 Ibid., p.54.
9 Nicolson, op. cit., pp.111–12
10 Lee, op. cit., pp.54–5.
11 Stahl, *The Diving Eagle*, p.60.
12 Broadcast of 11 September 1940: 'Every Man to his Post', His Master's Voice recording ALP 1436, quoted in Gilbert, *Finest Hour*, pp.778–9.

CHAPTER TWELVE: AIR SUPERIORITY

1 Churchill, *The Second World War*, Vol. II, pp.295–6.
2 Nicolson, *Diaries and Letters II, 1939–45*, p.116.
3 Collier, *Eagle Day*, p.260.
4 Rhodes (ed.), *'Chips' The Diaries of Sir Henry Channon*, p.266.

CHAPTER THIRTEEN: HITLER'S FIRST DEFEAT

1 Bickers, *The Battle of Britain*, p.242.
2 By John Ray, in *The Battle of Britain: New Perspectives*.
3 Ismay, *The Memoirs of General the Lord Ismay*, pp.181–2.
4 Keegan, *The Second World War*, p.81.
5 Lee, *The London Observer*, p.25.
6 Quoted in Richard Overy's 'The Few versus the Very Few', in *BBC History* magazine, June 2000.
7 Churchill, *The Second World War*, Vol. II, p.88.
8 Margery Allingham, *The Oaken Heart*, London, 1941, p.163. Quoted in Ferguson (ed.), *Virtual History*, p.320.
9 Bickers, op. cit., p.176.

Index